1

WARPLANES

PETER R. MARCH

Sopwith Triplane

WARPLANES

A HUNDRED YEARS OF
MILITARY AVIATION

PETER R. MARCH

CASSELL&CO

First published in Great Britain in 2000 by Cassell & Co
in association with the Royal Air Force Benevolent Fund

A CIP catalogue record for this book is available from the British Library
ISBN 1-85409-526-9

Book design by Graham Finch
Printed in Slovenia by DELO tiskarna
by arrangement with Korotan Ljubljana, Slovenia

Cassell & Co
Wellington House
125 Strand
London WC2R 0BB

CONTENTS

PREFACE

The development of military aircraft – from the man-carrying kites, flimsy reconnaissance balloons, and fragile wood and canvas biplanes and triplanes of the opening decades, to the sophisticated and stealthy F-117 and B-2 bombers, supersonic F-15 fighter and the multi-role Tornado, Harrier and F-16 fighter-bombers in the last years of the 20th century – show the enormous progress that has been made in aviation technology. An individual looking at road transport in 1900 and projecting forwards with a vision of vehicles in 2000, would probably not have been too wide of the mark. It is most unlikely that the same individual looking at powered flight (that did not first take place until 1903) could have realistically envisaged supersonic manned flight, cruise missiles, stealth bombers and fighters, vertical take-off and landing aircraft, spy satellites, space stations and man landing on the moon, within the century.

In this book I have taken a personal look, with considerable help from my colleagues Brian Strickland, Graham Finch and Robby Robinson, at some of the astonishing developments in military aviation that have taken place through the 20th century. No work of this kind can hope to be all-embracing. For every item that has been included there are alternatives that are of equal or greater merit in the eyes of other people, that have been left out or briefly touched upon. I have made my personal selection based on my perspective as an aviation journalist, photographer, civilian pilot and close observer of powered flying machines for the second half of the century.

Having always lived and worked in Bristol, England, where aircraft and aero-engine manufacturing remains one of the city's great industries (The Bristol Aeroplane Company, founded in 1910 at Filton, going on to spawn Bristol Aircraft and Bristol Aero Engines and leading to today's BAE Systems and Rolls-Royce at the same site), has kept me close to the dynamic face of aviation. In the last fifty years I have witnessed the faltering development of military helicopters, the thrust for more efficient and greater power from jet engines, the emergence of a practicable V/STOL fighter/ground attack aircraft, the technological triumph of the supersonic airliner and the vision of space travel.

International strife and conflict, whether on the scale of two world wars or more localised conflagrations in various parts of the globe, have inevitably had a major impact on military aviation. The use of the aeroplane as a weapon came with World War I, it became more sophisticated and developed its powers of mass destruction in World War II, honed them through the Cold War years and the conflicts in Korea and Vietnam, so that by the Gulf War in 1991, the military aircraft had achieved a pre-eminent position as a tool of war.

Like the narrative and chronology, the choice of illustrations is very subjective. Where possible I have selected photographs to give a view of an aircraft in its element or showing its special features. It is a mix of historic, contemporary and modern photographs of many of the important military aircraft types of the 20th century. I am indebted to the Royal Air Force Museum, British Aerospace (now BAE Systems), the Royal Air Force Benevolent Fund Enterprises, Royal Air Force Public Relations, Rolls-Royce and the many photographers who have given me access to their collections and provided me with a wide choice of subjects. This book would not have been possible without the extensive and careful research by Brian Strickland and the fastidious care in the presentation of the images by Graham Finch.

Military aviation has progressed from kites to satellites, and the aeroplane grown from faltering powered flight to today's stealthy electronic war machine, in less than a hundred years. Orville Wright succeeded in making man's first flight in a powered aircraft at Kill Devil Hills, Kitty Hawk, North Carolina on 17 December 1903, and this feat will be commemorated 100 years later by the roar of jet aircraft performing their salute overhead, and a cavalcade of machines tracing the fantastic story of flight. It will be left to others to chronicle the great strides that inevitably will follow through the decades of the 21st century, but one thing is certain – military aviation as we know it today will have been transformed beyond all recognition by the middle of the century, let alone 2100.

PETER R. MARCH

THE PIONEER YEARS
1900–1918

Royal Aircraft Factory SE.5a

BRITISH MILITARY BALLOONS

Below: A ground section of the Royal Engineers, pioneers of early British military ballooning.

Below: The Royal Engineers flew gas-filled balloons for battlefield observation purposes in a number of British military campaigns.

Balloons were used during the American Civil War and operated frequently over the lines, their observations being of value to Union commanders. The Confederacy used a few balloons in 1862, but changes in Union Army commands brought in new generals who were not particularly interested in them, and consequently the Balloon Corps was disbanded in 1863.

At this time, Captain F. Beaumont of the British Royal Engineers had observed the work of the Balloon Corps of the US Army on the Potomac. On his return to England he addressed a meeting at Chatham on 'Balloon Reconnaissance as practised by the American Army' and recalled seeing the fire of artillery being directed from a balloon. Artillery spotting eventually became destined to be one of the most vital of all duties for aerial observers.

During the following decade, similar craft were used in support of military operations in France. In 1870, Paris was surrounded by Prussian troops, and balloons were used to carry mail and despatches. Across in England, meanwhile, a chain of events had started which was subsequently to have a profound influence on the future development of aerial warfare. In 1862, the War Office commissioned Henry Coxwell – one of Britain's leading aeronauts – to make a series of ascents at Aldershot. The objective was to illustrate how captive balloons might be used for reconnaissance and signalling. Even the dropping of aerial torpedoes on 'enemy' forces was suggested, especially as this technique had been demonstrated by Coxwell in Berlin some years before.

It was another eight years before the British Army carried out further such experiments, at Woolwich Arsenal. The War Office allocated £150 for the construction of a balloon, and that named 'Pioneer' became the first to enter the Army's inventory in 1879. The first balloon to be actually used by the Army was 'Crusader', which entered service shortly afterwards. However, while balloons were powerless in flight they required a great deal of horsepower to transport them over land to their required location.

Soon afterwards, a balloon section was permitted to participate in manoeuvres at Aldershot. The results from these field trials convinced the Army hierarchy of the practical value of the balloon as a reconnaissance platform. After further evaluation, the Balloon Equipment Store was transferred from Woolwich to the School of Military Engineering at Chatham in 1882. Here a small balloon factory, depot and training school were established and led to the formation of a Balloon Section of the Royal Engineers in 1889, with proper funding and equipment.

In 1885 a balloon detachment had been sent to the Sudan, but it was unable to play a significant role in that conflict due to lack of support equipment - the major problem being getting hydrogen to remote areas. By the late 1880s three balloons, two officers and 15 other ranks went to war with the British Army – 101 years after a man had first become airborne in a balloon. They were sent to Bechuanaland, where dissidents had raised a republican flag at

Evaluation and field trials carried out in conjunction with the British Army led to the establishment of a Balloon Section of the Royal Engineers in 1889.

CHRONOLOGY

24 January 1900
During the Boer War (which commenced in 1889), the British Improvised Balloon Section took part in the Battle of Scion Kop by reporting enemy movements and directing gun fire.

15 February 1900
Kimberley in the Orange Free State, the western area of combat, was relieved when observers in balloons watched every move and reported the Boer evacuation.

26 February 1900
During the final Battle of Paardeberg, the Balloon Section made the biggest contribution to date in securing the important Boer War victory.

30 March 1900
The Third Balloon Section arrived in Cape Town for deployment in the field, for operations against the Boers.

17 May 1900
Balloons assisted the direction of heavy gunfire to secure the Relief of Mafeking after its siege.

5 June 1900
After a preliminary reconnoitre of the Boer defences by balloon, Pretoria was captured. The successful use of balloons for air observation by the British Army in the Boer War was the first key step in the development of military aviation.

2 July 1900
The German Count Zeppelin completed his first airship. It was successfully launched from Lake Constance.

February 1902
British Army estimates for 1902 requested six balloon sections, of which five were to be fully operational.

Mafeking. Order was soon restored without a shot being fired, giving the detachment little opportunity of proving its worth. This was probably just as well, as the rarefied atmosphere of Mafeking, high above sea-level, prevented the smaller balloons lifting a soldier off the ground.

In 1899, at the start of the South African War, a balloon was used to keep an eye on movements of the Boers besieging Ladysmith. When this conflict started, no-one could have foreseen that the success of balloons between 1899 and 1902 would revolutionise military ballooning in Britain. Both France and Germany were ahead in their work on airships, but it would be many years before these machines became an operational success.

On 7 March 1900, the 11,500 cu ft balloon 'Bristol' of the 1st Balloon Section of the Royal Engineers was attached to the Cavalry Division in South Africa, taking part in the advance on Bloemfontein and in engagements at the Vet and Zand Rivers.

FIRST MANNED POWERED FLIGHT

When the Wright brothers got off the ground on 17 December 1903 at Kill Devil Hills, Kitty Hawk, North Carolina, they were the first to make a controlled powered flight – but far from the first to take to the air. For more than a century, men had been going up in balloons, gliders and other assorted contraptions. The problem was not merely that of becoming aloft – the Montgolfiers had done that in hot-air balloons in 1783 – but rather to do it when you wanted to and be able to go where you wished. Predecessors had built kites and gliders and had studied and endlessly tried to emulate the motions of nature – indeed, the Wright brothers themselves were great bird

Below: Kill Devil Hills, Kitty Hawk in North Carolina at 10.35am on 17 December 1903 – aviation's premier moment. Orville Wright pilots the Wright Flyer as it leaves the launch rail under its own power.

Left: The Wrights' 1902 glider being tested in October 1903, ready for the engine and propellers. Their camp is visible on the desolate dunes below.

watchers. Within a period of four years' experimentation with gliders, using an intuitive scientific approach that achieved swift progress with spartan economics, the Wrights solved all the problems they encountered.

The actual event on 17 December 1903 passed almost unnoticed. The general ignorance surrounding matters aeronautical ensured that the occasion revealed only brief mention in the press, and it was even greeted with scepticism. It was entirely a private venture and had no military or government funding. They accomplished it at a time when the idea of manned flight was decried by science and by common sense.

The Wright brothers, Wilbur (above) and Orville (right).

Yet succeed the Wrights did – and though aviation began with them, it took on a life of its own as serious development moved to Europe. By making their aircraft practical they were in fact ten years ahead of the rest of the world. The real problem lay in controlling

the aircraft once it was in the air. The Kitty Hawk aircraft had incorporated just enough wing area, just enough power and just enough control to do the job; likewise, their succeeding aircraft did just enough to remain competitive.

Aviation's premier moment occurred on 17 December 1903 with the first successful take-off at Kitty Hawk of the Wright Flyer I. Making ready for its first flight, the brothers tossed a coin, and Orville won the honour of flying into history. The Flyer lifted from the

Orville Wright's description of the historic first flight on 17 December 1903

Orville's account of the historic day at Kill Devil Hills, one which they approached with some degree of confidence after the near-disaster of 14th December, when Wilbur had made the first attempt at flight.

"When we rose on the morning of the 17th, the puddles of water, which had been standing about camp since the recent rains, were covered in ice. The wind had a velocity of 22-27mph. We thought it would die down before long, but when 10 o'clock arrived, and the wind was as brisk as ever, we decided that we had better get the machine out. We lifted the Flyer onto the trolley, which was restrained by a wire until the critical moment when the engine had been run up to maximum rpm. First we set up the launch rail, only some 200ft (61m) distant from our workshop, and then signalled for our friends and helpers at the nearby Kill Devil Hill life-saving station to come and manhandle the aircraft into position. At last all was ready, the wind then fairly steady about 27mph (43km/h). As I had won the toss, it was my turn to fly and I shook hands with Wilbur – who reminded me of the sensitivity of the elevator."

"I took my position on the Flyer, the trolley was released as the engine raced and it lifted from the track after a 40ft run. The course of the flight up and down was excessively erratic. The control of the front rudder (elevator) was difficult. As a result, the machine would rise suddenly to about ten feet, and then as suddenly dart for the ground. A sudden gust when a little over 120ft from the point at which it rose into the air, ended the flight."

The memorable day was reported by Orville to his father in a telegram:

"Success four flights Thursday morning all against twenty one mile wind started from level with engine power alone average speed through air thirty one miles longest 57 seconds inform press home Christmas."

With Don Tate at left, Wilbur Wright observes the tethered flight of the 1902 glider. Once its vertical stabilisers had been made to pivot, increased control was possible.

Above: A windy site near Kitty Hawk was the chosen location for the Wright brothers' wooden hut, which served as both living quarters and workshop.

60ft (18m) wooden mono-rail and dolly to make the first ever successfully-controlled, powered and sustained flight, lasting for a distance of some 120ft.

Control in pitch was relatively simple, using a horizontal rudder (now known as an elevator) which could be fitted in front of, or behind the wings. A vertical rudder could cope with the yawing motion, but the problem of control in the roll was more difficult. Through observation of large birds, the Wright brothers saw the effects of differential warping of their wingtips, and decided to apply that principle to their aircraft.

In 1906 the Wrights patented a scheme for wing-warping including the opposed twisting of opposite wings as a means of providing roll control of an aeroplane. However, recent studies have shown that in England, Samuel Franklin Cody (who could not read or write, making written evidence scant) used wing-warping in 1903 for control of pitching. Two pusher propellers were used, driven from a single engine by means of chain drivers, one of which crossed so that the propellers were turning in opposite directions, thereby balancing the torque. The original engine was a light (weighing 179lb/81.4kg) but robust four-cylinder unit which delivered 12hp. The pilot lay slightly to the left of the centre line, with the engine a little to the off-side, the two weights balancing the other.

The Wrights were disappointed in the initial response to their achievement, and American aviation was rapidly being outstripped by European enthusiasm. In 1905 they felt that their aeroplane was good enough to offer the US Army. The reply received on 25 October was that, "The Board of Ordnance and Fortification does not care to formulate any requirements for the performance of a flying machine, or take any further action on the subject until a machine is produced which by actual operation is shown to produce horizontal flight and to carry an operator" – though the US Army did buy its first aeroplane from the Wright Brothers for $30,000 on 2 August 1909.

THE ZEPPELINS

Above: The naval Zeppelin airship L2 (LZ18), which first flew on 9 September 1913, incorporated a number of innovations including fully-enclosed cars attached directly beneath the hull. Conceived by Count Ferdinand von Zeppelin (inset, above) , it was the largest airship built before WWI.

T he wind of aeronautical change was beginning to blow in Germany, and in 1906 the War Ministry decided that the airship, whose performance up to this time had looked to have greater potential than the aeroplane, should be the vehicle adopted and developed for German military aviation.

Count Ferdinand von Zeppelin, who had been experimenting with airships for some years, launched his first dirigible airship LZ1 from Lake Constance on 2 July 1900. Carrying five people and operating from its floating hangar on Lake Constance near Friedrichshafen, the flight lasted about 20 minutes. The LZ1 comprised a lattice girder structure covered in cotton cloth, enclosing 16 balloons of rubberised cloth containing 400,000cu ft of hydrogen. Powered by two Daimler engines of 16hp, LZ1 was 420ft long and 36.5ft in diameter. On this first flight it ascended to a height of 1,300ft and travelled for less than a mile, its limited power making control difficult. LZ1 was later scrapped because of a financial crisis in 1902.

The second Zeppelin (LZ2, with more powerful engines of 85hp) made its first flight from Lake Constance on 17 January 1906, reaching a height of 1,500ft. Strong winds forced

Zeppelin LZ5 (Z11) was completed in May 1909. This rear view shows the multiple rudders and elevators as well as the chain-driven propellers.

CHRONOLOGY

16 April 1903
Samuel F Cody began naval trials of his man-carrying kite, towed into wind behind HMS *Seahorse*.

17 December 1903
At 10.30am at Kill Devil Hill, Kitty Hawk, North Carolina, Orville Wright made a flight of 120ft (36.5m), lasting some 12 seconds. It was the world's first manned, powered, sustained and controlled aircraft flight.

9 October 1906
German Zeppelin L3 took off for the first time on a flight of 2hr 17min carrying eleven people.

1907
The German military air force was founded when the army purchased its first Zeppelin dirigible.

1 August 1907
The Aeronautical Division of the US Army Signals Corps was created to study the flying machine and the possibility of adapting it for military purposes.

10 September 1907
At Farnborough Common, Hampshire, the first British military airship, *Nulli Secundus*, made its first public flight.

October 1907
Count Zeppelin's German airship travelled 320km (200 miles), making a complete circuit round Lake Constance in a flight lasting over nine hours.

it down at Kissleg for the night, but it was wrecked soon after its second flight in a storm that tore it to pieces. Its immediate successor, LZ3, flew on 9 October 1906, funded by a state lottery sanctioned by the King of Würtemberg. Stabilising wings were fitted in the pitch axis to reduce the wallowing motion encountered on the LZ1 and LZ2.

LZ4, the fourth built, made its first flight on 20 June 1908 and was 446ft long, with a diameter of 43ft and capacity of 519,000cu ft. Each engine developed 105hp, giving a top speed of 30mph. A special shaft allowed the crew access from one of the gondolas slung beneath the envelope to an observation post on top, in a position that could carry a machine gun in wartime. The two gondolas housed a total of ten crew members, six of whom were engineers.

On 4 August 1908, LZ4 set off across Lake Constance from Friedrichshafen and followed the Rhine towards Strasbourg and Mainz, which it reached at about midnight. On the return the engines, which had given problems on the outbound flight, once again malfunctioned and the airship was forced to land at Echterdingen, having spent over 20hr in the air and covering 436 miles. During the enforced stay a sudden squall lifted the ship from its mooring and, equally as quickly, dropped it whereupon LZ4 burst into flames and was destroyed. Though no crew were killed, von Zeppelin was devastated. He was practically penniless and his dreams for a rigid-type airship looked to have come to nothing. That said, more than any other event, this had demonstrated the awesome war capabilities of a machine that could roam across national boundaries at will.

However, his machines had captured the imagination of the German public to a greater extent than he ever realised, and within a short space of time over six million Marks had been collected in a national fund to establish the Zeppelin Airship Construction Company GmbH to build airships that were to become symbols of German pride and nationalism. LZ3 was handed over to the German Army as Z1 on 20 June 1909. Subsequently 'Z' became the prefix for German airships, while German Navy airships were given the prefix 'L'. The Military Aviation Service was established formally on 1 October 1912.

On 29 August 1909, von Zeppelin made a two-day flight in LZ5 to Berlin, and more than 100,000 people saw the airship coming in to land in the presence of Orville and Katherine Wright and the German Royal Family.

The use of the word Zeppelin became synonymous with all airships, meaning that other designs are usually ignored. Notable amongst these was the series of Schütte-Lang airships which first appeared in 1911. Dr Schütte was a teacher of ship construction at Danzig and had been attracted to the airship as a result of the disaster to the Zeppelin at Echterdingen. Like Zeppelin, he favoured the rigid type and his ideas gained the support of the industrialist Karl Lang, whose name was added to the title. The new design made its maiden flight on 17 October 1911.

The Zeppelin became the accepted military craft and both the Army and Navy used them in considerable quantities. Hindsight, though, shows them not to have made any major contribution to the development of German military aviation, either in terms of operational equipment or in the gaining of long-term useful knowledge.

US MILITARY FLYING

On 19 May 1908, Lieutenant Thomas Etholen Selfridge, after earlier unsuccessful attempts, became the first US military officer (serving with the US Army Signal Corps) to fly an aircraft. His mount was the White Wing, designed and built by Dr Alexander Graham Bell's Aerial Experiment Association (AEA). In an unfortunate twist of fate, however, he also became the first fatality suffered by an occupant of a powered aeroplane.

Lt Selfridge had designed the AEA Red Wing, powered by a Curtiss engine and with a span of 43ft (13.1m), and it was fitted with skids instead of an undercarriage, as it was tested from a frozen lake. Basically a Wright-type aircraft with tail surfaces, the Red Wing had an unusual wing layout – the lower wing having pronounced, curved dihedral, and the upper wing similarly pronounced, curved anhedral, so that the two wingtips came close to each other.

Orville Wright made an historic first flight, of an hour's duration, in 1908 at Fort Myer, Virginia, and seemed just about to secure the military contract that had been eluding the brothers. The Wrights had promised to deliver an aeroplane that would be able to carry two people with a combined weight of 350lb, with enough fuel to fly for 125 miles with a maximum speed of at least 40mph in still air.

All their hopes for the aircraft were dashed during US Army acceptance trials of the

Below: The aftermath of Orville Wright's crash at Fort Myer, Virginia in September 1908, when a guy rope snapped and damaged a propeller. This caused a control problem that led to the crash in which his passenger, Lt Selfridge, was killed.

Gallant Beginning by Keith Ferris depicts Benjamin Foulois flying a Wright Type A Biplane over Fort Sam Houston, San Antonio, Texas on 2 March 1910 – the first ever flight by a US military-trained aviator in a government-owned machine.

Wright Flyer A when a guy wire broke, damaging a propeller and causing a control problem which sent the aircraft crashing from about 75ft at Fort Myer. Lt Selfridge was accompanying Orville Wright on this 17 September 1908 flight and perished in the crash, after fracturing his skull when he hit one of the machine's struts. By the following year, Orville was flying again and had developed an aircraft to meet all the Army's requirements.

A few days earlier, an enthusiastic Orville had written to Wilbur (who was in France trying to interest the French Army in his machines) from Washington to say that he was 'getting a warm reception' and 'they all think the machine is going to be of great importance in warfare.' Glenn Curtiss, the second American serviceman to fly, had already sunk a battleship (or at least a simulation of one), on a lake in New York and had confidently reported that, 'the battles of the future will be fought in the air!'

In 1909, a young American Lieutenant, Henry H. Arnold, making his way home from duty in the Philippines, observed Bleriot's aircraft on display in Paris (soon after it had made the first flight across the English Channel), and wondered what it meant for the future.

CHRONOLOGY

December 1907
Samuel Cody began constructing a biplane at Farnborough. It received £50 funding from the British Army and used the 50hp Antoinette engine which originally powered the airship *Nulli Secundus*.

13 January 1908
The French company Voisin developed a biplane that was far more practical than the Wright biplane or European designs like the Voisin-Farman Ibis.

19 May 1908
Lieutenant Thomas E. Selfridge became the first US military officer to fly an aircraft, when he piloted White Wing designed and built by Dr Alexander Graham Bell's Aerial Experimental Association.

26 July 1908
First flight of *Nulli Secundus II* at Farnborough. It was only flown for a few weeks before the concept of using airships for military purposes was abandoned by the British Army.

21 August 1908
Wilbur Wright began demonstrating his Flyer A in Europe. He flew it from the artillery ground at Camp d'Auvres, near Le Mans in France.

September 1908
The Wright brothers demonstrated the Wright Flyer to politicians at Fort Myer, Virginia.

More Wright Flyers

On 6 May 1908, Wilbur Wright took to the air for the first time since 16 October 1905, when he last piloted the Flyer III at Huffman Prairie, near Dayton, Ohio. The Wright brothers were back at Kill Devil Hills, Kitty Hawk once again – the scene of their 17 December 1903 flight. This time they were testing the modified Flyer III prepared for the US Army trials, and Wilbur took off without a launching derrick for a distance of 1,008ft in 22sec. With a span of 41ft and powered by a 30hp Wright engine, it was capable of 40mph.

The Wrights returned to Fort Myer, Virginia in June 1909 with an improved version of their 1908 model which had crashed with Lt Selfridge at the controls. Cross-country and endurance flights were made during July, with Army pilots as passengers, demonstrating the utility of the design.

Though the US Army specification required a speed of 40mph, to guarantee the quoted contract price of $25,000 the Wright brothers were to receive an additional $2,500 for every 1mph they achieved above the specification. Orville averaged 42mph (67.6km/h) during a five-mile (8km) flight, winning a $5,000 bonus. The US Army accepted the aircraft on 1 August as 'Aeroplane Number One', Heavier-than-Air Division, United States Aerial Fleet. The Wrights were also contracted to provide an aircraft and pilot training for the US Army's Signal Corps, and to have their aircraft licence-built in France. These modified Flyer III designs were called Wright Flyer Model 'A's, with two upright seats and other refinements.

On 21 September 1908, Wilbur Wright made a significant long-distance flight in Europe, when he flew the Wright Flyer he was demonstrating from Camp d'Auvers in France. Covering a distance of 41.4 miles the flight lasted 1hr 31sec, by far the longest to date. By December he had made the first flight to exceed two

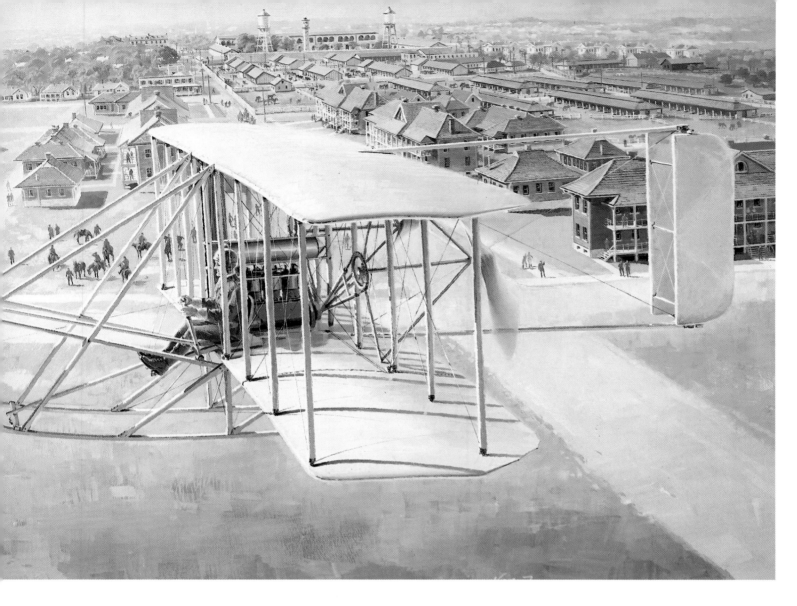

hours – travelling 100 miles at 33mph.

In early 1909, Wilbur Wright and Eustace Short of Short Brothers Ltd in England signed an agreement to build six Wright Flyers for members of the Aero Club under licence for a total cost of £8,400.

On 28 September 1909, Wilbur Wright flew around the Statue of Liberty at New York – the last public flight made by either of the Wrights.

The Wright Company was incorporated on 22 November 1909, with Wilbur Wright as its President. Orville began as Vice President (later becoming President when Wilbur died in 1912), and in September 1916, the Wright Company and the Glenn L. Martin Company merged to become the Wright-Martin Corporation of New York.

Wilbur Wright's flying demonstrations in France in 1909 were met by huge crowds. Here, horses in the paddock at Pau are steadied as the motorised aerial carriage passes overhead.

FIRST FLIGHTS IN BRITAIN

I n England the expatriate American (later naturalised British citizen) Samuel F. Cody (1861-1913) had developed the Hargrave man-lifting box-kite by giving its upper wings a true aerofoil, and the type had been adopted by the Army for observation purposes. The country was languishing in the aeronautical doldrums and only began to emerge through the efforts of two men – Cody and A.V. Roe.

Though the Wright brothers patented a scheme for wing-warping involving the opposed twisting of opposite wings as a means of providing roll control of an aeroplane, Samuel Cody claimed to have anticipated this for his kites in 1903, though this claim has not been entirely accepted by historians. Cody was unable to read and write, so there is an absence of any written records. Though the Wright brothers' invention went well beyond anything that Cody contemplated in 1903, it now seems certain that Cody did use wing-warping in 1903 for control of pitching.

The motor-kite was not quite a mythical bird, but of all Cody's creations it was by far

A. V. Roe's Triplane being prepared outside his railway arch workshop at Hackney prior to making its first flight at Lea Marshes, Essex on 13 July 1909. It had a JAP engine of notably low power-to-weight ratio.

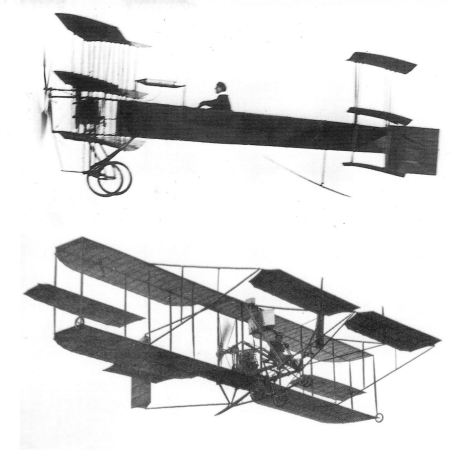

the most mysterious. The machine was a biplane with its upper span much greater than its lower (a configuration now known as a 'sesquiplane'). With a three-cylinder 12hp French Buchet engine, it did not carry a man on board.

Though not officially recognised, the first powered aeroplane flight (of 500ft/152m) in Great Britain, was almost certainly made by Horatio Phillips in a multiplane of 22hp. The aircraft was of his own design and featured narrow 'venetian blind' wings in tandem.

The first successful aeroplane flight in Britain was made by Cody (who had been involved in early airship development) in his British Army Aeroplane No. 1, powered by a 50hp Antoinette engine, on Farnborough Common on 16 October 1908. It had a span of 52ft, a wing area of 790sq ft and a fully-laden weight of 2,540lb. The flight lasted 1,390ft (424m), ending in a crash-landing, but without physical injury to Cody. At the time Cody was the Royal Engineers' Kite Instructor at the Royal Balloon Factory, Farnborough, and had been refused permission to build a heavier-than-air machine.

However, the first flight in an all-British aeroplane by a Briton is officially recognised as having been made on 13 July 1909 by Alliott Verdon Roe (later to become founder of Avro) at Lea Marshes, Essex in his 9hp paper-covered Roe I triplane. The Roe I had three 20ft span wings and three horizontal tail sections fitted to a covered fuselage with a triangular cross section.

In late 1908 Cody rebuilt his original machine into the Cody 2, with which he made over 30 flights in early 1909, the best of them covering four miles (6.4km). By the end of the year, following modifications to Cody 3, his aircraft was able to cover 40 miles (64km).

Early pioneers – Samuel Cody (above) in his British Army Aeroplane No.1 flying over Farnborough on 16 October 1908, and A. V. Roe (top) flying the second Roe I Triplane (identified by its cylindrical fuel tank) at Wembley Park on 6 December 1909.

Army Aeroplane No. 304 (Cody Type). These machines were large and sturdy, but clumsy in the air.

The 1910 Bristol biplane, familiarly dubbed 'Boxkite', was an unashamed copy of the Henri-Farman design – but the British version incorporated more refined metal fittings. (The replica aircraft illustrated here is flown by the Shuttleworth Trust at Old Warden in Bedfordshire).

Though his aircraft were somewhat large, they were sturdy, and illustrated that Britain could produce an aeroplane as well as the mainland Europeans. Cody's enthusiasm and determination spurred on the early British pioneers.

Initially, Roe was desperately short of money for his early machines and could only afford JAP engines with a low output. This meant that he could only achieve powered hops in his otherwise promising machines.

Prime Minister Herbert Asquith sent a letter on 30 April 1909 to leading British scientists, proposing that a committee of scientists should be formed to advise the government on aeronautical matters. The Advisory Committee of Aeronautics, a national institution, was soon formed with Lord Rayleigh as President – a man recognised throughout

the world as one of the greatest mathematical and experimental physicists, and one of the more successful in the way of original achievement.

The Committee engaged a young pioneer aviator, Geoffrey de Havilland, who had already made a somewhat imperfect but promising aeroplane to his own design, in its work. In December 1909, his initial aeroplane had made its one and only flight when it was run downhill into wind at Seven Barrows, near Newbury. Named the de Havilland Biplane No 1, the machine weighed 850lb and was powered by a 45hp, four-cylinder engine designed by himself and built by the Iris Motor Co of Willesden. De Havilland's wife assisted in producing the cotton covering of the wings and control surfaces. Soon after take-off though, de Havilland pulled up the nose too sharply, which caused the wings to fail, and it crashed.

EARLY NAVAL AVIATION

Above: American designer Glenn Curtiss, with US Navy support, developed new aircraft for operation from ships. Here a Curtiss 'Hydro-Aeroplane' is prepared for take-off in San Diego Bay in January 1911.

Main picture: Eugene Ely, in a Curtiss pusher biplane, makes the first take-off from the deck of the USS *Birmingham* on 14 November 1910. Despite touching the water and damaging a propeller, he managed to remain in control.

During the 1908 US Army trials of the Wright Flyer at Fort Myer, Virginia, representatives of the US Navy were present, and no doubt saw the potential for aviation in the sphere of naval operations. Flight from water actually dates back to the turn of the century, when American physicist Samuel Pierpoint Langley commenced experiments with large model aeroplanes catapulted from a houseboat on the Potomac River. In June 1901, Langley launched quarter-scale unmanned models from the houseboat, thereby recording the first sustained level flight by a petrol-fuelled aeroplane. Two years later, full-sized models were readied for manned trials but launching problems were encountered. After Orville Wright had piloted his aircraft into the history books on 17 December 1903, support for Langley lapsed.

When Wilbur Wright went to France in 1908 to give flying demonstrations, (regarded as sensational compared to those of their European counterparts) the US Naval Attaché to Paris was present at the first international aeroplane meeting to be held. So impressed was he with the flying that he recommended that the US Navy should convert a battleship and build other vessels to carry and launch aircraft – a suggestion that was immediately dismissed by the Department of the Navy.

Frenchman Henri Fabre became the first man to fly an aircraft from water on 28 March 1910 and, in the following June, Glenn Curtiss (who was the first American to fly a powered aeroplane after the Wrights) took the US Navy into the age of the aeroplane. He arranged the setting out of markers on Lake Keuka in the shape of a battleship, and then flew over the phantom vessel releasing lead pipe 'dummy bombs' in a simulated attack.

Through newspaper sponsorship, a race to become the first to fly an aeroplane from a ship now began. The US Navy hurriedly fixed a wooden platform on the cruiser USS *Birmingham* for this purpose. Civilian pilot Eugene B. Ely (who worked for Curtiss), in a Curtiss pusher biplane powered by a 50hp engine, made the first take-off from the *Birmingham* on 14 November 1910, whilst the cruiser was at anchor in Hampton Roads, Virginia. Ely took off safely from the 83ft (25m) long and 24ft (73m) wide ramp and landed at nearby Willoughby Spit – in time, this achievement would lead to the emergence of the aircraft carrier.

In the same year, a Royal Navy Officer had learned to fly on the Short S.26 – a Short derivative of the Farman biplane. Lt G. C. Colmore, RN was awarded his pilot's certificate on 21 June 1910, thus becoming the first naval officer in the world to qualify as a pilot. On 18 January 1911, Eugene Ely made the first landing on a ship – the armoured cruiser USS *Pennsylvania* in San Francisco Bay. The designated vessel was fitted with a 119ft 4in (36m) platform. He later took off for the return to Selfridge Field, thus becoming the first pilot to land and then take off from the deck of a ship.

The Royal Navy's Lt Charles Rumney Samson secretly flew from a platform erected over the foredeck on HMS *Africa* in a Short S.38 biplane while the battleship was anchored in Sheerness Harbour, near the Isle of Grain. Officially, he made the first British take-off from a ship on 10 January 1912, the Short S.38 again flying off the *Africa*. The aircraft had been prepared against the dangers of an accidental ditching by the temporary installation of inflated and streamlined air bags. After leaving the bow of the ship he climbed to a height of 300ft for the flight back to Eastchurch. These tests were part of concerted efforts to raise support for naval aviation in Great Britain.

In the following May, Samson (by then a Lieutenant Commander) flew a Short S.38 from the forecastle platform erected on the battleship HMS *Hibernia* while the vessel was underway. Steaming at 10kt during the May 1912 Naval Review at Portland, this was the first time an aeroplane had flown from a moving ship. As a result of this, Samson was appointed as the Commanding Officer of the Naval Wing, Royal Flying Corps the following October.

CHRONOLOGY

14 November 1910
Eugene Ely, in a Curtiss pusher biplane, made the first ever take-off from a ship – the cruiser USS *Birmingham*, at anchor in Hampton Roads, Virginia.

21 January 1911
The first use of wireless telephone conversation from an aircraft, flying over Selfridge Field, USA.

14 March 1911
The British War Office purchased four Bristol Boxkites in a military configuration for the Army.

23 October 1911
The first military mission with a powered aircraft – an Italian military Bleriot XI monoplane flying from Tripoli spied on Turkish forces at Azizia.

18 November 1911
An Avro Type D biplane fitted with floats was the first British seaplane to take off from water.

4 December 1911
First flight of the BE1 tractor biplane, the first in a long line of British reconnaissance biplanes to serve with the Royal Flying Corps (RFC).

10 January 1912
The world's first flying boat, the Curtiss No 1, made its maiden flight.

10 January 1912
Lieutenant Charles Rumney Samson RN became the first British pilot to take off from a ship, when he flew his Short S.38 biplane from a platform erected over the foredeck of HMS *Africa*, off the Isle of Grain.

13 April 1912
The Royal Flying Corps (RFC) was constituted in Britain by Royal Warrant.

9 May 1912
The world's first take-off from a ship underway was made by Lieutenant Commander Samson RN, flying from HMS *Hibernia* in a Short S.38 biplane.

7 June 1912
First firing of a machine gun from an aeroplane in flight (a Wright Model B biplane) in the US.

1 July 1912
Formation of the Aviation Battalion of the Italian Army – the requirements for aircraft, squadrons and personnel were to stimulate the development of many European air arms.

Ely's first take-off (and landing) from the deck of a ship took place on the USS *Pennsylvania* at the San Francisco Air Meet on 18 January 1911.

THE AEROPLANE GOES TO WAR

The first successful air raid on Germany was accomplished by two Sopwith Tabloids of the Eastchurch Squadron, Royal Naval Air Service on 8 October 1914. On the outbreak of WW1, naval squadrons took up patrol positions along the British east coast, waiting for the Germans to appear. The naval fliers soon became frustrated with the lack of activity and, when the German advance on the continent appeared as if it may force an evacuation from France of the British Expeditionary Force, it was suggested that naval squadrons should cross the Channel to counter this possibility.

The Navy jumped at the chance of some action. Commander Charles Rumney Samson RN, commanding the Eastchurch squadron of the RNAS, moved his force to Dunkirk in readiness. However, there was little aerial activity near the Channel ports and the weather was uniformly poor. Teaming up with a retired French infantry officer, who was acquainted with the district, he flew operational patrols to report the presence of German armoured cars.

Samson soon got the opportunity for genuine action when he took two Tabloids forward to Antwerp, where the Royal Marines and the Belgians were holding out. From that location he could reach Germany and, in retaliation for the Zeppelin attacks against the city, they tried their hand at bombing. Attacks on the German airship sheds at Cologne and Dusseldorf were made by four RNAS aircraft on 22 September. These proved unsuccessful, for although one shed at Dusseldorf was hit by three bombs, these failed to explode.

On 8 October, just as Antwerp itself was about to fall, one Tabloid hit Cologne's railway station. With German pressure on Antwerp growing by the hour, Samson wanted to make one more attempt from that airfield while strategic targets were still within range. Though withdrawing most of his unit from Antwerp, he temporarily left two Sopwith Tabloids there, with two pilots to fly them – Squadron Commander D. A. Spenser Gray and Flight Lieutenant 'Reggie' L. G.

The first successful strategic air raid on Germany, carried out by two RNAS Sopwith Tabloids on 8 October 1914, resulted in the destruction of the new German Army Zeppelin LZ25, which had been fully inflated inside its shed. (The photograph shows a replica Tabloid specially built in the 1980s).

In the opening phases of WW1, the Avro 504K was used by front-line squadrons in the RFC and RNAS for bombing and reconnaissance, but from 1915 onwards the type took on the training role. This modern replica carries an authentic colour scheme of the period.

Marix. A ground crew was left to service the aircraft, but were provided with a car in which to eventually withdraw. Fl Lt Marix reported on his action that day:

"When German shells began to fall on Antwerp, we dispersed our aircraft into the middle of the airfield in the hope that they would be safer. On the 8th the morning brought thick fog and it was not until midday that the two Tabloids could be prepared for take-off. I was airborne at 13.30hr and faced a flight of 104 miles to Dusseldorf. Though I suffered weather problems en route I was able to identify the target at Dusseldorf and I dropped my bombs from a height of about 600ft."

"Luck was with me, for inside one shed was the new army Zeppelin Z.IX (LZ25), fully inflated. It exploded violently, and as the roof collapsed flames rose to some 500ft, not only destroying the airship but the adjoining workshops. At once I was the target for a hail of machine-gun fire, but with the throttle fully open and weaving from side-to-side I was soon out of range and on course for return to Antwerp."

"Some 20 miles short of my destination the engine coughed and spluttered to a standstill. The fuel tank had drained, and with the sound of the wind whistling through the bracing wires I made a tricky landing near the Belgian side of the Dutch frontier. After walking for some distance I managed to borrow a bicycle, but finally regained Antwerp in the driver's cab of a train."

"I found that the ground crew had managed to render airworthy an unserviceable BE2 so that two pilots could fly out. Before that moment arrived, however, German shelling of

Air Warfare 1914-1916

When WW1 began in 1914, neither side really understood the implications of an air war. As the first months of the conflict progressed, deficiencies of immense size and importance were apparent in every aspect of aviation for every country involved.

The aviation mobilisation, such as it was at first, was executed by each respective General's staff. No-one had drawn the correct inferences from the very limited warfare that aircraft had been engaged in, and equally no-one had the slightest ideas of the enormous amount of equipment required in terms of both men and supplies, as well as the effort necessary to sustain a single aviation unit in operations.

No nation had any perspective of the wastage involved in aircraft operations. None had established an industrial base to sustain active combat operations. When war broke out, a mixed bag of some 25 aircraft landed in France – mainly a collection of English Blériots, Henri-Farmans, Avros and BE2/BE8s.

The Germans had some 450 aircraft, but little more than half were combat-ready. They also had eleven dirigible airships. The French were able to field around 300 front-line aircraft and five dirigibles. In further contrast, the British Royal Flying Corps had only 160 aircraft, of which only a third were 'front-line' quality, and they did not really come to grips with the dirigible question until after 1918.

German aircraft ranged from the graceful Taube monoplane to the very efficient Albatros biplane, designed by Ernst Heinkel. Germans machines tended to depend upon heavy, but reliable six-cylinder water-cooled automobile-type engines of around 100hp.

Although it cannot be said that aircraft won WW1 for the Allies, it is fair to say that they did prevent their immediate defeat.

The Morane-Saulnier Type N was armed with a fixed 0.315in Hotchkiss or 0.303in Vickers (or Lewis) machine gun. The RFC received 24 of the type.

the airfield damaged the aircraft and there was no alternative but to make good our escape by car, reaching the squadron's new base at Ostende on the following day." For his exploits, Marix was awarded the Distinguished Service Order.

On 21 November, three unarmed RNAS Avro 504Ks, each powered by a single 80hp Gnome rotary engine, made a successful attack on the Zeppelin sheds at Friedrichshafen on Lake Constance. Winston Churchill, the First Lord of the Admiralty, ordered four Avro 504s to be packed into unmarked trucks and driven to a base at Belfort near the Franco–Swiss border, where they were reassembled and made ready for a further such attack. Only three made it and, each carrying four 20lb bombs, set off on the long journey of over 250 miles there and back, arriving over Lake Constance without incident. Skimming the distance of the lake, they climbed before making their bombing run. The Germans were taken completely by surprise and the Zeppelin sheds were hit, destroying one airship. Squadron Commander E.F. Briggs, leader of the raid, was shot down and taken prisoner, but the others returned.

Early bombs were usually based on artillery shells with fins attached, and bombing sights were non-existent. Nevertheless, the will for action was there and these early examples of strategic bombing in the gestation period were a boost for morale.

GERMAN RAIDS ON BRITAIN

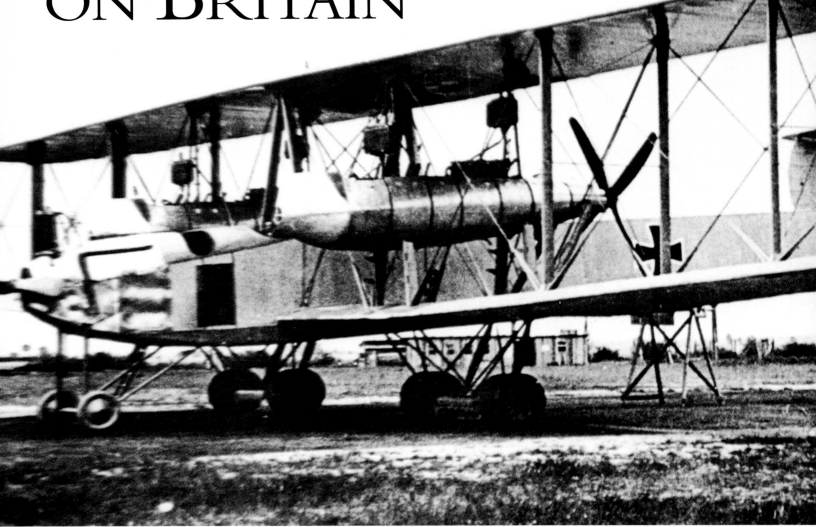

I n September 1914, German airships were used to drop small bombs and propaganda leaflets over Antwerp and Warsaw, and on 30 August four bombs fell on Paris, having been released from an aircraft. The leaflets probably had more effect on the civilian population than the bombs, but it was a start in involving civilians in front-line situations.

The formation of Major Wilhelm Siegart's (regarded as the Architect of German strategic bombing) Fliegerkorps des Obersten Heeresleitung in November 1914 had the sole object of attacking London with aircraft. The UK's geographical insularity, more than adequately guarded by the Royal Navy, would frustrate any attempts by sea. Through air attack, however, the nation might be bombed into submission and, it seemed, this aim could be achieved most rapidly by destroying London.

In the event, the first bomb to fall on British soil came down harmlessly near Dover on 24 December 1914, having been carried across the Channel by a C-type biplane. The first Zeppelin raid followed on 19 January 1915, when two airships dropped bombs in East Anglia

The collapse of Russian resistance on the Eastern Front led to the transfer of the larger R-planes such as the Zeppelin Staaken R.IV seen here to the Western Front, for use on raids over England. Based near Ghent in Belgium, these aircraft dropped 2,500kg bombs on enemy targets.

CHRONOLOGY

19 January 1915
Two Zeppelins operated by the German Navy made the first attack by an airship on Great Britain, when installations at Great Yarmouth were bombed.

15 February 1915
Ilya Mourmets bombers of the Imperial Russian Air Services went into action for the first time on an attack on Willenburg in East Prussia.

10 March 1915
The British Offensive at Neuve Chapelle commenced using maps which had been prepared solely from intelligence obtained by aerial photographic reconnaissance missions.

1 April 1915
A French Air Force Morane-Saulnier Type L parasol-wing monoplane shot down a German Albatros two-seater. This was achieved by the first use of a Hotchkiss machine-gun mounted to fire through the propeller arc.

25 April 1915
The first operational aeroplane mission by the US Navy, when a Curtiss AB-3 flying boat made a visual reconnaissance of Vera Cruz, Mexico for detection of possible mines.

30 April 1915
Allied aircraft were delivered to South West Africa to join the Union Expeditionary Force, and were used against German forces.

killing two civilians in Great Yarmouth and two elsewhere, and injuring sixteen. Several other raids followed and created little in terms of damage, but much public feeling. The raids highlighted the fact that the defences were quite inadequate – casualties among RFC and RNAS pilots trying to intercept the airships were quite high, simply because night flying was a skilled art that few had ever undertaken at that stage in the development of aviation.

Kaiser Wilhelm II initially would not allow the indiscriminate bombing of England, and it was in January 1915 that he relented sufficiently to allow Zeppelin raids – provided they were limited to dock installations and military establishments around the English coast and on the lower Thames. Under no circumstances was London to be bombed.

During the course of the war, the Germans dropped some 9,000 bombs on England, totalling some 280 tons. In just over 100 raids, they killed about 1,400 people and wounded 3,400 more, and caused £3m of damage in four years. In fact, though the Germans achieved little in material terms through Zeppelin attacks, they did have a disproportionate influence in Britain, forcing the British to keep aircraft and men home from France and other theatres.

By the end of 1915, the Germans were regularly attempting Zeppelin raids over England but it was not all plain sailing for the airship crews: night navigation was very difficult and they were often over 100 miles adrift from their scheduled targets. Bombing accuracy, once the target was located, was quite good, as the commander was able to slow or stop his ship directly above the objective, but the main problem was finding the target. Dead reckoning navigation and radio cross bearings were the accepted norms of the day, but the AA guns – forcing the airships higher, into cloud and unpredictable and unforecast winds – made this very much a hit or miss situation. Greater efforts were made to strengthen defences by increasing searchlight coverage, the quantity of guns, and more importantly, concentration on night flying techniques for fighter aircraft.

On 19 January 1915, three Zeppelins – L3 (LZ 24), L4 (LZ 27) and L6 (LZ 31) – took off from Fuhlsbüttel near Hamburg. The first two were to attack installations along the Humber Estuary and L6 was to engage targets on the lower reaches of the Thames. The commander of L3, Kapitänleutnant Fritz reported:

"We were still crossing the North Sea towards the Humber at 18.30hr, when a freshening wind made me decide instead to head for the secondary target of Great Yarmouth. Reaching the coast at 20.50hr I came low and dropped parachute flares to pinpoint my position. Identification of the lighthouse at Winterton enabled me to set course for Yarmouth, which I sighted at 21.20hr. Immediately, I dropped a parachute flare to dazzle the defences, this attracting the unsuccessful attention of an anti-aircraft battery. As we crossed the town from north to south, six 110lb bombs and seven incendiaries were dropped. I headed out across the North Sea, regaining our base at 09.40hr on 20 January, after being airborne for 22 hours 51 minutes."

Zeppelin raids on Britain became less frequent, especially as five airships were destroyed by fighters based in the UK between September and November 1916. The latest RFC fighters were able to outfly the later class of 'height-climbers', and incendiary ammunition made life intolerable for Zeppelin crews. Victory over the Zeppelin did not however end the fear of air raids - the big bomber was now ready to take over the task of strategic attack.

Germany commenced the development of the twin-engined Gotha AEG G.IV and Friedrichshafen G.III aircraft to take over strategic bombing from the Zeppelin in 1917. The much larger Staaken 'Giants' followed during 1918. Engine horsepower was considerably increased, strength-to-weight ratios improved, and steel tube welding replaced wood for airframe construction.

The first Gotha G.IVs carried six 110lb bombs and were able to attack from 15,000ft which meant that, in the absence of an effective air-raid early-warning system, they could drop their bombs and embark upon their return journey before RFC aircraft could climb to attack them. Operating from airfields in Belgium, the unit responsible for attacks on England was Bombergeschwader 3, which was established specifically on the orders of General Ludendorff with the prime objective of bombing London. This was to be a dual effort to undermine the determination of the public (who produced severe criticism of Britain's defences and thought that further attacks were inevitable) – the other element was the increasing use of U-boats to attack shipping in the hope of cutting supplies to Britain.

Mounting Zeppelin losses led to the employment of heavier-than-air aircraft in the strategic bombing role. The twin-engined Gotha G.IVs of Kagohl 3 proved particularly successful in their attacks on England.

CHRONOLOGY

31 May 1915
Zeppelin L.38 made the first bombing raid on London, when bombs were dropped on Stoke Newington.

1 August 1915
The first victory by an aircraft fitted with a forward-firing gun, firing through the airscrew disc, was made by a German Fokker E.III monoplane over the Western Front.

12 August 1915
A Short 184 seaplane from the seaplane carrier HMS *Ben-My-Chree* operating in the Dardanelles made a torpedo attack on a Turkish merchant ship – claimed to be the first ship sunk by an air-launched torpedo.

1 September 1915
The 'Fokker scourge' began and lasted through the winter, as Fokker monoplane fighters with synchronised machine guns shot down large numbers of Allied aircraft.

Combat Report – Zeppelin engagement, 1 October 1916

Flying a BE2c, Second Lieutenant W. J. Tempest of No 39 Squadron RFC gave a personal account of the destruction of Zeppelin L.31, commanded by Kapitan Leutnant Heinrich Mathy.

"About 11.45pm I found myself over SW London at an altitude of 14,000ft. There was a heavy ground fog on and it was bitterly cold, otherwise the night was beautiful and starlit at the altitude at which I was flying. I was gazing overhead toward the N.E. of London, where the fog was not quite so heavy, when I noticed all the searchlights in that quarter concentrated in an enormous pyramid. Following them up to the apex, I saw a small cigar-shaped object, which I at once recognised as a Zeppelin, about 15 miles away and heading straight for London. Previous to this I had chased many imaginary Zeppelins, only to find they were clouds on nearing them."

"It appeared to me that the Zeppelin had sighted me, for she dropped all her bombs in one volley, swung round, tilted up her nose and proceeded to race northwards, climbing rapidly as she went. At the time of dropping the bombs I judged her to be at an altitude of 11,000ft. I made after her at full speed at about 15,000ft altitude, gradually overhauling her. At this period the A.A. fire was intense, and I, being about five miles behind the Zeppelin, had an uncomfortable time. At this point my mechanical pressure pump went wrong and I had to use my hand pump to keep up the pressure in my petrol tank. This exercise at so high an altitude was very exhausting, besides occupying an arm, thus giving me one hand less to operate with when I commenced to fire."

"As I drew up with the Zeppelin, to my relief I found that I was free from A.A.fire, for the nearest shells were bursting quite three miles away. The Zeppelin was now nearly 15,000ft high and mounting rapidly. I therefore decided to dive at her, for though I held a slight advantage in speed, she was climbing like a rocket and leaving me standing. I accordingly gave a tremendous pump to my petrol tank and dived straight at her, firing a burst into her as I came. I let her have another burst as I passed under her tail and flying

along underneath her, pumped lead into her for all I was worth. I could see tracer bullets flying from her in all directions, but I was too close under her for her to concentrate on me."

"As I was firing, I noticed her begin to go red inside like an enormous Chinese lantern, and then a flame shot out of the front part of her and I realised she was on fire. She then shot up about 200ft, paused, and came roaring down straight for me before I had time to get out of the way."

"I nosed-dived for all I was worth, with the Zepp tearing after me, and expected every minute to be engulfed in the flames. I put my machine into a spin and just managed to corkscrew out of

German Naval Zeppelin LZ53 leaving its hangar for a night attack on England. The biggest airship raid of WW1 was on the night of 2-3 September 1916, when 14 crossed the English coast.

the way as she shot past me roaring like a furnace. I righted my machine and watched her hit the ground with a shower of sparks."

"I glanced at my watch and saw that it was about ten minutes past twelve. I then commenced to feel very sick and giddy, and I had difficulty finding my way to the ground through fog and landing, in doing which I crashed and cut my head on my machine gun."

On 25 May 1917, the bombers were ready to attempt their part of the task, twenty-three Gotha IVs setting out for London. En route they encountered deteriorating weather conditions and were forced to turn back when they reached Gravesend. Bombs were dropped on Folkestone, and one Gotha was shot down by an RNAS aircraft.

Two weeks later, on 13 June, twenty aircraft set out and this time fourteen reached their objective, dropping 72 bombs on the City of London. The result was far-reaching in terms of public reaction, which now reached a pitch well beyond that provoked by the airship night raids. These attacks resulted in the setting-up of three day-fighter squadrons with Sopwith Camels and Pups, and the re-organisation of anti-aircraft guns and searchlights into a command known as the Home Defence Brigade.

The new defences forced the Germans to use the cover of darkness, the last daylight raid on London taking place on 7 July 1917. Gotha daylight raids had killed over 400 civilians and injured a further 878, for an expenditure of twenty tons of bombs. The night campaign commenced on 3 September 1917, with the Friedrichshafen G.III being joined by an even more formidable heavy bomber, the four-engined Zeppelin Staaken R.IV.

The Staaken R.VI had a wingspan of 138ft and was the largest aircraft of the war. Fortunately for the British, only 18 of the 'R-planes' were built. One of them, in a raid on 16 February 1918, dropped the first blockbuster (2,000lb) bomb, hitting the Royal Hospital in Chelsea and causing heavy casualties. From their bases around Ghent, it was a mere 170 miles to London. Just as the Allies were improving their bomber capability, so were the Germans.

The German night bombers, never more than fifty in number, were tying down as many as 800 British fighter aircraft – machines that were urgently needed in France. Hugh Trenchard fumed at the dispersion of his aircraft, but the British public was still not satisfied. Anti-aircraft defences were considerably increased, and a new balloon barrage on the northern and eastern perimeter of London was set up. However, the German night bombing was less effective and by the end of 1917, equilibrium was being approached once again.

The Staaken VGO.II was the first successful R-plane and the first in a long line of giant Staaken bombers.

EARLY FIREPOWER

The Morane Type L flown by Frenchman Roland Garros
was equipped with a machine gun on the nose and steel
deflector plates on the propeller to prevent the bullets
from shooting off the blades.

A Nieuport 27 of No 1 Squadron RFC, which featured a
fixed forward-firing 0.303in (7.7mm) Lewis gun mounted
on the top wing, firing clear of the propeller arc.

T he French pilot Lieutenant Roland Garros, flying a Morane-Saulnier Type L parasol-wing scout monoplane, shot down a German Albatros two-seater on 1 April 1915. This was achieved by the first use of a Hotchkiss machine-gun mounted to fire forward through the propeller arc. Some of the bullets were a little late in firing, so the rear of the propeller blades were protected by steel wedge deflectors. Two or three more German aircraft fell to his gun in the following 18 days. Unfortunately he was forced down behind enemy lines and captured before he could destroy it on 19 April, thus enabling German engineers to discover the secret of his forward-firing gun.

The idea of a synchronising gear, however, was not new as many countries had experimented with such devices before the war. The original inventor was Franz Schneider, chief designer for the German LVG company, who patented his gear in 1913. Around the same time Lieutenant Poplavko hit upon a similar idea in Russia, as did the Edward Brothers in England, but their designs were simply filed by officials and forgotten. When the war commenced Raymond Saulnier, of the French Morane-Saulnier concern, had to return to using Hotchkiss guns which he had borrowed from the French government, and further work on his device ceased.

Right: The Nieuport 11 Bébé was an early WW1 French design with an 80hp (60kW) Le Rhône rotary engine. It had a high rate of climb and manoeuvrability, and in 1915 helped the Allies to gain temporary air superiority. (The 1990s replica shown here was built in the Czech Republic).

Below right: The RFC's first dedicated fighting scout was the Airco DH.2 (this is a replica constructed in the 1970s), initially delivered to No 24 Squadron based at Hounslow, commanded by Major Lanoe Hawker VC, late in 1915.

CHRONOLOGY

5 November 1915
The first occasion that an aeroplane was catapulted from a moving ship, when a Curtiss AB-2 flying boat was launched from the battleship USS *North Carolina* at anchor in Pensacola Bay, Florida.

1 April 1916
The Japanese Naval Air Corps was formed.

20 April 1916
The Escadrille Américans was established as an American volunteer unit flying on the Western Front – later becoming the famed *Escadrille Lafayette*.

28 May 1916
The Sopwith Triplane single-seat fighter first flew and production commenced for the RNAS. It was a formidable opponent for German types until superseded by the Sopwith Camel and SE5.

30 May 1916
The first of the Super-Zeppelin airships, the L.30 powered by six engines, joined the German Navy. It made nine major raids on England.

31 May 1916
German warships were shadowed by RNAS Short Type 184 seaplanes launched from HMS *Engadine* before and during the Battle of Jutland.

17 June 1916
The prototype RE.8 tractor two-seat biplane made its maiden flight at the Royal Aircraft Factory at Farnborough, Hants.

1 July 1916
The Battle of the Somme commenced in France and both sides fought to gain air superiority. It was the first major land battle where aircraft made a significant difference to the progress of a large military offensive.

16 August 1916
First flight of the Zeppelin Staaken R.IV bomber, which was later used alongside Gothas for raids on targets in England.

The system which made machine-guns on fighters really effective was the interrupter gear, or gun synchronising gear, which enabled bullets to pass between the blades of a propeller. The main early use of the interrupter gear was by the Dutch designer Anthony Fokker, who produced the E.I Eindecker for the German Air Force. This feature put the type so far in advance of its contemporaries in 1915 that it almost shot the Allied air forces from the skies over France. Fokker had devised a simple cam-and-pushrod linkage between the oil-pump drive of the Oberursel rotary engine and the trigger of an ordinary belt-fed Parabellum or Spandau machine-gun. This linkage pulled the trigger once during every revolution of the propeller, giving an average rate of fire of 400 rounds per minute. The gun fired so that the bullets passed between the propeller blades.

Lt Max Immelmann (known as the 'Eagle of Lille') scored the first victory with the interrupter gear on 1 August 1915, when he forced down an RFC aircraft that was bombing Douai airfield. His Fokker E.I monoplane was not fast, but it was manoeuvrable and its

Scourge of the Fokkers

Dutch designer Anthony Fokker was only 25 years of age at the outbreak of war but the Germans, somewhat reluctantly, had to seek his services. In experiments with interrupter gear for machine guns, firing through the propeller arc, the Germans simply shot the propeller off. Fokker rejected the primitive deflection systems and directed his staff to create a synchronising system for the Parabellum machine gun to be mounted on his new Fokker M.5k monoplane.

The synchronising system developed by the Fokker team momentarily interrupted the fire of the machine gun wherever the propeller blades were in front of the muzzle – therefore no bullets could hit the blades. Eventually the Allies did develop their own device, but not before Fokker's device gave Germany a significant advantage.

Fokker's M.5k was derived from an earlier French Morane-Saulnier, both owing much to the original Bleriot XI. It had a 80hp Oberursel rotary engine, copied from the French Gnome, and a top speed of 82mph. This tiny single-seat monoplane with its wingspan of only 28ft immediately became a world-beater. Fifty were ordered by the German High Command for immediate delivery, to be known as E.I Eindeckers.

In the hands of aces such as Oswald Boelcke and Max Immelmann, the threat of the Eindeckers had become known as the 'Fokker Scourge' by mid-1915. They greatly affected not only the air war on the Western Front, but also the subsequent development of combat aircraft, and the heavy losses that they inflicted were profoundly unsettling to Allied airmen.

At first, opposition to the Fokkers was light, but improved designs were being developed. From Britain, the Royal Aircraft Factory FE2b, Vickers FB5 Gun Bus and de Havilland DH2 – all pusher types to obviate the need for a synchronised gear – were only a start. The French responded to the Fokker threat with the Nieuport 11, known as the Bébé, which was very manoeuvrable, had a speed of 97mph and was armed with a Lewis gun mounted on top of the wing for the bullets to clear the propeller disk. These aircraft helped to elimate the menace of the Eindecker.

Though not an exceptional aircraft in terms of performance or agility, the Fokker E.III achieved results by means of its unique synchronised machine-gun. The photograph shows a 1970s replica Eindecker.

synchronised gun gave it a considerable advantage over opposing Allied aircraft and unchallenged control of the skies. The E.Is achieved air superiority for Germany from mid-1915 to mid-1916 and earned a fearsome reputation. Immelmann became the leading exponent of aerial dogfighting and went on to claim a further 14 Allied aircraft.

It was not until 1917 that the British developed an interrupter gear superior to that of the Germans. This had a Constantinesco gear by which the guns were fired by means of impulses transmitted through a column of liquid contained under pressure in a pipe. Using this system, no propeller blade was hit by bullets and, by overcoming the unreliability of mechanical gears, it was easily adaptable to many types of engine.

Immelmann and his compatriot Oswald Boelcke, another German Army Air Service ace, both showed a particular facility in handling the new system. They often flew together, displaying an uncanny co-ordination. For their leadership in clearing the skies of Allied aircraft, both were awarded the *Ordre Pour de Merite* – a medal that became known as the 'Blue Max' (after Immelmann), Germany's highest honour of the period. Both were killed in flying accidents in 1916.

The Allies had ample opportunity to copy the mechanism from captured Eindeckers, but for reasons still unknown this was not attempted. To give the RFC

Right: The British Lewis gun gave aircraft gunners lethal range and flexibility, but they were at the mercy of any sudden manoeuvring by the pilot.

The Sopwith 1½ Strutter was the first RFC/RNAS fighter to be provided with a machine gun synchronised to fire through a tractor propeller. With a gunner in addition to the pilot, it became the first British operational two-seat fighting scout and created a design formula that was to survive in the RFC (and subsequently the RAF) for more than a quarter of a century.

pilot the same facility with a forward-shooting gun that the Germans had, it was necessary to use either pusher aircraft (with the propeller at the rear) that could perform as well as a tractor aircraft (which were almost universal by 1915), or to site the gun on the top wing out of the propeller's arc. By 1916 the synchronised forward-shooting Vickers machine gun was introduced, transforming the fighting ability of the Sopwith Pups and Camels, together with the Nieuport 17, SPAD VII and XIII, and later the Royal Aircraft Factory SE5 and SE5a.

Despite the introduction of the new aircraft and the clear ascendancy over the German Army Air Service enjoyed by the Allies during 1916, it was not a happy time for British and French pilots and observers. The ground battles at Verdun and the Somme had required Allied aircrews to operate offensive patrols at full stretch over these two sectors for many months. Anti-aircraft fire, or 'Archie' as it was referred to by the RFC, was a constant inducement for fliers to keep as high as possible.

The RFC was so desperately short of aircraft during the Battle of the Somme that it appealed to the RNAS for help. The Admiralty agreed to part with large numbers of its invaluable Sopwith 1½-Strutters, which surprised the Germans when they discovered, to their cost, that it was the first two-seater with a synchronised front gun as well as the observer's gun.

AERIAL COMBAT

The main architect of aggressive policy by the Royal Flying Corps was General Hugh Trenchard, who since the beginning of the war had been a senior staff officer, but who subsequently became commander of the RFC in France. The Allied air forces had been reorganised into observation, bombing and reconnaissance units, and to these had also been added a fourth section – chase, hunting or fighting. Trenchard was determinedly offensive-minded, and insisted that the battle must be carried to the enemy. He wanted bigger squadrons, as well as more of them, and he gradually built up to totals of 18 aircraft per squadron. He rigidly adhered to his policy that the aircraft fly all the time, that losses be immediately replaced, and that there be no flagging.

By 1917 the Nieuports, DH2s and SPADS had mastered the Fokker Eindecker, but both sides had much more sophistication than they possessed earlier in the war, and were still fighting for mastery of the air. By early 1917 the German Albatros and Fokker Dr.1 Triplane fighters appeared, and during that year air fighting and the aces reached their zenith. The British fielded the Sopwith Triplane and Camel, soon followed by the Royal Aircraft Factory's SE5. The French had upgraded their Nieuports and SPADS. At the end of 1917 the German Jastas were equipped with Albatros D.I and then the D.II biplanes with in-line

The Sopwith Camel, arguably the finest British fighter of WW1, was a tricky and temperamental little aircraft to fly for a novice pilot, but it was unequalled in agility and overcame its lack of speed with this vital asset. This replica Camel is flying in the colours and markings typical of the 1917 period.

Left: In 1917, in an attempt to counter the improved performance of Allied fighters, Albatross initiated the development of the D.V and D.Va. Their widespread use was an attempt to overcome the enemy by sheer numbers rather than capability. However, they suffered heavy losses, not only from combat, but also as a result of being prone to structural failure of the lower wings. Illustrated here is an American-built replica.

Below: A British-built Nieuport 17 replica in RFC colour scheme. The Lewis gun mounted on top of the wing had a sliding mount, enabling it to be pulled down by the pilot and aimed upwards to make it possible to attack an enemy aircraft from below. The Nieuport rapidly made a name for itself and was the type flown by many WW1 aces.

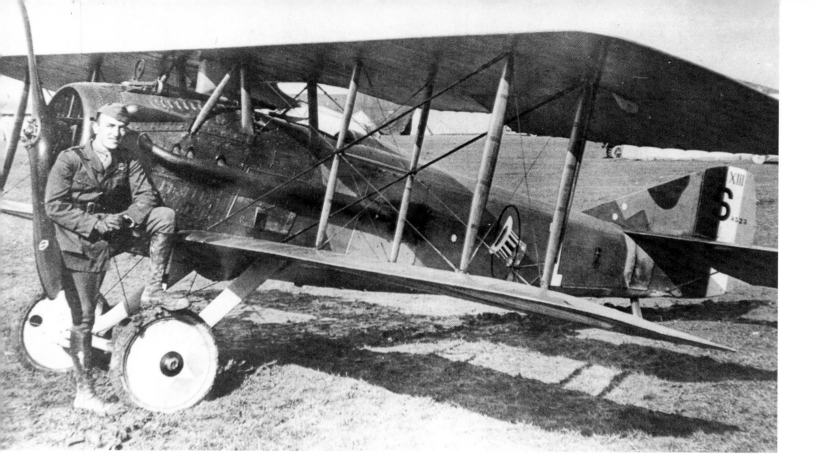

engines that provided stronger, better platforms for their two machine guns which gave them twice the firepower of Allied types. The Germans introduced new tactics – the swarm of fighters, the careful stalk for position and the approach from the sun.

The French tended to group all their best pilots into elite squadrons. Trenchard considered this strategy unwise, as it left the majority of the squadrons to cope with mediocre and poor pilots. Instead, he tended to build up each fighter unit round a few pilots of excellent capabilities in the hope and expectation that their skills would rub off on the other pilots – a system which in fact proved the most satisfactory of all.

By the 'Bloody April' of 1917, air combats had grown into massive affairs of up to 100 aircraft or more – a far cry from the individual combats of 1915 and early 1916. With the introduction of the SE5a, a higher-powered variant with two-gun armament, this then equalled the firepower of German types. The SE5a was soon joined by the French SPADS.XIII – an improved version of the S.VII, which also had more power and two guns. Phasing-in of the Sopwith Camel, a supremely agile aircraft, also provided the RFC with another twin-gun fighter.

A fourth type to end German dominance of the air was the Bristol F2b Fighter, which also entered service in 1917. With the performance and agility of a single-seater, the F2b was a formidable weapon with synchronised guns firing forward and a gun for the observer in the rear cockpit for defence. The Germans also continued to strive for improved aircraft. New versions of the Albatros arrived in 1918 – the D.V and D.Va – both of which had improved aerodynamics and a more powerful engine, but this fighter proved incapable of wresting from the Allies the superiority they enjoyed by the summer of 1917. The Fokker D.VII biplane and D.VIII parasol monoplane, both with excellent flying qualities, did not reach front-line service until very late in the war.

This was the era of great dogfights, and was also the period of WW1 when the first combat squadrons of the US Air Service began to see action, flying side-by-side with the weary French and British air forces. However, neither side won a final, clear-cut victory in the air over the Western Front.

Captain Eddie Rickenbacker, seen here with a SPAD XIII, was the top American ace of WW1, with 26 victories. He became a Commander of the 24th Aero Squadron, American Expeditionary Force.

CHRONOLOGY

16 August 1916
The Airco (de Havilland) DH4 day bomber first flew.

29 August 1916
The US Naval Flying Corps was formed, and preparations made for the deployment of naval aviation forces in operational roles, when needed.

9 September 1916
First flight of the Bristol F2a two-seater, which entered service on the Western Front in April 1917.

15 September 1916
The third phase of the Battle of the Somme opened, with waves of British and French ground attack and bombing flights over enemy lines.

21 November 1916
The French Breguet 14 bomber first flew. It was to become one of the most effective bombers of WW1.

28 November 1916
The first aeroplane raid on London was made by a German naval LVG C.II, six bombs being dropped on Victoria station in broad daylight.

AIR SUPERIORITY

The Allies wrested air supremacy from the Germans once and for all in the autumn of 1917, when a series of improved aircraft – some often dangerous to fly – reached the front. The Sopwith Camel was to kill more Germans than any other fighter. Another newcomer to service was the Royal Aircraft Factory SE5a, a conservative-looking fighter that pilots loved because of its forgiving flying qualities and stability as a gun platform. The Bristol F2b Fighter was coming into service and became one of the most effective weapons of the war, while the French-built SPAD XIII, which out-powered the SPAD VII, was good but, because of engine problems, was far less reliable.

Meanwhile, Fokker introduced the Dr.1. As agile as the Sopwith Camel, the Dr.1 Dreidecker (Triplane) arrived in relatively small numbers and served for only a year, but it rehabilitated Fokker's image as a fighter producer and led to the Fokker D.VII – an aircraft which represented a true departure from all previous aircraft designs of WW1 and which set

Right: The Sopwith Snipe was designed around the new Bentley rotary engine, and was intended as the ultimate successor to the Camel. Only 100 Snipes reached France before the Armistice.

Below: The Fokker Dr.I, conceived as a response to the Sopwith Triplane, was one of the most agile combat aircraft in history. Flown by such accomplished airmen as Manfred von Richthofen, they shot down many times their own number of enemy aircraft on the Western Front. The photograph shows a replica Fokker Dr.I.

Flying WW1 Aircraft

Piloting most aircraft of the 1914-1918 period was very demanding for a variety of reasons. Even at best, flying training was very limited by modern standards.

Pilots were generally able to fly anything with wings immediately, without specialised training, and yet the aircraft were more demanding than modern ones, because they required constant attention. Few machines had any trim devices at all, so control pressures varied continuously with variations in power and airspeed.

The German Gotha bombers were so tail-heavy that pilots became fatigued and often 'lost it' when trying to land. Rotary engines could be deadly on take-off and they demanded careful handling at all times. The Sopwith Camel, with its tremendous torque and a tendency for its engine to cut out, killed many unwary students during the climb-out.

However, some were delightful to fly. Those who flew the original Sopwith Pups agreed that it was a viceless aircraft. The Royal Aircraft Factory SE5a and Bristol Fighter also had good reputations, as did the Fokker D.VII.

The worst to fly were those types whose structural

capabilities always threatened the pilot and thus inhibited his capabilities to fight. The lower wing of the Albatros fighters could easily twist away in a dive, while Nieuport 28s had the habit of shedding the fabric on their upper wing surfaces.

The Fokker Dr.1 triplane (and later the D.VIII) suffered from quality control problems that caused the wings to

The Fokker D.VIII resulted from a fighter competition held in April 1918. Its performance was so impressive that it was put into immediate production. A British-built replica is shown here.

collapse in flight. Even the SPAD XIII, a type flown by most American pilots, had insoluble engine maladies and a poor glide angle, and many accidents resulted.

The Breguet XIV (illustrated here by a French-built replica) was perhaps the most famous French warplane of all time, and 5,300 examples were built up to December 1918. The pilot and observer/gunner were seated close together in open tandem cockpits.

the standard for the next decade of aircraft development. The D.VII became the standard fighter of the German squadrons for the last months of the war. It was the only aircraft specified by name in the Armistice Agreement to be turned over to the victorious Allies. As fine a fighter as it was though, the Fokker D.VII could do little to turn the aerial tide that crested over Germany's armed forces.

It was closely matched on the Allied side by the SE5a, the Sopwith Dolphin and Snipe and the prospect of the Nieuport 29 from the French. The German bombers (particularly Gothas) had become notorious, but the English equivalents – the majestic Handley Page HP 0/100 and 0/400 – were better aircraft. The Italians had success with the Caproni bomber and the excellent Ansaldo series of fighters and reconnaissance aircraft.

With the two-seaters, there was remarkable and often unremarked-upon successes, particularly by the Germans. The Albatros two-seaters were almost uniformly successful, as were the AEGs, DFWs, LFGs and LVGs. The French produced a number of excellent two-seaters, including the Breguet XIV, which sired a generation of able descendants; the Salmson II, an aircraft much-welcomed by American units; and the Caudron R.11, an elegant multi-place twin-engined aircraft.

When the Germans needed an armed reconnaissance
aircraft in 1915, LVG responded with the C.VI, which
entered service in 1918. Powered by a Benz IV engine,
armament was one forward-firing 0.31in (7.9mm) LMG
08/15 machine gun and a Parabellum gun in the rear
cockpit, and up to 243lb (110kg) of bombs. This original
airworthy LVG C.VI is preserved with the Shuttleworth
Collection at Old Warden.

AIRCRAFT AT SEA

By far the greater proportion of the RNAS effort in WW1 was by seaplanes or flying boats at coastal air stations, or landplanes at shore bases. The aircraft carrier as we know it today did not make its appearance until the closing phases of the war, evolving by gradual stages from the early seaplane carrier which originally had no take-off facilities – the aircraft being hoisted over the side to take off from the sea.

The early seaplane carriers were of limited value, as they were handicapped by their inability to keep station with the Fleet. They had to stop when hoisting their seaplanes aboard, and the seaplanes themselves could operate in only the calmest of waters because of the fragility of their floats. Following the Battle of Jutland in 1916, and the operational shortcomings it exposed, it was apparent that aircraft should be sent to sea as soon as possible. A Grand Fleet Aircraft Committee was formed to source a suitably fast large vessel, which could be requisitioned and then converted into an aircraft carrier.

HMS *Furious*, laid down shortly after the outbreak of war, was in the process of being built as a battle cruiser, but its 18in front gun turret was removed to facilitate a hangar and the flight-deck on the forecastle. This became the first warship to be built as an aircraft carrier for landplane operations, being launched on 15 August 1916. With a speed of 31kt she carried six Sopwith Pups in addition to four seaplanes.

Still, though, the problem remained of getting an aircraft back on to the ship, and, prior to developing techniques for landing Sopwith Pups on *Furious's* original deck, Squadron Commander E. H. Dunning was appointed test pilot. Flying his Pup on 2 August 1917, Dunning took up a position forward and starboard off *Furious*, which steamed at 26kt into a 21kt headwind. Side-slipping the Pup over the deck planking, he made an attempt to land while ratings on deck grabbed at straps on the fighter to bring it to rest, this being the first ever landing by an aircraft on a ship underway. On 17 August he tried again in even stronger winds, overshot, stalled, and was killed when his aircraft was blown over the side of the ship.

The first successful landing on a ship underway, when Sqn Cdr E. H. Dunning touched down in his Sopwith Pup on the deck of HMS *Furious* on 2 August 1917.

16 February 1917
First flight of the Fairey Campania, the first aircraft in the world to be designed and built specifically for operation from seaplane carriers at sea.

February 1917
The Junkers J4 armoured close-support biplane made its first flight, featuring corrugated duralumin skimming.

1 March 1917
The first production SE5 single-seat fighter was flown at the Royal Aircraft Factory, Farnborough.

1 March 1917
Approval was given to convert the battle-cruiser HMS *Furious* into an aircraft carrier.

6 March 1917
No 55 Squadron, RFC received the first aircraft fitted with the new Constantinesco machine gun with synchronisation gear.

21 March 1917
No 100 Squadron RFC was formed, the first to go to France specifically for night bombing operations.

4 April 1917
The British Air Offensive on the Western Front began, five days before the land engagement in the Battle of Arras.

30 April 1917
In what became known as 'Bloody April', the RFC lost 139 aircraft in combat, more than in any other month of the war; the Germans lost 72 aircraft and the French (who were less involved) lost 33.

25 May 1917
The first large daylight raid by enemy aircraft when 21 German Gotha G.IVs attacked targets in Kent.

28 May 1917
The U-36 was attacked by an RNAS Curtiss H.12, becoming the first German submarine to be sunk by an aeroplane.

5 June 1917
The US Army's First Aeronautic Detachment arrived in France and began training on Caudron biplanes.

13 June 1917
Fourteen Gothas made the first heavy daylight aircraft raid on London, causing many casualties.

July 1917
The Airco DH9 bomber made its maiden flight, an aircraft designed to carry heavier loads over greater distances than the DH4, although it was not a great success in its intended role.

26 July 1917
Formation of the German 'Flying Circus' under the command of Manfred von Richthofen.

The comparatively low speeds of aircraft at the time meant that take-off from a moving ship was not difficult. With the airstream provided by a vessel steaming into a strong wind, a small and lightly-loaded biplane could almost float off the deck. However, from the naval point of view, the need to steam into wind to launch an aircraft meant that, at a critical moment, it might be necessary for a ship to break station. This brought a suggestion that if some form of turntable could be provided it might be possible for an aircraft to take off into wind, independently of the ship's heading. Such discussion led to the provision of a short rotating platform over a gun turret, and this was first tested in June 1917 when Squadron Commander F. J. Rutland successfully took off from HMS *Yarmouth* in a Sopwith Pup.

On 1 October 1917 the same officer repeated his success by flying a Pup off a platform superimposed on the 15in gun turret of the battleship *Repulse*. The platform could be turned into wind without the ship altering course, and during take-off was in fact at an angle of 45° from the bow. Later experiments took place in April 1918 when the practice was extended to a two-seater aircraft, a Sopwith 1½ Strutter being flown off a turret platform aboard HMAS *Australia*. By the end of the war over 100 aircraft were being carried in this way by ships of the Grand Fleet. The first flight from a gun platform on an US battleship was made by US Navy Lieutenant Commander E.O. McDonnell in a Sopwith Camel, flying from the USS *Texas* anchored in Guantánamo Bay, Cuba on 9 March 1919. This success led to the installation of similar platforms on a large number of battleships and large cruisers.

However, unless the ship was near land there was nothing but the sea upon which an aircraft could alight. The death of Dunning brought landing-on experiments to an end for a few months, but his attempts had shown that the concept was realistic. This led to the development of practical aircraft carriers, a weapon that was to prove of decisive importance in the years ahead.

Another method of using aircraft at sea was the towed lighter. These were designed to be

A Sopwith Camel is prepared for take off from a towed lighter underway. This method provided some capital warships with the capability for aircraft operation. The 2F.1 Camel was developed essentially for naval use with seaborne forces.

towed behind a destroyer, measuring 58ft in length and 16ft wide and could reach 21kt without throwing up sheets of spray. Initially used to convey large flying-boats across the North Sea so as to increase their radius of action over the Heligoland Bight area, eventually in 1918 it was discovered that they could also be used with 30ft-long take-off platforms for launching single-seat fighters. The first successful take-off, using a Sopwith 2F.1 Camel, was by Lieutenant Stuart D. Culley on 31 July 1918, who a few days later destroyed the Zeppelin L.53 (LZ100), having flown off such a vessel.

Dunning's earlier experimentation led to the provision of a 284ft long flying-on deck on *Furious*, aft of the superstructure. This deck was fitted with an early form of arrester gear comprised of longitudinal wires and transverse ropes weighted with sandbags. There was also a rope crash-barrier to protect the superstructure, and the wires were engaged by spring-clip hooks on the aeroplane's axle and a further hook engaged the transverse ropes. The system was not particularly successful, owing to eddies and hot-air currents set up by the funnel and superstructure, which led to *Furious* eventually having a flush deck extending from bow to stern. Nevertheless, *Furious* was able to claim to have been the only carrier in WW1 to have launched a major air action when, on 19 July 1918, seven Sopwith Camels flown off its deck made a successful attack on the Zeppelin base at Tondern, destroying L.54 and L.60.

Above: A Sopwith Pup piloted by Sqn Cdr Rutland gets airborne over the 15in guns of the battlecruiser HMS *Repulse* on 7 October 1917. The flying-off platform seen here was an experimental downward-sloping ramp mounted on the warship's 'B' turret.

This Sopwith Pup came to grief whilst attempting a landing aboard HMS *Furious*. Pups were fitted with a sprung-skid undercarriage for carrier landings.

BIRTH OF THE ROYAL AIR FORCE

Above: The Handley Page V/1500, the largest British bomber of WW1, and the first with four engines, was designed to bring Berlin within range of RAF bases in East Anglia.

Opposite page: A line-up of No 85 Squadron's SE.5As in France in April 1918. The famed RFC unit flew the type under the command of Colonel 'Billy' Bishop and Major 'Mick' Mannock, both holders of the Victoria Cross.

The Royal Air Force was born at a time when the Germans had already launched the first of their great offensives, and when the western front was reeling and wide open as it had not been since 1914. Both the RFC and RNAS had performed well since the outbreak of WW1 and neither saw the need for amalgamation and a new air arm, but there were considerable elements of political horsetrading behind it – especially as the scheme had its origins in the German bomber campaign of 1917, and the unremitting pressure that the newspapers put on the government because of it.

Following a report to the War Cabinet by General Jan Smuts which favoured the amalgamation into one Royal Air Force, that would then be able to operate independently as an equal with the other services, the service chiefs of both the Army and Royal Navy gave the plan their guarded approval. Both Lloyd George and Winston Churchill (now back in the cabinet as Minister of Munitions) were in favour of the amalgamation. Trenchard was brought home from France and appointed as Chief of the Air Staff. The new Royal Air Force was officially born on 1 April 1918.

The Gotha raids of 1917 had not only triggered the eventual separate air force, but they had also brought the question of a British bombing of Germany to the table. Trenchard was subsequently offered command of the bombing effort, to be known as the Independent Air Force. It had four squadrons when Trenchard arrived and eventually worked up to nine (five

The Bristol F.2b Fighter, known affectionately as the 'Brisfit', became one of the mainstays of the RAF in its formative years. As soon as pilots began to adopt single-seater tactics, using the forward-firing Vickers gun as the main offensive armament, the F.2b became one of the most effective fighters of WW1.

night and four day) – but that was hardly an overwhelming force with which to take on industrial Germany.

Bombing did not play much of a role in WW1, though attempts to build aircraft capable of carrying substantial loads did advance aviation technology, particularly in 1918. In retaliation for the desperate German bombing of Paris and London, the British developed their largest aircraft of the war – the Handley Page 0/100, known as the 'Bloody Paralyser'. It could carry over a ton of bombs, including a single bomb of 1,650lb (748kg) that could devastate an entire factory.

Nearly 100 of these Handley Pages eventually became available, and these were used for both day and night operations against German targets. They struck at night against cities along the Rhine and in six months of operations they dropped over 600 tonnes of bombs,

1 April 1918
The Royal Air Force was formed by the amalgamation of the RFC and RNAS.

1 April 1918
The best German fighter of WW1, the Fokker D.VII biplane, entered service on the Western Front.

5 June 1918
The Independent Air Force was set up for the strategic bombing of Germany.

6 June 1918
The Fairey IIIA two-seat naval light bomber made its maiden flight.

1 July 1918
Zeppelin L.70, the first of a planned new class for the German Navy, made its first flight at Friedrichshafen. It had a top speed of 81mph and was the fastest of all Zeppelin's wartime airships.

1 August 1918
The British North Russian Expeditionary Force, including air units, arrived at Archangel with Fairey Campania seaplanes aboard HMS *Nairana*. They were to be employed against Bolshevik forces.

5 August 1918
During the last airship raid on Britain a German Navy Zeppelin (L.70) was destroyed by fighters.

8 August 1918
A continuous day and night bombing offensive was mounted by the RAF over the Western Front, in support of the Allied efforts to cut off the German retreat from France.

September 1918
RAF aircraft in the Palestine campaign attacked and destroyed the retreating Turkish Seventh Army at Wadi el Far'a.

14 September 1918
Forty Handley Page 0/400 heavy bombers attacked German targets using new 1,650lb (748kg) bombs.

4 October 1918
The Curtiss NC-1 flying boat, a US Navy anti-submarine aircraft powered by three (and later four) Liberty tractor engines, made its first flight.

12 October 1918
The first US night operations in France were flown by the 185th Aero (Pursuit) Squadron.

10 November 1918
The last major raid of WW1 was carried out by the Independent Air Force by No 55 Squadron, RAF when eleven DH4s attacked railway sidings near Cologne.

11 November 1918
The Armistice ends WW1 at the eleventh hour of the eleventh day of the eleventh month.

mostly high explosives and some incendiaries. The de Havilland DH9 squadrons, operating in daylight, suffered brutally heavy losses, but it was light bombers that played an important part in land operations during the closing stages of the war.

Britain's first four-engined bomber, the Handley Page V/1500, was a larger development of the 0/400 and was meant to be able to reach Berlin from bases in East Anglia. Able to carry three tons of bombs for 1,200 miles, only three of the great bombers were ready for service, and they never did bomb Germany. The 'Bloody Paralyser' remained the Independent Air Force's standard equipment, and forty of the type took part in the largest 'strategic' raid of the war in September 1918, when the Saar area was bombed from bases near Nancy.

The Armistice was signed on 11 November 1918, and it would be another 22 years before strategic bombing of Germany occurred again.

BETWEEN THE WARS
1919–1939

Fairey Flycatcher

TRANSATLANTIC NON-STOP

The Vickers Vimy taking off from Newfoundland on 14 June 1919 at the beginning of Alcock and Brown's historic flight to County Galway, Ireland – the first direct Atlantic flight. The aircraft is currently exhibited in the Science Museum in South Kensington, London.

The first non-stop crossing of the North Atlantic, from west to east, was achieved in a Vickers Vimy with extra fuel tanks, flown by two ex-RAF officers, Captain John Alcock and Lieutenant Arthur Whitten Brown. Flown between Lester's Field, near St John's, Newfoundland and Clifden, County Galway, Ireland on 14-15 June 1919, the total flying time for the 1,890 mile (3,034km) journey was 16hr 27min, at an average speed of 121mph (195km/h). The following day, the first mail to cross the Atlantic by air was delivered in London after being transferred to England by boat. The two men encountered appalling weather conditions and fought against the most unexpected odds. It was also a test of endurance for the Vimy and its two Rolls-Royce Eagle engines. Six times Brown had to climb out on to the wings to attend to the engines. Alcock related the trip thus:

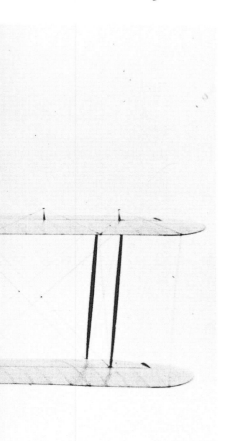

"After gaining height over Newfoundland, we set the Vimy on course for Ireland over St John's where we crossed the coast at Conception Bay at 16.27hr GMT. The weather was excellent and the Vimy slowly gained height. Despite the pain of his crippled legs, Brown took frequent sun sights and drift measurements, which involved a lot of movement. No sooner had the Vimy entered a thick bank of fog, than the radio transmitter went out of service because the propeller of the wing-generator had sheared off."

"At about 18.00hr the starboard engine suddenly began to sound sick. A section of the inner exhaust pipe was splitting away from the engine casing and vibrating in the wind. Flames were belching out and were blown backwards in a long fiery streamer by the wind. The noise prevented any conversation."

"We then discovered our only source of artificial warmth, electrically heated waistcoats, were useless because the battery to power them had failed. We faced the daunting prospect of a night to be spent at a height of more than 5,000ft in an open cockpit."

"Shortly after 03.00hr on the 15th, the Vimy flew into an electrical storm, so violent that the aircraft was thrown out of control and spiralled towards the ocean with engines racing. When we came out of cloud, dangerously near the water, the aircraft was in a steep bank. Only by a miracle was I able to avert disaster and start climbing again."

"The engine air intakes began to get clogged up with snow and ice as we entered a second storm of torrential rain. Brown, realising that only he could remedy the situation, clambered out onto the port wing. Five more times Brown had to climb out onto wings to clear ice from the air intakes and engine dials, mounted on the inside of the nacelles. On at least two occasions, Brown made what he thought would be a last entry into the flight log and stuffed it into his shirt,

CHRONOLOGY

2 January 1919
An RAF DH9, fitted with the first production Napier Lion engine, flew to a record height of 30,500ft.

1 April 1919
Imperial Japanese Army Air Division established.

23 May 1919
Immediately after the German Navy scuttled its fleet at Scapa Flow, technicians at the German Navy airship bases of Nordholz and Wittmundhaven destroyed seven front-line airships, almost all that remained of their Zeppelin fleet.

28 June 1919
Treaty of Versailles forbade Germany from supporting any military air forces and called for the destruction of all air material.

29 September 1919
A fully integrated air force was formed in Poland – the Polskie Wojska Lotnicze, which included volunteer US Army Air Service pilots.

January 1920
The RAF dispatched a squadron of DH9A bombers to British Somaliland as the 'main instrument and actor' in the overthrow of the 'Mad Mullah'.

1 February 1920
Emanating from the squadron which had been attached to the RFC in WW1, the Suid Afrikaanse Lugmac was formed as the South African air arm.

20 August 1920
Prototype Fairey IIID, developed as a general purpose land or floatplane, made its first flight at Hamble, initially powered by a Rolls-Royce Eagle engine.

6 June 1920
The US Army Reorganisation Act made the Air Service a combatant arm of the US Army – deferring hopes of an independent air arm similar to the RAF.

22 June 1920
A Sopwith Pup became the first aircraft to successfully take off from the deck of a Japanese ship underway, from the seaplane carrier *Wakamiya*.

19 July 1920
Airship R80, designed by Barnes Wallis as the first streamlined British airship and the last to be planned during WW1, made its maiden flight.

October 1920
The first trans-Canada proving flight of 3,265 miles in a flying time of 45 hours was completed by a Canadian Air Force Fairey seaplane.

1 April 1921
Royal Australian Air Force formed, created out of the Australian Air Corps.

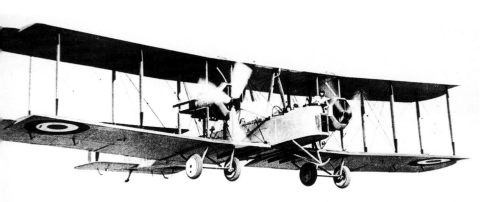

Vimy IVs of No 216 Squadron in Egypt operated some of the mail services between Cairo and Baghdad until August 1926. A direct development of the Vimy was the Vickers Virginia (opposite), represented here by a Virginia X flying in the markings of No 500 Squadron based at RAF Manston.

hoping his experience would be of use to later aviators if his body was ever found. Meanwhile, ice was making enormous difficulties for me. The ailerons were becoming iced up, making lateral control impossible, and the other controls became very heavy."

"Then came the first light of dawn in the sky ahead, and with it the realisation that we had probably faced the worst of our trials. One question remained – how good had been the navigation of Brown?"

"Certainly it was good enough, for just before 08.30 we could see land ahead. In fact it was remarkable, for despite our problems we crossed the Irish coastline only a few miles north of our intended track. The clouds were low and the terrain ahead was hilly and I thought it would be folly to fly on. Then came the anti-climax, our landing at 08.40 being in a peat bog, rather than on the smooth green meadow we had thought it to be. This was the Derrygimla Bog, at Clifden, County Galway. Although the Vimy was badly damaged, as we had removed the front landing gear before the flight we were both uninjured."

One more milestone in aviation's progress had been reached. Both men were rewarded with a Knighthood for their gallantry, and the Daily Mail prize of £10,000. Tragically, Alcock was killed in an accident when flying over France on 19 December 1919.

Airship Challenge

The first airship crossing of the North Atlantic was made by the British R-34, between East Fortune, Scotland and New York during 2-6 July 1919.

Having arrived at Mineola, Long Island, with 30 crew members aboard, it then completed the first double crossing by returning to Pulham, Norfolk (to where it was diverted), between 9-13 July – little more than 75hr later, assisted by the prevailing winds, after a trouble-free flight.

Post-war, when thoughts turned to commercial aviation, it seemed that airships might yet have a role, and that Britain might realise Count Zeppelin's dream of passenger-carrying airships circling the globe. To some people the arguments were conclusive – airships took longer, but aeroplanes had shorter ranges and were noisy and draughty. Airships combined the luxury of an ocean liner with a little more speed and they could operate directly between the great population centres of the world, either inland or on the coast. In 1919 the airship appeared to have a bright future.

The R-34, commanded by Major G H Scott, RAF had

70 tanks with 5,880gal of fuel, in addition to 2,760gal of oil and three tons of water. Construction of the R-33 and R-34 was based on data gathered from the German Navy Zeppelin L.33 (LZ.76) which, damaged by gunfire, had been forced down virtually intact in Essex on 24 September 1916. R-33 was built by Armstrong Whitworth

and R-34 by William Beardmore and Company during the latter stages of WW1. Both were 'normal' metal ships, with a length of 643ft and diameter of 76ft, which gave this class a capacity of 1,950,000cu ft in nineteen gas-bags. Powered by five 240hp Sunbeam Maori 4 engines, their maximum speed was 62mph,

with a disposable lift of 26 tons.

R-34 commenced its trials at Inchinnan on 14 March 1919, and the Royal Navy accepted it in late May 1919, when it was flown to the East Fortune base. In company with R-29, it took part in a six-hour flight around the Firth of Forth in June. This was followed by a 56-hour

In July 1919, the British airship R34 flew from East Fortune, Scotland to Long Island, New York before completing a successful return trip to Pulham in Norfolk. As a result, R34 had achieved the first east-west crossing, the first successful airship crossing and the first return crossing of the Atlantic.

flight around the Baltic coast of northern Germany, fully armed, as part of a series of measures to 'persuade' the German Government to sign a peace treaty. This flight augured well for the Atlantic crossing.

The outward flight to the USA took 108hr 12min and the crew were treated like royalty. Moored to a three-wire system for three days, some anxious moments arose and when the mooring rope nearly broke on the 8th, Captain Scott decided to leave the next day.

Returning to East Fortune, R-34 underwent a refit before returning to Pulham in February 1920. It was permanently assigned to Howden the following month, and modified to take a mooring mast attachment, but this was never fitted. In January 1921, R-34 was damaged beyond repair after it had struck a hill in fog and was broken up – a sad end for an excellent airship that had flown over 400 hours.

SILVER WINGS OF MERCY

T he link between the RAF and humanitarian relief has always been strong, and among the occasions on which the air arm has participated in this role to particularly vital effect was during the siege of the ancient capital of Afghanistan, Kabul, in the winter of 1928-29.

British influence in the Middle East grew out of an Empire which, in that part of the world, was already on the wane by the beginning of this century. After WW1, local tribesmen sought greater powers of control, even autonomy, over disparate groups populating the region. To maintain control, the British Government sought ways to suppress insurrection and terrorist activity, planning to use troops in a policing role. Fortunately for the future of the nascent RAF, post-WW1 demobilisation left the Army pitifully short of the manpower essential for the occupation of such large territories. The geographical area of Iran, Iraq and Afghanistan was more than ten times that of the British Isles.

Immediately after the war the Chief of the Air Staff insisted that the RAF should have a global role and argued against reducing the RAF to a token force, which had been the intention of many in high places. Sir Hugh Trenchard spoke for a reduced RAF bearing greater global responsibility for Britain's interests. Trenchard knew that the way to consolidate the future of the RAF was to abandon claims for peacetime expansion, which a war-weary British public would not tolerate, and transfer the onus for growth to politicians.

In proposing that the RAF take responsibility for policing these regions, Trenchard gave the Government an economic and manageable means of extending its influence against objections from the Army and the Navy. So it was that the RAF received a boost, without expansion, and gained its remit to police the Empire the best way it could with some ageing aircraft.

It was a daunting task and one few relished. Using WW1 aircraft, and with little prospect of new equipment, the RAF was asked to take charge of regions devoid of local government and intentionally-recognised boundaries, to police frontiers hotly contested by local tribes and militia, oblivious to the influence or interests of the British. As for aircraft, squadrons were to be equipped with Bristol F2b Fighters, and de Havilland DH9 and DH9A bombers. Larger types such as the troop-carrying Vickers Vernon, its successor the Victoria, and the Vickers Virginia (a descendant of the wartime Vimy) were also in service.

Following a brief operation in Somaliland during 1919, it was to Mesopotamia (Iraq) in 1920 that the RAF first went on a permanent policing role. Trenchard worked out that one

Above: A Vickers Vernon ambulance over Iraq in 1926. Sick soldiers could be evacuated to base hospitals in Baghdad in a matter of hours, saving many days of uncomfortable travel by surface transport that would otherwise have been involved.

bomber squadron could do the work of 1,500 men on the ground and proved his point in December 1919 with 12 DH9s of 'Z-force'. Several months later, a pitifully small force of less than 24 aircraft in two squadrons, covering an area exceeding two million square kilometres, was supplemented by a third squadron equipped with DH9As brought across from Ramleh in Palestine.

With territory so vast and unmapped, navigation was a real problem. On cloudy nights flying was almost impossible. Gone were the railway lines, rivers, lakes, towns and cities by which pilots would navigate their way across Britain and continental Europe, yet communication across these vast distances was essential. By the end of 1920, two more squadrons had been assigned duty in Iraq and in June 1921, DH9As began a routine mail service between Cairo and Baghdad.

Aircraft and engine reliability was crucial at all times despite the challenges presented by desert flying in hot conditions. The RAF's role in the Middle East was reinforced by decisions made at the Cairo Conference of 1921 to reinforce Britain's air presence in the

The original Handley Page Hinaidi, doped aluminium for tropical service, at Risalpur in January 1929 during the relief of the British Legation at Kabul.

CHRONOLOGY

20 October 1922
RAF aircraft were sent to the Dardanelles to face the Turks in the Chanak crisis.

28 November 1922
The Fairey Flycatcher – the first naval aircraft to be built to withstand catapult launches – made its first flight.

9 January 1923
The Cierva C4 autogiro made its first flight near Madrid, Spain – one of the most important contributions to the development of rotary-wing aircraft.

1 February 1923
A substantial force of Kurds and hill Arabs began advancing on Kukuk and the RAF responded by mounting the first-ever airlift of troops, using Vickers Vernons.

23 March 1923
The Regia Aeronautica was formed as the first Italian independent air arm, equipped with the Ansaldo A.300/4 general-purpose biplane.

2 May 1923
The first non-stop crossing of the USA by an aeroplane was made by a US Army Air Service Fokker T2, flying from Roosevelt Field, Long Island to Rockwell Field, California.

region and to places further east in India.

Across the border in Afghanistan, toward the end of 1928, trouble brewed up at the hands of rebels intent on overthrowing the Afghan ruler, himself energetically committed to transforming his country into a modern, European-style state. When the road from Kabul to the Khyber Pass – the only route from Afghanistan into India – was cut, the British Legation became a refuge for diplomats and their families. Situated barely three kilometres outside Kabul, it was a safe haven so long as the rebels remained outside. However, the only aircraft in the region were two-seat DH9As, while Vickers Victoria transports were more than 2,300km away in Baghdad.

Eventually, the Victorias, three DH9As, and a Handley Page Hinaidi were used to airlift 586 people and ten tonnes of baggage in 84 flights on journeys across mountainous country totalling 43,315km. In one of the worst winters on record, over some of the world's most inhospitable terrain, the RAF carried evacuees in total safety from a far-flung trouble spot. It was a precedent the RAF would continue in succeeding years in many countries, conducting

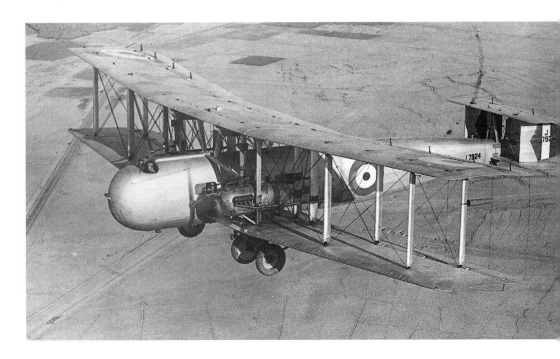

Big Russians

In the Soviet Union, Andrei Tupolev, working in conjunction with Junkers of Germany, designed a twin-engined (680hp/507kW M-17 engines) all-metal monoplane, the ANT-4 (TB-1) of 1924, and this was followed by the four-engined ANT-6 (TB-3) in December 1930. These were significant aircraft of their day – especially for the Soviets.

A low-wing monoplane, the ANT-4 made its first flight (on ski-landing gear) on 26 November 1925. Intended for the heavy bomber role, it was of all-metal construction with open cockpits for a crew of six, with corrugated metal sheet covering (as used by Junkers) and a glazed nose section. It was the first twin-engine, all-metal cantilever monoplane to go into production in the world. It could be equipped with either wheel or ski undercarriage. The first aircraft was completed as a propaganda aircraft – named *Strana Sovietov* (Land of the Soviets) and it was planned to fly across Siberia and on to New York, but the aircraft was damaged in a forced landing. A later aircraft completed the 13,199 miles (21,242km) between Moscow and New York in 1929.

When production ceased in 1932, a total of 216 had been built, forming first-line bomber units for many years before being relegated to the transport role. The TB-1P was a seaplane version for the Navy, with floats bought from Short Brothers in England. Many were used by Aeroflot as freighters and also by the Soviet Arctic Aviation Authority (Aviaarktika). Trials were also made with parasite fighters. The final examples were grounded in 1945.

The ANT-6 (TB-3), developed from the ANT-3, was the most advanced four-engined heavy bomber in service in the early 1930s, but still retained open cockpits for the crew of ten. It first flew on 22 December 1930 and 818 were built before production ceased in early 1937. It also demonstrated national capability to produce and develop over many years. For a long period the ANT-6 was the backbone of the V-VS (Soviet Air Force) heavy bomber units. Equipped with eight machine guns for defensive armament it was able to carry 4,409lb (2,000kg) of bombs. Some were used as transports in the Arctic. Used operationally against the Japanese during border incidents in the late 1930s it was also involved in the 'Winter War' with Finland in 1939/40.

Other uses included night bombing and transport of all kinds – vehicles or tanks could be

The Tupolev ANT-6/TB-3 heavy bomber was one of the greatest achievements in aviation. Unlike other giant aircraft of the late 1920s, it was designed to meet a real need.

carried between the landing gear legs. It was also used for Zveno parasite fighter experiments, and could carry two Polikarpov I-15 fighters above the wings and two I-16s beneath for air launching.

During the German invasion of Russia in 1941 (Operation *Barbarossa*) a few ANT-6s remained in service as glider tugs and para-troop transports. The design was under constant revision during the production run and as new versions appeared so even more impressive height-with-load records were set up. In October 1936 an ANT-6 set an altitude record of 23,071ft while carrying a 22,046lb (12,000kg) load.

Left: Vickers supplied fifteen Victoria IIIs to the RAF from May 1925. This is the fourth production aircraft, and shows the dihedral on the upper and lower wings. As replacements for Vimys and Vernons with Nos 70 and 216 Squadrons in the Middle East, they virtually doubled the load-carrying capacity of these squadrons.

evacuations, airlifts and relief flights that helped forge new airways across the world.

Of the Kabul operation *The Times* correspondent wrote:

"In those winter weeks – surely destined to be famous forever in the history of the Royal Air Force – the great aeroplanes went to and fro in all weathers over mountainous country of the most forbidding kind, where landing was practically impossible and any sort of failure in skill or material must have meant disaster. There was no disaster. In more than seventy journeys, nearly 600 men, women and children were rescued, and not one suffered injury. It is a great thing to have won the Schneider Trophy. It is a greater thing, greater for the country and for the future of travel by air, to have effected the rescues from Kabul."

SCHNEIDER RACING

The Schneider Trophy, or to give its full title, *La Coupe d'Aviation Maritime Jacques Schneider*, was announced in 1912 as the prize for a new international air race specifically for seaplanes. The man behind the trophy was Jacques Schneider, a wealthy French industrialist and amateur pilot, who envisaged that seaplanes would provide the means of global transportation and commerce in the future. The rules of the contest, which included navigability and watertightness tests, were aimed at discouraging 'freak', one-off aircraft with no developmental future, and to spur on the advancement of viable commercial machines. The contest was to take place over the open sea, along a course of not less than 150 nautical miles in length. Any aero club affiliated to the Fédération Aéronautique Internationale could compete, and winning countries staged the following year's race. Any nation winning the contest three times in five years (or three times in five contests when the race went biennial after 1927) would win the Schneider Trophy outright.

The first race, in 1913, was held in Monaco, and was won, for the only time, by France. The aircraft, piloted by Maurice

Above: Lt James Doolittle with his Curtiss R3C-2 during the 1925 Schneider competition, which was won by the Americans for a second time.

Above: The streamlined Macchi M.67, an unsuccessful contender in the 1929 Schneider competition.

Left: The ill-fated Supermarine S.4 at Baltimore in 1925. Designed by R. J. Mitchell, the S.4 was ahead of its time and was the world's fastest floatplane. During practice, however, the S.4 crashed into Chesapeake Bay and was written off, although pilot Henri Biard escaped unhurt.

Prévost, was a Deperdussin, the foremost racing aircraft of its day. Monaco was again the venue for the 1914 race, and Britain recorded its first win, with Howard Pixton flying the Sopwith Tabloid to great effect – both the Deperdussin and Tabloid were little more than landplanes on floats.

World War I interrupted the sequence, with Britain hosting the event at Bournemouth in 1919. The event was poorly organised, with spectators damaging aircraft, and fog causing the contest to be declared void. Although disqualified from the 1919 race, Italy staged the next contest.

Italy won both the 1920 and 1921 contests in Venice, with no overseas competition at all, and needed only one further victory to take the Trophy permanently. Britain fielded the Supermarine Sea Lion II at Naples in 1922 to attempt to keep the Trophy alive. Despite the tactics of his three Italian opponents, Henri Biard flew the aircraft to victory, denying the Italians the Trophy and giving Supermarine and its chief designer, R. J. Mitchell, their first victory.

The 1923 contest, at Cowes in England, saw a new development. America fielded a Navy team with a new racer, the Curtiss CR–3. Based on its successful landplane version, it was a streamlined floatplane unlike the British Sea Lion III and the French CAMS 38. With a superior aircraft and tightly run crew, the Americans won comfortably.

The years 1924-1926 saw American dominance. In 1924, no country could develop an aircraft to match the Americans, and at the request of the British, the Americans sportingly cancelled the contest. This allowed Britain and Italy to develop new designs. The Italian Macchi company produced a sleek flying boat monoplane, while the British Gloster concern continued its development of the biplane and Mitchell at Supermarine produced the radical S.4. America again won and was now poised with two of the three required wins to take the trophy in perpetuity. They were thwarted in 1926 by the Italians, who won with the Macchi

Right: The Supermarine S.6B, designed by R. J. Mitchell, which won the Schneider Trophy outright for Britain in 1931 and laid the groundwork for the future Spitfire.

M.39 floatplane monoplane. 1925 was, therefore, the last time a biplane won the Schneider Trophy, and was the last time an American team competed.

1927–1931 was the closing era of the Trophy, with Britain winning in 1927, 1929 and 1931 (the event became biennial from 1927) to take the trophy permanently. The 1927 contest was held in Venice. R. J. Mitchell of Supermarine worked on correcting the design faults of the ill-fated S.4 and produced the S.5. Gloster continued with the biplane configuration, producing the Gloster IVB – perhaps the ultimate biplane aircraft – and Italy fielded the Macchi M.52. The British S.5s took first and second places, all other aircraft retiring.

The Solent saw the 1929 contest, with the start and finish off Ryde Pier. Mitchell made a break at this stage and switched from engine manufacturer Napier to Rolls-Royce in order to obtain a more powerful engine. The aircraft he designed to take this new powerplant was the S.6, and one of the two examples which competed took the Trophy for the second time.

The Supermarine S.6 and its Rolls-Royce 'R' engine were both refined further to produce the S.6B for the 1931 race. In the absence of Italy's challenge (due to fatal engine problems in their Macchi MC.72) this ultimate racing floatplane design retained the Schneider Trophy for Britain in perpetuity.

The techniques used by Mitchell in designing the S.4, S.5, S.6 and S.6B were later used in the design of the Spitfire and development of the Merlin engine. Schneider's dream of seaplane dominance did not come true, but his Trophy spurred on aircraft development at a key moment in history.

Outright Winners

During practice, the Schneider machines were flown in turn by Stainforth, Long, Boothman and Snaith. The increasing strain on those involved in preparing the racers became very obvious. Major G. P. Bulman recalled:

"On 7 September, the S.6Bs were withdrawn to have their racing engines fitted. The night before the contest nerves were taut. R. J. Mitchell and I walked from the RAF Mess to see the new engines doing their final run. Jimmy Ellor of Rolls-Royce dashed to us in a panic to announce that the wing radiators were stone cold and the system was not working. The effect on poor Mitchell was appalling. He spluttered "This is the end", and said he had been a fool to go ahead with this

wing-cooling idiocy and we would be the laughing stock of the world. But by the time we got to the S.6s gleaming under the floodlights, the engines were being gradually opened up. All panic had subsided – the radiators were fine."

Using the ultimate R engine, averaging a fantastic 407.5mph in four runs, Stainforth described the sequence of his speed record flight: "Opened up quickly and got nearly full revs very soon, but did not get full power during take-off. Swung too much to left but brought her back before porpoise could develop. Slight porpoise damped out after throttling slightly. Felt fore and aft instability a little just after getting into the air. Machine accelerated rather slowly and was tail heavy. Engine got really going after ASI read 200mph, and tail heaviness disappeared. Started

runs at Warner Lightship at one end and Hythe pier at other. Visibility not good, but kept line by use of clouds. Landing OK except for slight swinging from side to side."

Another aircraft pioneer wrote of the world-speed record success by the S.6Bs:

"This ought to be a wonderful spiritual tonic to the people of this country. We seem to have an inferiority complex. We begin to wonder if anything will ever go right and we can compete with other nations. But here, in a new development which is science, art, and industry in one, not only can we hold our own with other nations – we are left absolutely unchallenged."

The victorious Flight Lieutenant John Boothman is held aloft by his groundcrew in front of the winning aircraft.

ENGINE DEVELOPMENT

The 1923 Schneider Trophy Race held in England was won by an American Curtiss R-3 Navy racer at a speed of 177mph, powered by a 450hp Curtiss D-12 twelve-cylinder Vee liquid-cooled engine with a very small frontal area. The cooling radiators were of the surface type, forming part of the wing leading edges.

British aircraft manufacturer Richard Fairey had observed the Curtiss in the air at Portsmouth and saw immediately that this was the way in which performance of military aircraft could be improved. Though the British Air Ministry failed to support his ideas, Fairey raised the money as a private venture and negotiated with the Americans for the right to use the D-12 engine, the Curtiss-Read metal propeller, high-efficiency aerofoil sections and wing-surface radiators. Fifty D-12s were imported and installed in the Fairey Fox. So impressed was he with the 158mph speed of the Fox in 1925, that Air Chief Marshal Hugh Trenchard immediately ordered a squadron of the type.

The clean lines of the Fairey Fox, in comparison with other RAF aircraft of the period, are demonstrated by these early production Fox Is of No 12 Squadron.

Rolls-Royce was working on a new V-12 aero engine in the late 1920s, to compete with the Fairey Felix unit, which was basically the licence-built Curtiss D-12. When the Fairey Fox first entered service it was an embarrassment to the RAF because of its superior speed compared to other types, and Trenchard used the occasion as a stick with which to beat Rolls-Royce (and also Napier).

Initially the new Rolls-Royce engine was called the 'F', and each bank of six cylinders was a monobloc aluminium casting, with thin steel open liners of 5 x 5.5in in size (1,296cu in). At its first test in 1927 it was producing 490hp at 2,350rpm and in the following year geared 'F's appeared. In 1930 the engine was named the Kestrel.

A ram air inlet was installed which added 10mph to Kestrel-powered aircraft. During the 1930s full supercharge, automatic boost control and 87-octane fuel were added for improved performance, and final marks of Kestrel were rated at 745hp at 3,000rpm at 14,500ft. Total production of the Kestrel numbered 4,750.

The Hawker Fury biplane fighter, which first flew in 1928, ranks among the most elegant aeroplanes of all time, for in its day it epitomised the compact single-seat interceptor fighter with the clean lines of the finely cowled Kestrel engine. The Fury was the RAF's first front-line aircraft capable of more than 200mph in level flight. During the final years of the Fox in service it is fitting to note that the aircraft were re-engined with the Kestrel.

In the late 1930s, the Kestrel was modernised into the smaller Peregrine, which was rated at 885hp at 3,000rpm, but was not a success when fitted to the Westland Whirlwind. The same cylinder blocks were used in the later Vulture engine, having four Peregrine blocks arranged in X-24 form, but endemic conrod failures rated this engine as a disaster, though 508 were produced, all being fitted to the ill-fated Avro Manchester.

The Hawker Fury, powered by the finely-cowled Rolls-Royce Kestrel in-line engine, must rank amongst the most elegant aircraft of all time. In its day, the Fury epitomised the compact single-seat interceptor fighter. This stacked formation is made up of Furies from No 1 Squadron, RAF.

Record-breaking Flights

In the period between the two World Wars there was much prestige to be gained in record breaking flights. The Schneider Trophy contests led the way in speed, but there were many individual aircraft used in attempts to set new long-distance and height records. They varied from modified production aircraft to new types designed specifically for the task. All these had an influence on the development of military aviation and political implications.

The Fairey Long-Range Monoplane, of which two examples were built, was designed to meet AM Spec 33/27. Wind-tunnel tests with models convinced Fairey that a high-wing cantilever layout would be most advantageous. The first example flew at Northolt on 14 November 1928, powered by a single 570hp (425kW) Napier Lion XIA engine. The specification had required a

range of 5,000 miles (8,045km) and by the time that the Monoplane flew the world's absolute distance record in a straight line was 4,466 miles (7,187km), set by an Italian Savoia S.64.

The original record attempt was to have been made between Cranwell and Cape Town, but because of delays and weather conditions it was decided to try for Bangalore in India. But various problems were encountered before and during the flight, which ended at Karachi. A distance of 4,130 miles (6,647km) had been covered in 50hr 37min. There was insufficient fuel to complete the flight, but this was the first non-stop flight from the UK to India. In December 1929, an attempt was made to Cape Town, but the aircraft flew into high ground near Tunis, killing both of the pilots.

As a result of experience with the first aircraft, a revised Specification was issued for the second. Flown on

The Fairey Long Range Monoplane was the outcome of the Air Ministry's decision to purchase a special aeroplane to capture the world long-distance record for Britain in the late 1920s.

30 June 1931, it had an automatic pilot developed by RAE Farnborough, and carried an impressive array of instrumentation. On 6 February 1933, it left Cranwell and flew 5,410 miles (8,707km) to Walvis Bay, South West Africa in 57hr 25min, to set a new record. Three months later though, that record was smashed by a Blériot-Zappa 110 flying from New York to Syria, a distance of 5,657 miles (9,104km).

Engine designers were continually striving to improve high altitude performance, and there was both technical merit and commercial advantage to be gained by the attainment of still greater heights. In Britain pressure mounted for an attempt to regain the record held by Italy and in June 1934 Bristol received an invitation to tender for two prototypes of a suitable aircraft.

The Bristol 138A was a low-wing monoplane of wooden construction in order to minimise weight, and a simple, fixed undercarriage was selected for the same reason. Power was by a specially adapted Bristol Pegasus engine with a two-stage supercharger. The cockpit was covered by a hinged plastic canopy, which had hot-air demisting.

Sqn Ldr F. R. D. Swain was selected for the attempt, made from Farnborough on 28 September 1936, and he attained an FAI-homologated height of 49,967ft.

Although the Italians regained the record in May 1937 with a flight to 51,362ft, minor improvements were made to the Type 138A to enable Flt Lt M. J. Adam to raise it again to 53,937ft on 3 June 1937.

The Bristol Type 138A high-altitude research aeroplane, which reached nearly 54,000ft in 1937. At the time it was the largest single-seat aeroplane in the world, with a span of 66ft.

THE BIPLANE ERA

Throughout the 1920s and early 1930s, the biplane was the norm. Most were of wooden construction, though some eventually had steel-tube fuselages. Up to this time the monoplane formula had made little headway in the military field. Development in Britain had never recovered from an official ban on the monoplane enforced temporarily in 1912, after a series of accidents involving aircraft of this type. Initially air arms had to make do with obsolete wartime equipment – the biplane had been established as the predominant configuration, and there was little incentive for change.

Elsewhere, relatively slow biplane fighters were preferred to monoplanes because of their excellent manoeuvrability. Biplane fighters reached their zenith with the Hawker Fury of 1929, which was the first military aircraft to exceed 200mph (323km/h) – and the Gloster Gladiator, the last biplane to enter RAF service.

Most of the Fairey IIIDs served with the Fleet Air Arm as twin-float seaplanes. The IIID MkIIIs (illustrated below) were mainly employed by the RAF with No 202 Squadron at Kalafrana, Malta during the early 1930s.

Westland Wapiti IIAs served with No 601 'City of London' Squadron, Royal Auxiliary Air Force at RAF Hendon from 1929 until 1933.

Military aircraft were more or less standardised in the late 1920s. The classic fighter was a biplane, with either a radial or an in-line engine and carried two rifle-calibre machine guns. It had a top speed of something between 150-200mph and a range of some 250 miles.

In the US there was the beautiful Curtiss B-2 fighters and the sturdy little Thomas Morse MB-3A, together with designs from Boeing and Grumman. In Britain notable biplanes of the period included the Bristol Bulldog, Fairey Fawn, Flycatcher, Fox and Swordfish; De Havilland DH9A; Westland Wapiti and Wallace; Hawker Fury, Hart, Hind, Demon, Kestrel, Osprey and Nimrod; Handley Page Hyderabad, Hinaidi and Heyford; Vickers Valencia, Victoria, Virginia and Vernon. French designs included the Breguet 19 and Nieuport-Delage Ni-D.29 and 62.

Left: Converted from a Wapiti IIA, the first production Westland Wallace (K3562) flying low over Westland's airfield at Yeovil in 1931.

Right: Entering service in 1929, the Bristol Bulldog was the RAF's principal fighter through the early 1930s. This example has been recently restored for display in the RAF Museum.

Right: For over a decade, from 1923 to 1934, the Fairey Flycatcher was a standard first-line fighter of the Fleet Air Arm. This flying replica was built in the 1970s.

The Hawker Hind general purpose light day bomber, a development of the Hart, was in its heyday during the early phase of the RAF expansion scheme in the mid-1930s. This ex-Afghan Air Force example flies regularly at Old Warden as part of the Shuttleworth Collection.

The Gloster Gladiator – the last of the RAF's biplane fighters, 490 of which were delivered to the service in the late 1930s.

These were lovely aircraft, carefully crafted and lavishly maintained – often painted in bright squadron colours and brought out for display at air shows and inspections. Many manufacturers resolutely ignored the old adage 'If it looks good, it will fly' – and they draped spars, struts, wheels, gun bins and other protrusions on their aircraft, with total disregard of drag and wind resistance.

The 1929 Handley Page Hinaidi looked like an angry bulldog and many bombers and transports looked like flying barns with a question mark for a fin. The large British flying boats such as the Supermarine Southampton, Stranraer, Walrus and Sea Otter; Short Rangoon, Sarafand and Singapore; Saro London; Blackburn Iris and Perth – looked very much like blue whales with wings attached – which may have been appropriate as they were operating from water.

The absolute prize for ugliness probably went to the French – for they produced the Bloch, Potez and Lioré et Olivier series of bombers – all slab-sided, square wings, engine nacelles, turrets and landing gear sprouting everywhere. For many, this was the 'golden age' of aviation, an era abruptly curtailed by the onset of World War II.

POLISH FIGHTERS

The Polish Air Force received 175 examples of the PZL P.11c, which featured a Skoda-built Bristol Mercury engine. The gull-wing configuration was chosen to give the pilot better-than-average forward vision. This P.11c (No.1) is the leader's aircraft of No 113 (Warsaw) Squadron, 2nd Air Regiment.

The Polish nationalised company Panstwowe Zaklady Lotnicze (PZL, or National Aviation Establishment) was formed on 1 January 1928 and its first design was the PZL L.2, a braced high-wing monoplane, accommodating a crew of two in open cockpits, used for reconnaissance/liaison purposes. The L-2A entered service with the Polish Air Force in 1931. The PZL L.5, which first flew in July 1932 was a biplane primary trainer for the Polish Air Force and some were still in service in 1939.

PZL designer Zygmunt Pulawski sought to provide the fighter pilot with a better than average forward view and designed a gull-type high-wing monoplane configuration – later known as the 'Pulawski wing'. This wing was tapered both in chord and thickness and incorporated thin-section sloping inboard panels, giving the pilot a clear view between them.

The P.7/I with a 450hp (336kW) Bristol Jupiter engine was first flown in October 1930 and had a maximum speed of 199mph (320km/h). The armament was two 7.7mm (0.303in) Vickers Type E machine guns. It had an all metal construction with aluminium-alloy sheet covering. The subsequent P.7/II with revised rear fuselage structure and other refinements went into production at the Warsaw factory. The Polish Air Force acquired 150 examples, the type entering service in late 1932.

Aerodynamics and Alloys

In the pioneering days of aviation, the principal requirement of an aircraft was that it should fly, and aerodynamic considerations made the methods of construction a secondary problem. With biplanes, in addition to providing rigidity, bracing wires allowed the structure to be 'rigged' into the correct shape by tightening or loosening appropriate wires.

From the early days, aviators sought to reduce drag (air resistance). The fundamental method of achieving this objective is by streamlining, or making all parts of the shape of a streamline, the path a streamline followed by smoothly flowing particles of air. Drag reduction depended on changes to structure, and real advances were made only with the adoption of the stressed-skin, all-metal airframe. Smooth metal skins, flush rivets, carefully streamlined cockpits and retractable undercarriages, wing fillet shapes and engine cowlings all made major contributions.

The high-speed Schneider racers, mainly British, American and Italian, pointed the way to the fighters of the future and provided ample opportunity for developing strong and light metal structures, perfecting streamlining and evolving powerful engines. The growing use of steel and aluminium alloys led to the general adoption of semi-monocoque stressed-skin construction, first with a mixture of wood and metal, and then with metal alone.

An aluminium derivative, Y alloy, was of great importance for aero engine pistons. Specialists in their forging was Peter Hooker Ltd, the wartime British licensee for Clerget rotaries. Following the collapse of the airship programme and the proposed new Stromboli engine, Wallace Devereux – who had extensive knowledge of processing alloys, decided to launch on his own.

Tom Chapman, who went to Armstrong Siddeley Motors from Armstrong Whitworth at their amalgamation and ultimately became managing director recalled:

"Devereux boldly came to old man Siddeley and said 'If you are going to continue with aluminium pistons there is one thing you have to do – give me £10,000 so that I can buy part of this business and establish it for the particular job you need me to make'."

"Devereux quickly spent that £10,000 and went back to the old man and got another £10,000 and when that went, still another – and that was the start of what became the famous High Duty Alloys Ltd. With that first £10,000, he bought most of the specialist piston forging plant when Hookers was put up for sale, and installed it in a rented building on the Slough Trading Estate. By vigorous salesmanship, he gained increasing markets at home and abroad for forged pistons, extending to all forms of duralumin forgings and extrusions".

By the autumn of 1933 Poland had become the first nation in the world to have a first-line force of all-metal monoplane fighters. Over 100 P.7s were still in service at the outbreak of WW2 and some 50 were flown out to Romania when Poland collapsed in late September 1939. Around the same number were captured by the Germans and subsequently used, after refurbishment, as trainers by the Luftwaffe.

The PZL P.11 was a subsequent version fitted with a more powerful engine – a 530hp (395kW) Bristol Mercury IVA, enclosed in a long chord Townsend ring. Fifty early P.11bs were delivered to the Romanian Air Force. The P.11/III was the production prototype and competed in the American National Air Races in Cleveland during August 1932.

The P.11c was produced for the Polish Air Force and 175 were delivered by the end of 1936, replacing the P.7 as the standard fighter. It had a maximum speed of 242mph (390km/h) and had the same armament plus underwing racks for lightweight bombs. They were very manoeuvrable, compact and sturdy. Twelve squadrons were so equipped at the outbreak of WW2 and it was claimed that 126 Luftwaffe aircraft were shot down for the loss of 114 of their own number. Surviving P.11s flew to Romania, which eventually used them alongside their P.11Fs against the Soviet Union in 1941.

CHRONOLOGY

30 March 1927
A flight of No 47 (Bomber) Squadron Fairey IIIFs took off from Cairo to fly to Cape Town and back.

27 May 1927
France's first aircraft carrier *Bearn* was completed.

28 July 1927
A US Army Fokker C-2 monoplane completed the first successful non-stop flight from the continental USA to Hawaii, a distance of 2,407 miles, in a flight time of 25hr 50min.

1 November 1927
The USS *Saratoga*, the US Navy's first fleet-sized aircraft carrier was commissioned on the east coast, followed soon afterwards by the USS *Lexington*.

FLYING BOATS

Above: The Italian Savoia-Marchetti S.55 series was one of the most successful flying-boat designs of the 1920s and '30s. The S.55M military version featured uncowled engines and gunners positions at the front of each hull.

During WW1 a number of successful flying boats were developed to meet combat requirements. Some were amphibians and often featured a short hull with the tail surfaces supported by booms. In the 1920s, thoughts turned to a rebirth of international contests to replace international combat, and the Schneider Trophy evolved as a race for waterborne aircraft. However, with a generous oversupply of military aircraft of all types left over from the 1914-18 conflict, aviation was almost at a standstill throughout the 1920s.

In England, the experience gained from the design of the Supermarine Swan civil transport flying boat was put to good use in the design and production of the Supermarine Southampton. Wooden hulls were still the standard construction, and with biplane construction the engines were exposed to the slipstream which contributed to aerodynamic drag and accounted for their slow speed.

The decade between 1930-1940 was a period of development for flying boats, and the

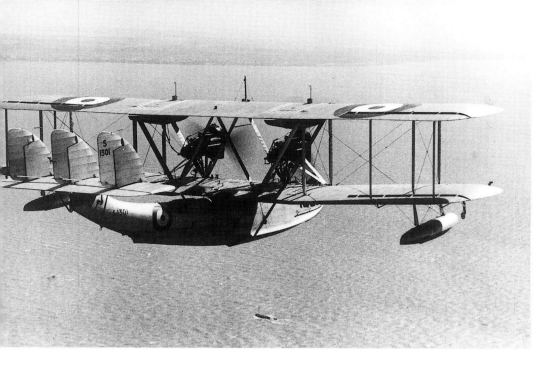

The Supermarine Southampton military flying boat
embodied all the experience that the manufacturer
had accumulated and set a new standard for marine
aircraft. Southamptons served with the RAF for over
a decade – a record of longevity for flying boats
surpassed only by the Sunderland.

CHRONOLOGY

3 February 1928
The Boeing F3B-1 naval fighter made its first flight.
Designed as a multi-capability naval fighter-bomber
it was able to operate with floats or fixed
undercarriage.

June 1928
The prototype Hawker Hart light bomber, one of
the most famous British aircraft of the period, made
its initial flight from Brooklands.

23 December 1928
The RAF undertook to evacuate civilians from Kabul,
Afghanistan during tribal disturbances. The aircraft
flew a total of 28,160 miles without any loss of life.

26 March 1929
The first all-metal version of the Fairey III, the Mk IIIF
two-seat reconnaissance spotter, made its inaugural
flight, powered by a 570hp Napier Lion XIA engine.

24 April 1929
The first non-stop flight from England to India
was undertaken by an RAF Fairey Long-Range
Monoplane, a flight of 4,130 miles (6,647km) in a
flight time of 50 hours 37 minutes.

7 September 1929
The 1929 Schneider Trophy Contest held in the Solent
was won by a Supermarine S6 of the RAF High Speed
Flight at an average speed of 328.63mph.

2 October 1929
The 722ft-long, diesel-powered Airship R-101, built
under state management, was unveiled at RAF
Cardington. It made its first flight on 14 October.

16 January 1930
A patent for a new kind of aircraft engine was filed
by a junior RAF officer – Flying Officer Frank Whittle
– who had been unable to arouse any interest from
the RAF, the Air Ministry or the aircraft industry.

29 April 1930
One of the most famous biplanes of its day, the
Polikarpov I.5, powered by a 450hp supercharged
Jupiter VII radial engine, made its first flight.

12 June 1930
First flight of the Handley Page Heyford, the RAF's
last heavy bomber of biplane configuration.

5 October 1930
The British airship R-101, on a proving flight to India,
crashed on a hillside near Beauvais, northern France
and only eight of the 54 passengers and crew
survived – an event which shattered British faith in
long-distance passenger-carrying airship flights.

bases from which they operated. Transition from wood to metal structures began in the early
1930s and the Blackburn Iris II, III and IV were produced. At the beginning of this period
there were companies who specialised in military marine aircraft – notably Shorts,
Blackburn, Saunders Roe and Supermarine in Britain; Dornier and Rhorbach in Germany;
Macchi and Savoia-Marchetti in Italy; Breguet and Latécoère in France; Beriev in Russia; and
Sikorsky, Boeing, Martin and Consolidated in the USA.

Two design characteristics had to be reckoned with in each design. One was the
necessity to mount the engines and propellers in
a position high enough to keep the propellers
clear of the spray pattern generated by the
aircraft movement through the water. The other
was the requirement for improved lateral stability
when on, or in contact with, the water surface.
Each company approached these requirements in
a slightly different way.

In England the flying boats were used for
North Sea patrols, to 'show the flag' in the
eastern Mediterranean and Far East, and when
the Spanish Civil War broke out, to ensure the
safety of British shipping. The Supermarine
Stranraer, which entered service in 1936, was the
last biplane flying boat with the RAF.

The mid-1930s produced a variety of flying
boats. They were one of the best vehicles for
service in remote areas where acres of concrete
runways were not practical for economic and
environmental reasons. In the US the Grumman

The Saro London was one of a number of biplane flying
boats still in first-line service with Coastal Command in
September 1939. This is an early Mk.I converted to
Mk.II standard in 1937, with Bristol Pegasus X engines,
circular cowlings and four-blade propellers.

Above: A silver-finished Grumman J2F-6 Duck, built by Columbia Aircraft Corporation after Pearl Harbor. An amphibian, the main-wheels retracted into the sides of the main float. In various versions, the Duck (which first flew in 1933) served throughout WW2.

J2F Duck was entering service – an unusual 'spoon-bill' amphibian with the bow of the single-float projecting under and well forward of the propeller. The latter half of the 1930s saw the design and early testing of flying boats that were the mainstays of the flying fleets of WW2. Among these were such famous designs as the Short Sunderland, Supermarine Walrus, Consolidated PBY Catalina, Dornier Do18, Kawanashi H6K–5 'Mavis' and H8K 'Emily'.

The Sunderland benefitted from the extensive aerodynamic and hydronamic studies carried out during the design and construction of the Empire flying boats. Its duties ranged from coastal patrol, long-range convoy patrols, sea-rescue aircraft and transport. The PBY Catalina, in its many variants, was eventually produced in greater numbers (3,290 in total) than any other flying boat.

As war approached in Europe in 1938, several flying boat designs emerged, probably in anticipation of military conflict. These included the German Blohm und Voss Bv138, Dornier Do18 and 24; the Italian Macchi C.94; and the Russian Beriev MDR.6.

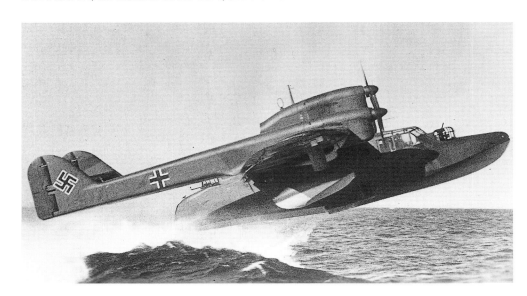

The Blohm und Voss Bv138A was widely known as the 'Flying Clog'. Most operated in the harsh environment of the northern oceans, seeing much service around the Norwegian coast.

AERIAL REFUELLING

The development of an air-to-air refuelling system was pioneered by the United States Army Air Service (USAAS) in 1923 using a pair of DH4Bs. The system was later developed by Britain's Sir Alan Cobham, who carried out early experiments with DH9 and Handley Page W.10 biplanes in 1932-33. On 24 September 1934, Cobham and Sqn Ldr Helmore took off from Portsmouth in an Airspeed Courier, which then took on 275 gallons into overload cabin tanks before attempting to fly to India, with further aerial refuelling from RAF aircraft en route. The British Air Ministry and Imperial Airways encouraged further experiments by Sir Alan's company.

In Britain, a refuelling method was developed by the RAF and patents were granted to Flt Lt R. L. R. Atcherley in 1935, and these were assigned to Flight Refuelling. In 1935 two

During early flight refuelling experiments a Vickers Virginia X acted as the tanker, passing fuel through a flexible hose to several different types of receivers during the course of many flights. Here it is refuelling a Westland Wapiti as part of the aerial demonstrations at the 1936 Hendon Air Display.

Seen refuelling the Short flying boat *Cambria* over Southampton Water on 20 January 1938, the sole Armstrong Whitworth AW.23 bomber-transport had been seconded by the Air Ministry to Flight Refuelling Ltd for use as a tanker trials aircraft.

RAF Vickers Virginias demonstrated air-to-air refuelling. By 1937 faster tankers, in the shape of the prototype Armstrong Whitworth AW23 and Handley Page HP51 transports, were made available. On 20 January 1938, the AW23 refuelled flying boat *Cambria* for the first time in a storm – rain, low cloud and even fog.

In April 1939, tests were carried out with two of the larger Short S.30 Empire flying boats – *Caribou* and *Cabot* – refuelling in the air from Handley Page Harrow II tankers. Then three Harrow bombers were made available, equipped as tankers carrying 900 gallons of fuel as transferable cargo. Two were shipped to Hattie's Camp, Newfoundland (later to become known as Gander) and the third to Rineanna (now Shannon) in Eire.

By August 1939, the first weekly scheduled transatlantic service from Southampton began, calling at Foynes and being refuelled after take-off for Botwood, Montreal and New York. A total of eight crossings in each direction were made until the service was suspended because of the outbreak of WW2. The actual refuelling process only took eight minutes to pass 800 gallons after the three to seven minutes spent in making contact and linking hoses.

FIGHTER REVOLUTION

T he most significant change in aircraft design to take place in the 1930s was the appearance of monoplanes in quantity. There had been earlier fighters, but their performance had not been significantly better than contemporary biplanes. They had suffered some disadvantage in requiring a longer take-off and landing run than was provided by small airfields of the period. In the event of war, units would have to operate from bases that were available – and this often meant open fields, patches of flat desert or other undeveloped sites.

Increases in range, speed and load carrying capacity of new bombers had outstripped traditional fighter designs, and many fighters then in front-line service could be outrun. A radical change was inevitable, and in several countries the first of the fighters which were to gain fame in WW2 were on the drawing board in the initial half of the 1930s.

The destruction of attacking bombers was an essential task, especially in view of the pessimistic forecasts, then prevalent, of the havoc that a bomber offensive would wreak upon cities. The development of new fighter designs was hurried forward and replacements for fixed-undercarriage biplanes with two or four guns evolved as low-wing monoplanes with retractable undercarriages and much heavier armament.

The French Dewoitine D.520 was roughly comparable with the RAF's Hurricane. It was the only French fighter regarded as modern, but proved no match for the Bf 109 and was unable to turn the tide in 1940.

The prototype Hawker Hurricane during its first flight on 6 November 1935.

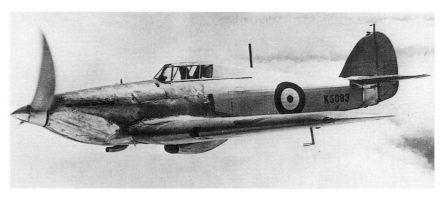

Focke-Wulf's Fw187 had a narrow fuselage, short nose and powerful engines. Armament consisted of MG 17 machine guns on the fuselage sides and MG FF 20-mm cannon under the lower fuselage. The type was not put into production, and the few that were built were used for weapons trials.

Twin-engined Fighters

The twin-engined fighter came to the fore in the 1930s, while the use of a turret on a single-engine fighter to give it all-round fire was also a logical development of the successful two-seat fighters of WW1 and the intervening period. Boulton Paul's Defiant, with a four-gun turret behind the pilot, entered service in 1938, but by 1940 it was deemed a failure for day operations.

In the late 1930s a number of air forces were developing 'heavy' fighters, and these tended to be twin-engined aircraft with their obviously extended range. Their role was to include bomber escort, while in the defensive role their combat radius could allow them to intercept incoming bombers, before they came within the range of single-seat interceptors. It so happened that these early 'heavy' fighters were used in a variety of roles to which they were unsuited, most becoming night fighters, though some excelled in this role during the war years.

In Germany the Messerschmitt Bf110 was the first twin-engined fighter for the Luftwaffe, but it proved very vulnerable to Allied single-seaters. The faster Focke-Wulf Fw187 bomber destroyer was not put into production since the Luftwaffe planners believed the Bf110 would be adequate in serving this category of fighter. In France the Potez 630 and 631 were of a similar design. The Potez 540, built as a long-range fighter, was relegated to a night bomber role.

For light-bomber duties, the RAF used the Bristol Blenheim, fitted with a 4 x 0.303in gun pack under the nose, until the emergence of the Bristol Beaufighter in

The Bell FM-1 Airacuda was designed as a long-range escort fighter. Pusher engines allowed the engine nacelles to be modified into gunnery compartments, but the concept was not a success.

late 1940. The Westland Whirlwind single-seat twin-engined fighter, with four Hispano 20mm cannon, appeared in early 1939, but the type was plagued by underpowered and unreliable engines.

The Americans experimented with the Bell FM-1 Airacuda (FM standing for Fighter Multiplace), which had a crew of five and featured two pusher engines in nacelles, each of which contained a 37mm cannon. This was abandoned after only thirteen had been built. Another interesting machine hailed from the Netherlands – the Fokker G1, which entered service in 1938, featured a central crew nacelle, with the tail unit mounted between twin booms that carried the engines ahead of the wings.

CHRONOLOGY

3 April 1933
Two RAF Westland Wallace aircraft made the first flight over the 29,028ft peak of Mount Everest.

4 April 1933
Buffeted by severe winds, the US Navy airship *Akron*, one of two designed to carry parasite aircraft, crashed in New Jersey with the loss of 73 lives.

21 June 1933
The prototype Supermarine Seagull V amphibian, built for the Royal Australian Air Force, made its first flight and after trials by the RAF it was produced as the Walrus for air-sea rescue duties.

1 July 1933
A mass formation of 24 Savoia-Marchetti S.55X flying boats left Rome on a flight to the World's Fair at Chicago, via Iceland, as a demonstration of Italy's aeronautical progress.

7 September 1933
Six Consolidated P2Y flying boats of the US Navy flew non-stop from Norfolk, VA to the Panama Canal Zone, a distance of 2,059 miles in 25hr 20min, to demonstrate long-range deployment.

15 October 1933
The Rolls-Royce Merlin aero engine, which had its origins in the P.V.12 (designed and developed as a private venture), made its first test run.

October 1933
The Polikarpov I-15 'Chaika', developed from the I-5 and featuring a gull configuration on the upper wing, made its first flight.

31 December 1933
Initial flight of the Polikarpov I-16 'Rata'. The following year the type became the first monoplane fighter with an enclosed cockpit and retractable undercarriage to enter service with any air force.

1 March 1934
The first Boulton Paul Overstrand medium bomber entered RAF service, being the first bomber to incorporate a power-operated gun turret.

19 July 1934
An operational test was made of parasite fighters carried beneath the airship USS *Macon*, when two Curtiss F9C-2 Sparrowhawks, without landing gear, were launched and later 'hooked' on again.

20 July 1934
The British government proposed the expansion of the RAF by 41 squadrons, together with 820 new aircraft, over the following five years.

Stressed-skin construction began to appear on many fighters, but there was still reliance on fabric covering for parts of the airframe. This permitted simpler production methods and easier repair of battle damage – both vital considerations in the period of 1930s expansion.

When the Hawker Hurricane was announced, albeit as a private venture, it had an unprecedented armament of eight 0.303in machine guns and able to exceed 300mph in level flight. An armoured bulkhead was fitted behind the engine, later to be followed by a bullet-proof windscreen and another slab of armour behind the pilot.

In-line engines were being preferred by designers, but being water-cooled made them more vulnerable to gunfire than air-cooled radials. However, performance at that time was of paramount performance. The more advanced Supermarine Spitfire, the epitome of the single-seat fighter, followed soon after with stressed-skin construction. The Dewoitine D.520 was designed in France, but was in service in only small numbers during the Battle of France.

In Germany, the Messerschmitt Bf109 replaced the interim biplanes of the Luftwaffe, and this rugged monoplane was further developed remaining in service throughout WW2. Poland meanwhile produced the excellent PZL P.7. However, in the US designers had settled for air-cooled radials for their new monoplanes but still retained the two machine gun armament that had been standard throughout the 1920s. Resulting from this, the performance of the Seversky P-35 (predecessor of the P-47 Thunderbolt) and Curtiss P-36 (forerunner of the P-40 Warhawk) fell well below contemporary European standards. Since no hostile bomber could reach continental American targets from existing bases, the status quo was maintained.

Russia had introduced the Polikarpov I-16 monoplane in 1936, which in its time was quite an advanced aircraft. The Mitsubishi A5M carrier monoplane fighter of the Imperial Japanese Navy was also a forward-looking design, used in action against the Chinese in 1937.

Left: The Boeing P-26A of 1934 was the link between old and new concepts of fighter design – combining outdated features such as an open cockpit, external bracing and fixed landing gear with a new all-metal low-wing monoplane design.

AMERICAN INNOVATION

The world was crippled by an economic depression from 1929 (following the stock market crash) until the mid-1930s, and this particularly affected the United States. Millions were unemployed, industries were failing in every country and governments appeared powerless to alter or redirect the blind forces of the market.

In America, the Morrow Board report entitled 'Is the US in danger by air attack from any potential enemy of menacing strength?', the answer to the question was a resounding 'No!'. The general reaction was that a country that had no enemies, and that had two great oceans between it and any conceivable trouble spots in the entire world, did not need an air force. The US Army Air Corps, newly created from the old air service in 1926, languished throughout the late 1920s.

Until air forces could find a viable reason for their existence, they were to remain the 'stepchildren' of the older services. However, throughout the 1920s, aircraft were getting bigger, better and faster. All-metal construction was becoming the accepted norm, as was aerodynamic streamlining and stressed skin, retractable landing gear, rotating turrets and leakproof fuel tanks. There were many other ideas, together making for a revolution in the aircraft industry, especially in the United States.

Below: The Douglas C-47 enjoyed a long operational career, and was used in every combat area of WW2. This example is an early C-41 variant.

Above: The Martin B-10, the US Army's first all-metal monoplane bomber, featured internal bomb stowage, a retractable undercarriage, and had the first gun turret ever fitted to an American bomber.

CHRONOLOGY

12 September 1934
The prototype Gloster Gladiator, the last of the RAF's biplane fighters, first flew as the Gloster SS37. Armed with four machine guns it had a top speed of 253mph, entering service in February 1937.

7 October 1934
One of the most important Soviet bombers of WW2, the Tupolev ANT-40 (SB-2) made its initial flight. In production until 1941, over 6,600 were built.

4 November 1934
The Junkers Ju86 bomber made its first flight, representing the resurgence of the German aircraft industry during the 1930s.

4 February 1935
The Mitsubishi A5M, powered by a 550hp Nakajima Kotobuki 5 radial engine, made its maiden flight at Kagamigahara, Japan.

24 February 1935
The Heinkel He111c prototype was flown for the first time. Publicised as a twin-engined transport for Lufthansa, it had been designed for and was intended to serve with the then secret Luftwaffe.

26 February 1935
A Handley Page Heyford bomber flew across a special test range at Daventry where short-wave radio transmitters had been set up, and scientists saw an oscillograph of the aircraft on a cathode ray tube.

9 March 1935
Formation of the Luftwaffe, a new national air force, was announced in Germany.

24 March 1935
The Avro 652A prototype was flown for the first time, entering RAF service as the Anson. It was the RAF's first monoplane aircraft with retractable landing gear, albeit hand cranked.

28 March 1935
The Consolidated P3Y-1 flying boat produced for the US Navy, and subsequently named as the PBY Catalina, made its initial flight.

In the early 1930s the revolution began. Designers, with new materials and manufacturing techniques, together with the development of new engines, began the transition to the next generation. There was a quantum leap forward and factories started to turn out the designs that would fight in the early stages of WW2. The Martin B-10 bomber entered service in 1935 and was an all-metal, mid-wing monoplane with enclosed cockpits, retractable undercarriage and internal bomb-carrying capacity. With a maximum speed of 207mph (333km/h) the pattern for future bombers was established, eventually leading to the B-17 Flying Fortress and B-24 Liberator.

Many of the new bombers came from the development of commercial aircraft – in spite of the recession and what it did to travel generally, there was a slowly growing market for air travel. Airline routes also had potential military uses. In the twin-engine airline business Boeing produced the Model 247, Douglas the DC-1, DC-2, DC-3 and military derivatives, and Lockheed were developing the Model 12 Electra. Variable-pitch propellers were coming into use, together with the introduction of landing flaps. Within a relatively short period all the ingredients required of fast, modern aircraft were coming to fruition in the United States.

Right: The revolutionary Boeing 247 was the first American low-wing multi-engine transport with clean aerodynamic design. This 247D was impressed into the RAF early in WW2 and was used for research into instrument and automatic landing systems.

SPANISH CIVIL WAR

Crucial to the development of modern aviation technology and operational practice was the civil war in Spain, which broke out in July 1936. The country was split between radical left and revolutionary right, and after a long series of riots and abortive risings, a bitter struggle finally broke out. From the beginning the forces of the two dictators of Germany and Italy – especially their air forces – were seen in impressive action, while democracy was once more impotent.

The Spanish Air Force was small and its equipment outmoded, comprised mainly of some 40 Nieuport Di.D-52 fighters and 60 Breguet XIX light bombers. It was less the Spaniards themselves than the foreign intervention that became significant, and in this the air war reflected the entire conflict. Germany and Italy intervened blatantly on the side of the Nationalists, while France sided surreptitiously and the Soviet Union more openly with the Loyalists. The British 'wrung their hands' ineffectively around the edges.

The Nationalists were able to use DC-2 and Fokker transports to fly their units of the Spanish Foreign Legion and Africa colonial soldiers across the Straits of Gibraltar. Later the Germans provided Junkers Ju52 transports to aid in this task.

Within a month the German Condor Legion was a fully-fledged air operation and the pilots got good combat experience that stood them in good stead at the beginning of WW2 – lessons that the British and French pilots still had to learn in 1940. The Germans were able to refine and test new equipment, and by the end of the war the Heinkel He111,

Twelve Savoia-Marchetti SM.81 bombers, together with a similar number of CR.32 fighters from Fascist Italy took part in the Spanish Civil War. As with the early Heinkel He111, the SM.81 carried its bombs vertically stowed, resulting in an untidy trajectory which did not help the aiming accuracy.

Japan and China at War

Just before the World Disarmament Conference opened in February 1932, fighting broke out between Japan and China in Shanghai, and rapidly escalated. The world was shocked by newsreel images of repeated air attacks on densely populated towns, and by the vigorous bombing by Japanese naval aircraft of Chinese positions in the Chapei district of Shanghai.

In 1931, the Japanese had taken over Manchuria, which they set up as a puppet state the next year, and withdrew from the League of Nations. Then for several years there was growing tension as Chinese Generalissimo Chiang Kai-shek tried to pull his faction-ridden country together. In July 1937 open, if undeclared, war broke out and the Japanese launched a full-scale invasion of north China.

The Chinese could oppose this onslaught with manpower, but not much else. They only had a few obsolete aircraft, flown as often as not by foreign mercenaries. The Japanese took the old capital of Peking and the new one of Nanking, where they bombed the American and British gunboats in the Yangtze River, sinking the USS *Panay*. Everywhere the

The Mitsubishi A5M2 was the forerunner of the 'Zeke' and featured an open cockpit and fixed undercarriage.

Japanese bombed and strafed, their aircraft usually unhindered in the sky. To meet the occasional fighter opposition, they developed long-range escort fighters. They hacked out emergency forward airstrips where the fighters could quickly refuel and rise to fight again.

By late 1938, the Japanese controlled most of the coast and all of China's main ports, starving the Chinese of outside help, but they could not finish the war with airpower alone. By 1939, they were forced to change their strategy to one of occupation and attrition.

Nevertheless, the Japanese had learned valuable lessons on the use of airpower. New aircraft and new techniques had been developed. The Mitsubishi A5M fighter and G3M2 bomber had proved excellent aircraft for their purpose, and their high-level bombing and fighter techniques were more than a match for anything done in Spain.

War was in the air by the late 1930s, and everywhere totalitarian powers were aggressive and demanding air power. Its potential for destruction was a hot topic, overtly used as a propaganda tool.

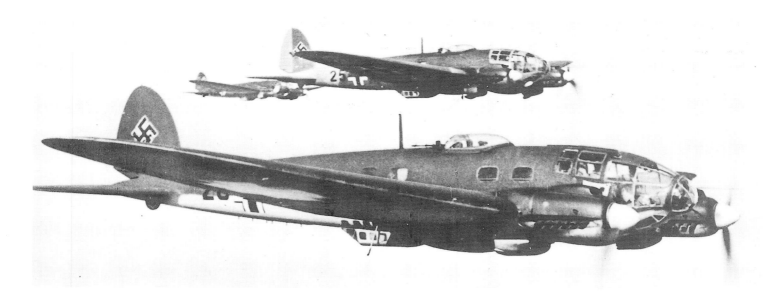

Four bomber Staffen of Kampfgruppe 88 used the Heinkel He111E-1 in the Legion Condor in Spain during 1938. The He111P shown here was introduced in 1938 and was the first to feature the smooth nose profile.

Messerschmitt Bf109 and Bf110, Dornier Do17 and Junkers Ju87 'Stuka' were in action in Spain – aircraft types that would fight much of WW2. Italy sent 763 aircraft for operations, including Fiat CR.32 biplane fighters, and for the bomber role Savoia-Marchetti SM.79 and SM.81 trimotors and Fiat BR.20s. The French supplied some 200 aircraft – an *Escuadra España* was formed at Toulouse, with Dewoitine D.272 parasol-winged fighters and Potez 540 twin-engined bombers being used.

The largest supplier of aircraft to the Republicans was the Soviet Union, and some 1,400

Right: The Soviet Union, demanding full payment in gold, supplied a large number of Polikarpov I-15 biplanes, most of which were deployed on the Madrid front, where the Nationalists threatened the capital.

Bottom: The Junkers Ju87B was the first of its type to drop bombs in anger, whilst serving with the Staffel 'Jolanthe', a very active Legion Condor unit.

CHRONOLOGY

12 April 1935
The first flight of the Bristol 142, subsequently called the *Britain First* took place at Filton This aircraft was eventually developed into the Bristol Blenheim.

15 April 1935
The Douglas TBD-1 Devastator torpedo bomber made its first flight. It served in the US Navy until 1942.

1 May 1935
A new scheme of RAF Expansion, known as Scheme C, was announced to raise the aircraft strength of the Home Defence air force to 1,500 by March 1937.

15 May 1935
The Curtiss P-36 metal monoplane fighter made its first flight and served as a stop-gap fighter until the P-40 Warhawk was developed.

28 May 1935
The Messerschmitt Bf109 prototype was flown at Augsburg, heralding the start of a successful Luftwaffe fighter dynasty.

23 July 1935
A report on Radio Direction Finding, known later as Radar, was presented to the British Air Defence Research Committee.

6 November 1935
The first flight of Hawker's first monoplane fighter (later named Hurricane) took place at Brooklands.

12 November 1935
The British Government approved plans to build five radar early warning stations between Bawdsey and South Foreland, protecting the Thames Estuary and the approaches to London.

9 December 1935
The Curtiss SB2C Helldiver carrier-based scout bomber, made its first flight.

2 March 1936
RAF officer Frank Whittle set up Power Jets to develop a turbojet aircraft engine.

3 March 1936
A British Government White Paper proposed an increase from 1,500 to 1,750 RAF first-line aircraft for home defence.

Russian machines went to Spain. These comprised mainly the Polikarpov I-15 biplane fighter, but when this became outclassed by newer Western types, they sent the Polikarpov I-16 monoplane, together with the Tupolev SB2 bomber. A few American 'volunteer' pilots went to Spain, mainly using the Grumman G-23 (an export version of the US Navy FF-1 fighter built in Canada), which had been intended for Turkey.

Condor Legion aircraft successfully bombed and put out of action the Spanish battleship *Jaime I*. Throughout the war tactical deployment of aircraft continued to demonstrate the value of air power. The widespread bombing of cities, by both sides, caused considerable concern throughout the world. Gradually the war burned down; the Nationalists slowly improved their strength and their territorial holdings, while the Loyalists fought bitterly amongst themselves. Barcelona fell in March 1939 and the Nationalists stood triumphant, though exhausted, while the foreign and International Brigade returned home.

BIGGER BOMBERS

In the 1920s, with 'the war to end wars' only a few years in the past, the idea of another major conflict looked somewhat remote. Only France, who had retained a large air force as a continuing deterrent to Germany, remained a potentially serious enemy to Britain in the event of a seismic deterioration in relations. Thus, in Europe, the bomber threat was still mainly academic.

In the United States, General 'Billy' Mitchell, who commanded a tactical bomber group in France towards the end of WW1, was a strong believer in strategic bombing. Mitchell's propaganda kept the concept of the bomber in existence in the US in the inter-war years.

The use of the bomber in colonial wars, in which the defences were negligible or non-existent, tended to draw attention away from the problems that would be met if such attacks were to be made on a sophisticated and industrial nation. There was a growing belief that the bomber would always get through. The depressed economic climate of the late 1920s and early 1930s encouraged disarmament – money was scarce and little thought was given by any other nation to the building of a bomber force.

The Handley Page Heyford, together with the Vickers Virginia (well past its useful life by the end of the 1920s) remained the backbone of the RAF's bomber force until 1937. By then the Fairey Battle, Bristol Blenheim and Armstrong Whitworth Whitley monoplanes were

This overall-black Armstrong Whitworth Whitley V was flown by No 78 Squadron based at RAF Dishforth. The Whitley was the slowest of all the British bombers but was a rugged bomb carrier.

91

When the Boeing B-17B entered service in 1939 it was the fastest and highest-flying bomber in the world. The USAAC had embarked on a major programme to perfect long-range strategic bombing by day, relying on the massed firepower of large formations of aircraft like the B-17 to counter the threat from any attacking enemy fighters.

entering service. The French meanwhile had tended to look on the bomber as an army support weapon, and in the Far East, Japan (who had been fighting China since 1931) had used its aircraft almost entirely in support of her armies.

In the US, there was a move to evolve a strategic bomber doctrine, and Boeing decided on a military version of its all-metal Model 307 Stratoliner monoplane transport. By the late 1930s, the B-17 Flying Fortress prototype had flown, a revolutionary four-engined aircraft that could fly at 25,000ft – a height which provided considerable protection from fighters. The Douglas B-18 of the USAAC meanwhile used the wings and tail unit of the DC-2 transport.

The revolutionary Norden bomb-sight enabled bombing from this height with a high degree of accuracy. At this time strategists and politicians in America, protected on one coast by the Atlantic and the other by the Pacific, felt that strategic bombing was at that time neither necessary or acceptable. There the role of the bomber was primarily that of attacking any enemy fleet which might have the nerve to approach the coastline of the USA.

From the mid-1930s it was Britain alone that

Below: From 1937, the German Dornier Do17 (dubbed the 'Flying Pencil') was one of the most notorious and active fast bomber/reconnaissance aircraft in the world. Early variants of the Do17 had a maximum bomb load of 2,205lb (1,000kg).

5 March 1936
The Supermarine Spitfire prototype was flown for the first time, powered by a Rolls-Royce Merlin engine and armed with eight machine guns.

17 March 1936
The first flight of the Armstrong Whitworth Whitley bomber. It became one of the mainstays of RAF Bomber Command in the early years of WW2.

12 May 1936
The Messerschmitt Bf110 twin-engine strategic fighter made its initial flight. Ineffective on daylight operations, it became a formidable night fighter.

15 June 1936
The prototype of the Westland Lysander was flown for the first time. It was the first monoplane to join Army Co-operation squadrons.

15 June 1936
The Vickers Wellington, the best of all the RAF's night medium bombers in the early years of WW2, made its first flight.

21 June 1936
The Handley Page Hampden twin-engined bomber made its maiden flight. It was the last of the twin-engined monoplane bombers to enter service with the RAF during the expansion and rearming of Bomber Command in the late 1930s.

18 July 1936
The Spanish Civil War began and Germany, Italy and the Soviet Union sent aircraft and personnel to the war zone.

16 October 1936
The Short Sunderland four-engined flying boat made its first flight.

2 December 1936
The first Boeing Y1B-17 four-engine bomber, which was eventually developed into the B-17 Flying Fortress, made its initial flight.

21 December 1936
First flight of the Junkers Ju88, the Luftwaffe's most adaptable and widely used medium bomber of WW2.

1 January 1937
One of the most effective carrier-borne torpedo bombers in the world, the Nakajima B5N, first flew.

was building a heavy bomber force specifically designed to carry a bombing war to enemy industry. By 1937, the RAF had the Vickers Wellington, with an armament of six machine guns and capable of carrying 4,500lb of bombs over 1,200 miles – a far cry from the biplanes of only a few years earlier. The RAF decided to eliminate the light bomber (Hawker Harts and Hinds, whose bomb load was 500lb) in favour of 'mediums' (Blenheims and Hampdens) and 'heavy mediums' (Wellingtons and Whitleys). No thought was given for a modern light bomber, a shortfall which WW2 quickly made apparent.

Left: The three-engined Savoia-Marchetti SM.79 came to represent for Italy what the Spitfire meant to the British and the B-17 to the Americans. Achieving success as a torpedo-bomber in the Mediterranean, it was a rugged adversary that proved difficult to shoot down.

In 1937 new 'shadow' factories came into production by fits and starts, and British rearmament really began to get under way. However, by 1936 the RAF had already started planning four-engined bombers, the first being the Short Stirling, which initially flew a few months before the outbreak of war.

Germany was considering the concept of the 'Ural' long-range strategic bomber to enable the Luftwaffe to strike any corner of Europe, with Junkers and Dornier building prototypes of their Ju89 and Do19 respectively. These were followed by the Ju86 (and later Ju88), Do17 and Heinkel He111, as well as the Junkers Ju87 dive-bomber.

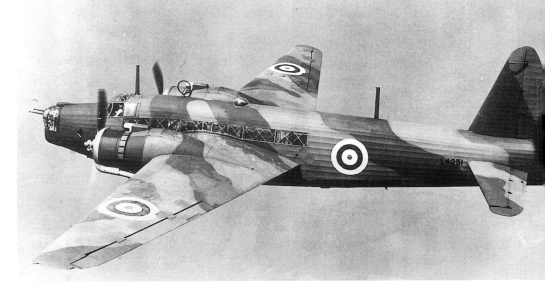

With its unique geodetic 'basket weave' method of construction, the Vickers Wellington bomber (widely known as the 'Wimpey'), was the backbone of RAF Bomber Command early in WW2 until four-engined heavy bombers became available in large numbers.

In Russia the Tupolev SB twin-engined bomber entered service in 1935, and Italy was producing the Savoia-Marchetti S.79 (a tri-motor) and the Fiat BR.20. The Japanese had two Mitsubishi twin-engined bombers in service, in their war against China, in the late '30s – the Army Ki21 and the Navy G3M series. In Poland the PZL P.37 Los was entering service, as was the Fokker TV in Holland. The French produced two fast streamlined medium bombers – the Amiot 350 and the Lioré-et-Olivier 451, but very few were in service by 1939.

CHRONOLOGY

1 April 1937
The Junkers Ju87 'Stuka' was delivered to the Luftwaffe for the development of dive-bomber tactics, and these were put into practice when three aircraft were despatched to Spain later in the year.

12 April 1937
The Whittle turbojet engine was successfully tested for the first time at the British Thomson Houston (BTH) factory in Rugby, Warwickshire.

30 April 1937
An early illustration of the battleship's vulnerability to air attack was given when the *Espano*, being operated by the Spanish Nationalist forces, was sunk by Republican aircraft.

7 May 1937
A milestone in the evolution of pressurised aircraft when the Lockheed XC-35 (adapted from the Model 12 Electra) made its first flight.

30 June 1937
The US Navy received the four USAAC airships in its inventory when the Air Corps abandoned its airship programme.

4 July 1937
The German Air Ministry set up a rocket aircraft research programme called Project X.

Radar

The Air Ministry was making intensive efforts, as far as finances allowed, to establish direction-finding (DF) facilities. Initially a Marconi-Adcock 'anti-night effect' Direction Station was established at Pulham, Norfolk. Mastery of the skies depended on aircraft equipment – and a greater measure of that mastery was made possible by radio.

Patrick Blackett, who was Professor of Physics at Manchester University, spoke at the Tizard Memorial Lecture at the Institute of Strategic Studies in 1960:

"The appointment of Henry Tizard as Chairman of the Air Ministry's Committee for the Scientific Survey of Air Defence was a major event in our history. It led of course to radar and the first effective system of air defence."

"It was due to Tizard's personal initiative as early as 1936 that civilian scientists were attached to the fighter station at Biggin Hill to study the art of controlled interception, as it would have to be done, when a year or two later the radar chain would become operational.

This experiment seems to have been the first official recognition that the actual operations of modern war are so complicated and change so fast that the traditional training of the serving officers and personnel is inadequate."

Airborne radar was developed from the autumn of 1935 but here progress was slower, partly for reasons of priorities and also partly because of the difficulty of accommodating apparatus of sufficient power within the restricted space of an aeroplane. The breakthrough came with the development of an improved form of the magnetron valve.

In the spring of 1939 Watson-Watt persuaded a number of high-level physicists to spend their long vacations at radar stations. Among them were Professors Oliphant and Randall and Dr Boot from the University of Birmingham who, over the course of the next six months, produced the resonant cavity magnetron which was soon developing astounding power in a device a few inches in size.

ENTER THE MERLIN

I n the late 1920s Rolls-Royce decided that its future lay with the monobloc petrol aero
engine. To power the large flying boats then being designed, an enlarged 'F' engine was
developed in 1927 as the 'H', later named the Buzzard. A geared and supercharged
engine of 2,239cu in, and weighing 1,460lb, it produced 925hp at sea level. Only a limited
number were built but, in 1928, it formed an admirable base for the Rolls-Royce 'R' unit to
contest the 1929 Schneider Trophy, and pressure on the firm by the Air Ministry provided the
incentive to develop a racing engine.

The 'R' was also later used to set both land and water speed records. A double-sided
supercharger was installed between the V-block on the 'R', and the highly stressed parts were
strengthened. When first run in May 1929, it produced 1,800hp for a period of one hour at
2,900rpm and fitted to the Supermarine S6, it won the 1929 Schneider race.

The British government refused to give any funding to the staging of the 1931
Schneider, but the day was saved by a £100,000 donation by Lady Houston. Spurred on by
this gesture, Rolls-Royce made a supreme effort to increase the power of the 'R' engine, and
by August 1931 it was producing 2,350hp at 3,200rpm. The engine duly delivered the 'goods'
and Great Britain won the Schneider Trophy outright.

In 1928 a special 'F' had been designed to use steam cooling and this was developed into
the Goshawk, but flight testing revealed many problems. Though tried in twelve different
aircraft, only twenty-four Goshawk units were manufactured.

After the outstanding Schneider success – and a world speed record attained with the S6

Early Hurricane Is of No 87 Squadron at RAF Debden in
the summer of 1939. Low visibility national markings
were introduced after the Munich crisis of 1938.

CHRONOLOGY

7 July 1937
Japan began a full-scale invasion of China.

15 July 1937
The Blohm und Voss Bv138 twin-boom long-range
maritime flying boat made its first flight.

11 August 1937
The Boulton Paul Defiant fighter, the first with a
four-gun power-operated turret and no forward
armament, made its maiden flight. The concept
proved fatally flawed, but the Defiant did prove a
useful night fighter in the early stages of WW2.

2 September 1937
First flight of the Grumman F4F-2 monoplane fighter,
the prototype of the Wildcat – the first in the
Grumman 'cat' series of famous naval aircraft.

CHRONOLOGY

18 January 1938
Eighteen PBY Catalina flying boats of the US Navy left San Diego for a non-stop flight to Hawaii, which they completed in 20 hours flying time.

20 January 1938
An Armstrong Whitworth AW23 transport was used in the first UK flight-refuelling tests, with a Short Empire flying boat over the Solent.

6 April 1938
The Bell P-39 Airacobra, a fighter with tricycle undercarriage designed with the engine installed mid-fuselage to make room for a centrally-mounted 37mm cannon, firing through the propeller boss, made its first flight. Many went to Russia under Lend-Lease.

23 May 1938
In the belief that the biplane fighter still had a future in a modern air force, Fiat in Italy developed the CR42 Falco, which made its first flight on this day.

11 July 1938
The Soviet Union deployed large numbers of bombers and fighters against Japanese forces in a territorial dispute on the borders of Korea, Manchuria and Siberia.

11 October 1938
The Westland Whirlwind, to be the RAF's first single-seat twin-engined fighter, made its maiden flight. It proved to be underpowered and plagued by troublesome engines.

14 October 1938
One of the great American fighters of WW2, the Curtiss P-40 Warhawk, made its initial flight.

15 October 1938
The RAF's first twin-engined monoplane torpedo bomber, the Bristol Beaufort, made its first flight. Despite its designated role, the Beaufort was more often in action dropping conventional bombs on ports and installations and on mine-laying sorties.

26 October 1938
One of the most important twin-engined light bombers of WW2, the Douglas DB-7, first flew. It became the Havoc night fighter and Boston bomber in the RAF, and was the most-produced of all aircraft procured by the USAAF in the 'Attack' category.

7 November 1938
Two RAF Vickers Wellesley light bombers established a world long-distance record flight of 7,158 miles from Ismailia, Egypt to Darwin, Australia.

12 January 1939
US Congress approved authorisation of $300m on a force of a maximum of 6,000 aircraft with $180m of the total spent on combat types.

in the same month – the British Air Ministry refused to give any funding to develop a new engine. By late 1932, the company itself decided to develop one as a private venture, but as a conventional V-12, and the first PV12 unit test ran on 15 October 1933.

The initial engine was installed in a Hawker Hart, making its inaugural flight on 12 April 1935. With the start of the RAF Expansion Scheme, the Air Ministry then decided to support the new engine, and this was then named as the Merlin. The initial Merlin Is (of which 180 were delivered) were committed to the Hawker Hurricane fighter being developed by Sidney Camm, and the Fairey Battle light bomber.

The Merlin G had an improved flat head cast integral with the block and with all four valves parallel. It became the Merlin II in early 1937, by which time it was producing 1,030hp at 3,000rpm. The Merlin X, fitted with a two-speed blower, entered production for the Armstrong Whitworth Whitley and Handley Page Halifax bombers.

When a new supercharger was fitted, the Merlin XX was built for the Hurricane II, and the Mk45 for the Spitfire V. The high-altitude Merlin 60 series doubled the power at height, adding 10,000ft to the Spitfire's service ceiling, together with an increase of 70mph to its top speed. Merlins, which many regard as the world's most famous piston engine, were also used in the Boulton Paul Defiant, Bristol Beaufighter II and Vickers Wellington II, while the conversion of the Avro Manchester into the highly-successful Lancaster was made possible. With the advent of the Merlin-powered P-51 Mustang, the engine was licence-built in the US with 55,523 being produced by Packard. UK production totalled 112,517 units.

The Merlin reached the peak of its development midway through WW2, when the improved Griffon, a scaled-up version of the Merlin with 36% greater capacity, was introduced, transforming the performance of the Spitfire.

The Fairey Battle was one of the key types chosen by the Air Ministry to equip the rapidly expanding RAF of the late 1930s. Fitted with a single Merlin engine, the Battle proved to be grossly underpowered for its intended role as a day bomber.

Fieseler's Storch

Without doubt, the Fieseler Fi156 Storch (Stork) was the foremost example of an army co-operation and observation aircraft and certainly the design by which other types operating in this role (including those used by the Allies) were judged. First flown in 1936, it was a remarkable STOL (short take-off and landing) braced high-wing monoplane with a long-stroke main landing gear. Its extensively glazed cockpit provided an excellent view for the three-man crew. It was probably the only Luftwaffe aircraft demonstrably better than any Allied counterpart.

For with little more than a light breeze blowing, it needed a take-off run of less than 200ft (60m) – and could land in a about a third of that distance. Such performance was accomplished by the Storch's high-lift devices – a fixed slat extending over the entire span of the wing leading edge, together with slotted ailerons and slotted camber-changing flaps occupying the entire trailing edge.

Regarded as a 'go-anywhere' aircraft, the Storch was found virtually wherever German forces were operating in WW2, performing tactical reconnaissance, emergency rescue (mainly in North Africa), liaison, staff transport and various other roles.

Wartime production totalled 2,900, and a number were supplied to Axis satellite and neutral air forces. In WW2, the Storch was also built for the Luftwaffe by Morane-Saulnier in France (as the MS500/501/502 Criquet series) and by Mraz in Czechoslovakia (as the K-65 'Cap').

It had a fuselage of welded steel construction with fabric covering and the wings were made of wood with a fabric covering. The bracing struts were of steel tubing. The STOL capability was substantially enhanced by its very strong undercarriage, whose energy-absorbing oleos could withstand the high vertical sink rates that were imposed by steep approaches.

Powerplant was a 240hp (179kW) Argus As10C-3 inverted Vee-8 air-cooled piston engine, which gave a maximum speed of 109mph (175km/h). Its incredible

The Fieseler Storch, with its STOL capability, was by far the best liaison and spotter aircraft of WW2.

slow-flying capability was its best defence against attacks by enemy fighters, but it could be equipped with an aft-firing 7.9mm MG 15 machine gun, firing through a transparent panel in the top decking.

Storchs played a vital role in the German invasion of France in May 1940 when they landed shock-troops ahead of armour in Belgium and Luxembourg to secure lines of advance. Better-known exploits included the rescue of Benito Mussolini from imprisonment in a hotel amid the Appenine mountains in northern Italy on 12 September 1943, landing on the tiny terrace at the back of the hotel. Severely overloaded, it took-off over a sheer edge. There was also the flight of General Ritter von Greim (piloted by Hanna Reitsch) into beleaguered Berlin to take charge 12 days before the German surrender in May 1945. At least 47 airworthy Storchs were captured in the Mediterranean theatre and were used by RAF front-line squadrons.

MITCHELL'S SPITFIRE

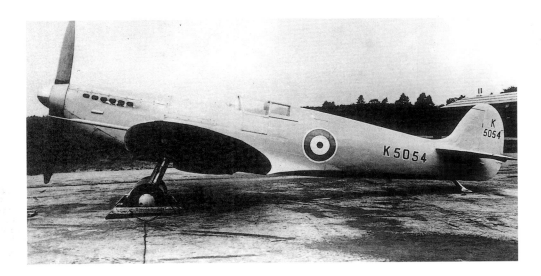

J oseph Smith, who succeeded R. J. Mitchell as Chief Designer at Supermarine, speaking to the Royal Aeronautical Society, said: "The Spitfire, with its Rolls-Royce engine – and its family – will always be regarded as a classic example of British aeronautical achievement, proved and tested over eleven years of production and Service use. Originally designed by the late R. J. Mitchell in 1935, the prototype Spitfire first flew in 1936; since then, over 22,000 have been manufactured in 33 different types. This remarkable aircraft remained a front-line fighter throughout the whole period of the war."

The legendary Spitfire was created by a design team led by Reginald J. Mitchell, and was the outcome of a process of development and refinement of a single-seat fighter design which Mitchell originally conceived as a private venture, because he was dissatisfied with a Goshawk-powered fighter he had proposed to a rigid 1930 Air Ministry specification. The prototype Spitfire was of such advanced conception that an Official Specification (F.37/34) had to be virtually 'written round' it when the Air Ministry contract was produced in the winter of 1934/35. It made its maiden flight on 5 March 1936, some four months later than its great contemporary, the Hawker Hurricane, and production aircraft began to enter RAF service with No 19 Squadron at Duxford in August 1938.

By the outbreak of WW2, nine full squadrons of Spitfires were in the front-line, and on 16 October 1939, Spitfires of No 603 (RAuxAF) Squadron became the first UK-based aircraft to shoot down an enemy machine since hostilities began. When the Battle of Britain commenced the following summer there were nineteen squadrons fully-equipped with Spitfires. At that time, the Spitfire was the only RAF fighter capable of meeting the Messerschmitt Bf109E on truly equal terms, and the part it played in saving Britain from invasion is now history.

Supermarine's chief designer Reginald J. Mitchell (left) with Sir Henry Royce in the early 1930s. The Rolls-Royce PV.12 engine (subsequently named Merlin) was crucial to the Spitfire's development.

Above: The first production Spitfire I was flown on 14 May 1938, and the aircraft is seen here over the south coast shortly afterwards with Jeffrey Quill at the controls. It was almost identical to the prototype, the only difference being the method of construction.

Top left: The prototype Spitfire (K5054) first flew on 5 March 1936 from Eastleigh airfield, near Southampton.

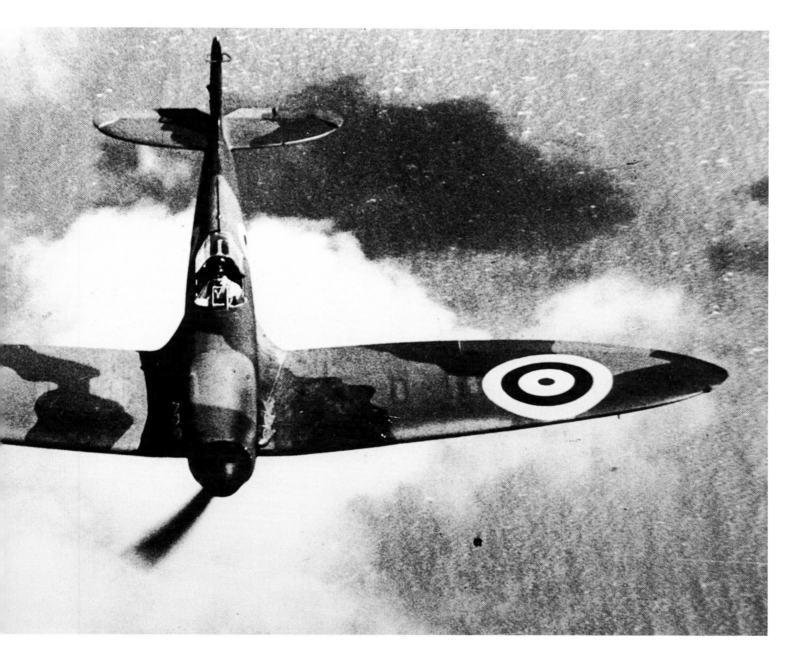

The Spitfire was operational throughout the war and served with distinction on every major battlefront, its various roles including those of fighter-bomber and reconnaissance aircraft. To meet ever-changing and increasingly exacting operational requirements it underwent continuous development and adaptation. Unfortunately Mitchell never heard more than a tiny fraction of the praise which was lavished on the Spitfire, for he died of cancer in June 1937 at the tragically early age of 42 – only fifteen months after the prototype flew from Eastleigh. It was the only Allied fighter to remain continuously in production throughout the war. When production ceased in October 1947, 20,351 had been built. In addition, 2,408 navalised Seafires had left the production lines.

Born on 20 May 1895, Mitchell left school at sixteen and served an engineering apprenticeship with a locomotive product company. In 1916, he obtained a position with Supermarine Aviation works at Southampton. Within three years he was in the drawing office as chief designer and, in 1920 (at the age of 25) became overall chief designer.

The firm was taken over by Vickers in 1928 and Mitchell was appointed director and chief designer, posts he held until his death in 1937. He was elected a Fellow of the Royal Aeronautical Society in 1929, and in 1932 was awarded the CBE. Mitchell was a member of the Air League of the British Empire and a founder member of the Hampshire Aeroplane Club, obtaining his pilot's licence in 1934.

A further quote from Joseph Smith: "Foremost among his characteristic ways was a clear thinking ability to create, which made him a designer in the truest sense of the word. This ability was the driving force of his life – and resulted in a tremendous output of new types of aircraft in an incredibly short span of years. No other man, in my experience, has produced anything like the number of new and practical fundamental ideas that he did during his relatively short span of working life. The wholehearted and continuous appreciation of this genius was an inspiration to all who worked with him."

All the forethought of Mitchell and the ambition of his design team to exploit their Schneider Trophy successes by developing a front-line fighter would have been fruitless if a corresponding advance had not been made in powerplant design – the Rolls-Royce Merlin. Sir Henry Royce summed up 'R. J.' as 'a man slow to decide and quick to act'.

As production of the Spitfire was stepped up, various improvements were introduced – the most important of which was a three-bladed, variable-pitch constant-speed propeller. This is a Spitfire IA, armed with eight wing-mounted machine guns. By mid-1940, nineteen squadrons were equipped with the type.

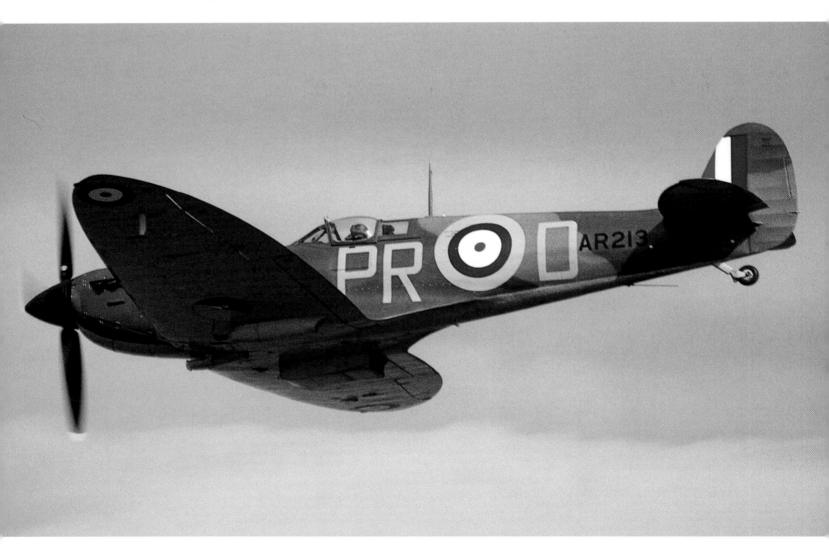

The purely experimental Heinkel He178 was notable as the world's first turbojet-powered aircraft to fly. It took to the air in 1939, nearly two years before the Gloster E.28/39 in Britain.

The Dawn of the Jet Age

Von Ohain in Germany had obtained a patent in 1935 for his turbojet, with an axial-plus-centrifugal compressor and inward radial turbine, and he was engaged by the Heinkel company in 1936 to develop a turbojet to power its He178 research aircraft.

At the same time that work was in progress on the He176 rocket aircraft, Heinkel was developing the He178, which featured the company's HeS 3b (S for Strahl, meaning jet) engine. By September 1937, a hydrogen-fuelled demonstration engine was being bench-tested, and in March 1938 the HeW 3 engine, using petrol as a fuel, was developing about 1,100lb st (4.89kN). The first example, the HeS 3, was air tested slung beneath He118 D-OVIE in May 1939.

The He178 became the world's first turbojet aircraft to fly when Flugkapitän Erich Warsitz made a circuit of the factory airfield at Rostock-Marienche on 27 August 1939, nearly two years before the Gloster E.28/39 became airborne in Britain. Its development was very much on a private venture basis and it was not until 28 October 1939 that Luftwaffe official observers were to see the He178 in flight. The project attracted little interest at the time and work was discontinued in favour of the He280, and the He178 flew seldom thereafter.

The He178 was a shoulder-wing monoplane of composite construction. The jet engine was mounted in the fuselage, with a nose air-intake duct passing beneath the pilot's seat and a long tailpipe discharging from the fuselage tailcone. A retractable tailwheel-type landing gear was installed.

Subsequently the He178 was donated to the Berlin Technik Museum, but was destroyed during a wartime air raid. The He280 was a more advanced twin-engine design by pairs of the new Heinkel turbojets, the HeS 8 and HeS 30. The first powered flight was on 2 April 1941, but suffered from wholly inadequate power. Nine prototypes were built for research purposes, but the rival Messerschmitt Me262 was chosen for production.

In England, Frank Whittle was the man most deeply involved with jet engine research. In 1928, whilst a Flight Cadet, he wrote a thesis at the RAF College, Cranwell in which he described how gas turbines and jet propulsion would free aircraft from the existing limitations on flight performance. He obtained a patent in 1930, but neither the British Air Ministry or industry showed any interest at that stage.

By 1935, Whittle was to obtain capital to form Power Jets Ltd, and BAH (British Thomson-Houston) were contracted to build a single engine with a double-sided centrifugal compressor and single-stage axial turbine. The first unit was ready for testing on 12 April 1937.

Work continued with the original engine and it was not until the greatly improved W1X first ran on 14 December 1940 that the Air Ministry was prepared to give financial help. A contract was placed for an engine to power a research aircraft (the W1) together with that for the Gloster E.28/39 airframe itself.

CHRONOLOGY

27 January 1939
The Lockheed P-38 Lightning twin-engined, twin-boom fighter made its first flight – one of the best-known USAAF fighters operational in WW2.

1 April 1939
The Mitsubishi A6M1 single-seat fighter prototype first flew, adopted by the Imperial Japanese Navy in July 1940 as the Type '0' carrier fighter – an aircraft better known as the Zero.

11 May 1939
Air units of the Imperial Japanese Army AF went into action against Russian forces when fighting broke out on the Manchuko border with Outer Mongolia.

14 May 1939
The Short Stirling four-engine heavy bomber prototype made its first flight. It was the first four-engine monoplane bomber to enter RAF service and the first to be used operationally.

1 June 1939
The prototype Focke-Wulf Fw190 made its first flight at Bremen – the aircraft which is now regarded as the outstanding radial-engined fighter and attack type of WW2.

17 July 1939
The Bristol Beaufighter, the RAF's first purpose-designed twin-engined night fighter, and the first effective production aircraft in this role to be equipped with airborne interception (AI) radar, made its first flight.

20 July 1939
The first Kawasaki Ki-48 prototype twin-engine light bomber made its initial flight.

17 August 1939
The first military version of the Douglas DC-3 was ordered by the USAAC as a command transport. Designated C-41, it subsequently became the C-47.

20 August 1939
The first reported example of air-to-air combat using rockets fired from a fighter, when five Polikarpov I-16s attacked a formation of Mitsubishi A5Ms over Manchuria during the Russo-Japanese war.

24 August 1939
General mobilisation of the Royal Air Force.

27 August 1939
The world's first aircraft to fly purely on turbojet power, the Heinkel He178 with a Heinkel HeS3b engine, was flown at Heinkel's Marienche airfield.

Boeing B-17G Flying Fortress

SECOND WORLD WAR
1939–1945

THE BATTLE OF BRITAIN

Right: The Dornier Do215B-1 was a development of the Do17 with DB 601A engines, mainly used for long-range reconnaissance during the Battle of Britain.

Below: A pair of Hurricane Is of No 501 Squadron scramble from RAF Hawkinge on 15 August 1940 to intercept another German bomber formation.

In the mid-summer of 1940, after the fall of France, the British braced themselves to meet the full brunt of the German Luftwaffe. It was crucial for the British to control the English Channel to stop the Germans from mounting an invasion. The resulting Battle of Britain became the first independent air battle in history, though it was not intended to be so. At the time it was regarded by both sides as a prelude to invasion, and only when the Germans failed in their objectives was it realised that the air battle was going to be the whole of the campaign.

Had it been solely a question of numbers, the RAF would have been in serious difficulties right from the start. In 1938, the RAF had believed it needed a minimum of fifty-two fighter squadrons for home defence against the Luftwaffe. By June 1940, it only had thirty-two as a result of the campaign in France – and in particular the effort to protect the Dunkirk evacuation. Of these squadrons, only twenty-five were made up of Hurricanes and Spitfires – less than half the strength the British had thought necessary. On 8 August 1940, the RAF had 654 aircraft in Fighter Command; the Luftwaffe had 1,971, including 594 of their best fighter, the Messerschmitt Bf 109E. The Germans outnumbered the RAF's strength by roughly three to one.

Initially, the Germans began attacking Channel convoys and ports, but it was the RAF that had to be the Luftwaffe's real target – the Channel battle served only to cost Fighter Command aircraft that they could not afford to lose. The British had two radar networks – a

A formation of Spitfire Is from No 65 Squadron at RAF Hornchurch led by F/O Bob Stanford-Tuck, who became one of the first RAF pilots to claim five victories in the Battle of Britain.

high-level one that could cover the enemy coast from Rotterdam to Cherbourg, and a low-level one that reached out some thirty miles to sea – and these were the next German targets.

On 15 August, the Luftwaffe launched its main attack – 'Eagle Day'. It was intended as the great knockout blow, but it turned out to be a disaster. The Luftwaffe lost a total of 75 aircraft, while the RAF lost 30 in the air and another 24 machines on the ground. The last weeks of August and the first of September proved the crucial time for the RAF, as during this period the Germans finally got their priorities correct and went for the whole structure of Fighter Command – namely the airfields, radar stations and control mechanisms.

In a two-week period the RAF lost 264 fighters, though many of the pilots parachuted or crash landed on their own territory and lived to fight again. On 7 September, Goering threw victory away by believing the exaggerated claims of his pilots, and decided the British were already finished. Had the RAF been beaten in the air, everything else would have followed as a matter of course.

Sporadic air attacks on the UK continued until 15 September, when the Luftwaffe

The Heinkel He111 was the Luftwaffe's most successful bomber throughout the Battle of Britain. This is a Merlin-engined example built by CASA after the war.

Above: During the Battle of Britain, the RAF's Hawker Hurricanes destroyed more enemy aircraft than all the other defences put together.

launched its heaviest daylight raid on London. The RAF, which had gained sufficient respite to replenish some of its squadrons, met the onslaught and inflicted heavy casualties. On 17 September, Hitler made the decision to postpone indefinitely Operation *Seeloewe* (Sealion) – the intended invasion of the UK. Casualties had been heavy for both sides – 1,882 Luftwaffe aircraft, and 1,017 aircraft and 537 pilots of RAF Fighter Command.

The last word on the Battle of Britain must be for the men who fought and won it in the sky – the pilots of Fighter Command: "They were a remarkable breed, not quite like any other set of British fighting men. They cultivated a rakish and light-hearted approach to life. They affected to despise the external manifestations of Service discipline and disregarded the more pompous conventions of King's Regulations whenever possible." Squadron Leader G. A. L. 'Minnie' Manton of No 56 Squadron based at RAF North Weald recalled: "I don't think any of us (and I was older than most) really appreciated the seriousness of the situation. When we could be scared to death five or six times a day and yet find ourselves drinking in the local pub before closing time on a summer evening, it all seemed unreal".

Dogfights over England

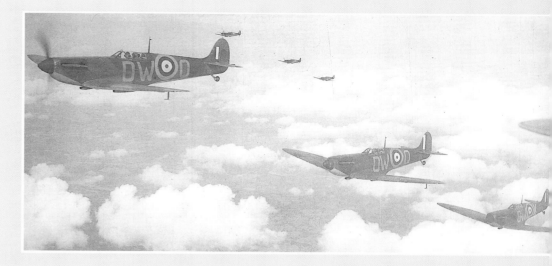

The King has been graciously pleased to approve the following award in recognition of gallantry displayed in flying operations against the enemy:
Bar to the Distinguished Flying Cross to Acting Wing Commander Paul Jones DSO, DFC. This fearless pilot has recently added a further four enemy aircraft to his previous successes. In addition, he has probably destroyed another four and damaged five hostile aircraft. (AIR MINISTRY COMMUNIQUÉ)

"I would like to tell you something about my boys in my squadron. They are grand lads, every one of them. Since the war started they have shown that they can fight as well as they fly, and between them they've already won six of the nine DFCs that have been awarded to the squadron. There has never been a happier or more determined crowd of fighter pilots, and, as an Englishman, I'm very proud to have the honour of leading them."

"There is one curious thing about this air fighting. One minute you see hundreds of aeroplanes in the sky, and the next minute there is nothing. All you can do is to look through your sights at your particular target – and in your mirror too, if you are sensible, for any Messerschmitts trying to get on your tail."

"Another day we like to remember – what fighter squadron who was in the show doesn't! – was Sunday 15 September 1940, when 185 enemy aircraft were destroyed. Our squadron led a wing of four or five squadrons in two sorties that day, and we emerged with 52 victories for the Wing, twelve of them falling to our squadron. On the first show that day we were at 20,000ft and ran into a large block of Ju88s and Do17s – about 40 in all and without a single fighter escort. This time, for a change, we outnumbered the Hun, and no more than eight got home from that party. At one time you could see planes going down on fire all over the place, and the sky seemed full of parachutes. It was sudden death that morning."

"The other day I led two of the latest recruits to the squadron on a search for a Ju88 off the East Coast. We found it 50 or 60 miles out to sea, and I led an attack from below. Suddenly the raider jettisoned his bombs and two of us had to duck out of the way. We know some of the tricks to try to get rid of our fighters, and at first I thought he was throwing out some new kind of secret weapon to bump us off. Then I realised he had let them go to help his speed."

"I kept with him and told the other two boys to go in and have a crack. Their shooting was amazingly accurate, and for the first time I saw bullets other than my own going into the fuselage of an enemy bomber.

Spitfire Is of No 610 Squadron from RAF Gravesend flying in battle formation. The larger roundels and squadron codes on the fuselage had been introduced in June 1940.

I watched them cracking in. The bomber pilot tried to get away and made for cloud. He went in, while one of my boys cruised around on top and the other waited below. Either the pilot of that Ju88 was a fool or he just could not help it, but he came flying out of the cloud at the other end on a straight course. The people below went up – it was almost like watching an event at a coursing meeting. When they had finished their ammunition those two Canadians left the bomber in a pretty bad state, and all I had to do was finish him off."

During the Battle of Britain, the Messerschmitt Bf109E proved to be generally superior to the Hurricane and Spitfire. This version is a restored Spanish-built Hispano HA.1112, modified with a Daimler Benz engine to represent a Bf109G.

TARANTO

The island of Malta was a vital staging post in the Mediterranean, and in 1940 there was growing concern that it was inadequately defended and within reach of attack by the Regia Aeronautica. The island, and its supply convoys, were threatened by the powerful presence of the Italian Fleet, a formidable fleet of warships divided between the naval bases of Naples and Taranto.

The British Admiralty had concluded that the wide expanse of Taranto harbour would present the best possible target for torpedo bombers. Admiral Cunningham decided to use HMS *Illustrious* and the Mediterranean Fleet with its Fairey Swordfish aircraft to attack this stronghold.

On 10 November 1940, a Martin Maryland of No 431 General Reconnaissance Flight at Malta reported a full complement of the Italian fleet, including six battleships, at anchor at Taranto. The next day, Nos 815 and 819 NAS, already embarked on *Illustrious*, together with Nos 813 and 824 NAS (flown on from HMS *Eagle*, which was out of action because of bomb damage), launched a night attack in two waves.

The attack began when two Swordfish strung a line of flares around the harbour and dropped bombs on an oil storage depot. The biplanes came in low, twisting and turning to avoid barrage balloon cables and the long line of warships spitting a deadly hail of fire from anti-aircraft weapons and machine guns. Cranking up to full power and diving so low over the water that some spun their wheels on the wave tops, the Swordfish bore steadily in. Disregarding the enemy, they fanned out, aligned on their targets, dropped their torpedoes and pulled up steeply, dodging the deadly web of balloon cables.

Few could have expected the Swordfish – not the most daunting weapon with which to challenge the Italian Navy, with a maximum speed of only 130mph (209km/h) – to accomplish such a task. A key element was the superb manoeuvrability of the 'Stringbag', but surprise was also essential for a successful result. All the aircraft survived to launch their weapons and escape. The following morning, Marylands on recce sorties from Malta confirmed an heroic achievement. Four battleships, a cruiser, two destroyers and two auxilary vessels had been severely damaged, and none would present a threat to the Royal Navy for many months. In a brief moment, 21 fragile biplanes and 42 gallant men (with each Swordfish loaded to its maximum, one of the usual three-man crew had to be left behind) had, at a single stroke, decisively altered the balance of power in the

The Fairey Swordfish was designed to be flown at very slow speeds, specifically for carrier operations. With a single torpedo carried under the fuselage, it had a range of 546 miles (879km) and proved ideal for the attack on Taranto.

Mediterranean. For the eventual loss of two aircraft, the British left the Italian Fleet in ruins behind them. The biggest problem with the attack had been getting the torpedoes to work in very shallow water, but the RN had successfully resolved it.

At the time, this outstanding success did not receive the accolades which it deserved. Cunningham, not a strong advocate of naval air power, made no recommendations for awards for aircrew gallantry. Nevertheless, the Japanese noted the success of the operation and it no doubt influenced their planning of the attack on Pearl Harbor which took place thirteen months later. The Swordfish went on to outlive the aircraft designed to replace it – the Albacore – and served throughout the war.

BOMBER FORCE

In 1941, RAF Bomber Command was struggling to expand but was continually beset with difficulties and frustration. Although the first really 'heavy' bombers were introduced from the winter of 1941/42, technical problems repeatedly caused their withdrawal from operations. There were serious delays in the production of these new types with the result that Vickers Wellingtons, together with obsolescent Hampdens, Whitleys (at that time still classed as 'heavy' bombers) and Blenheims continued to fly the majority of sorties throughout 1941. The Wellington – reliable, but slow and poorly armed – was the backbone of Bomber Command until well into 1942.

The first of the four-engined bombers to enter service was the Short Stirling, which went to No 7 Squadron at RAF Leeming in late 1940 and became operational from RAF Oakington, Cambs in February 1941. Undercarriage collapses and frequent belly landings were all too prevalent in the early

days. It lost popularity with crews for it was unable to fly at more than 18,000ft when fully loaded with bombs, and indeed was often hard put to reach 12,000ft. It was also handicapped by its inability to carry bombs larger than 2,000lb (909kg). By late 1943, the Stirling was on the wane – being completely outclassed by the Lancaster – and was then allotted only the less difficult targets.

The second of the new 'heavies' to enter service was the twin-engined Avro Manchester which joined No 207 Squadron at RAF Waddington in November 1940, and commenced operations in February 1941. Underpowered and suffering overheating with its unreliable Rolls-Royce Vulture engines, the Manchester fleet was grounded for several weeks at a time.

The Manchester was one of the RAF's biggest disappointments – yet, if it had not existed, the highly successful Avro Lancaster would not have been developed from it.

The Handley Page Halifax was the next to become operational in this bomber sequence, which joined No 35 Squadron at RAF Leeming in December 1940, and went into action in March 1941. Hydraulic problems dogged the Halifax during its early months in service. Early operational experience showed that the bulky and weighty dorsal turret, and its equally cumbersome nose turret, produced so much drag that they were a serious handicap to performance. Later marks operated with only the four-gun tail turret, and the large 'square' fins replaced the earlier triangular ones. Nevertheless, the Halifax proved its ability to withstand heavy damage and still get home safely. Bomber Command's Halifaxes flew 82,773 operational sorties during WW2 and dropped 224,207 tons of

The RAF's first four-engined bomber, the Short Stirling, was flown mainly by No 3 Group, Bomber Command during 1941-42. Although agile for its size, the Stirling suffered from being underpowered when fully laden. This is an improved Mk.III version in late 1942.

Above: Vickers Wellingtons had a long and successful period on night operations, with heavy attacks on all the main targets in Germany and others in Italy.

Opposite page: The Handley Page Hampden, operating from airfields in Lincolnshire, was the standard bomber of No 5 Group from mid-1939. These aircrew are with No 50 Squadron, based at RAF Waddington.

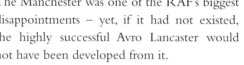

CHRONOLOGY

25 November 1940
The de Havilland Mosquito, conceived as an unarmed light bomber whose defence lay in its very high speed, was first flown.

25 November 1940
The Martin B-26 Marauder made its initial flight.

January 1941
The Japanese Kawanishi H8KI long-range flying boat (Allied code name *Emily*) made its first flight.

9 January 1941
The prototype Avro Lancaster made its maiden flight – the best-known and most successful of the RAF's wartime heavy bombers.

10 February 1941
The first British airborne forces operation of WW2 was supported by Armstrong Whitworth Whitleys, which dropped paratroops to destroy a viaduct at Tagino in Italy.

11 March 1941
The US Lend-Lease Act was approved by President Roosevelt – the UK, in particular, received greatly increased supplies of American aircraft.

Above: A founder member of the Pathfinder Force (PFF) was No 35 Squadron, whose Halifax 'P-Peter' was one of the PFF's earliest casualties, lost during a raid on Nuremburg on the night of 28-29 August 1942.

'Bomber' Harris

Group Captain Ken Batchelor OBE, DFC, RAF(Retd) recalls Marshal of the RAF Sir Arthur Harris Bt, GCB, OBE, AFC, LLD C-in-C Bomber Command:

"As a bomber squadron flight commander in 1940-41, I was well aware of our shortcomings and difficulties in pressing home our attacks effectively. Forced to fly at heights which often involved flying in bad weather rather than over it and without radar navigational aids, concentrated damage to targets was the exception rather than the rule. A hundred bombers over a main target was a maximum effort."

" The idea of self-defensive formations for attacks in daylight on naval shipyards and other primary targets proved to be disastrous and caused the loss of many of our pre-war professional crews. It also forced us into night operations without any long-range fighter cover. Even so there is a regrettable tendency to forget that for nearly four years Bomber Command alone was the only means of taking the offensive war into our enemy's homeland ."

"No one was more acutely aware at that time than Arthur Harris, then Air Officer Commanding No 5 Group with twin-engined Hampden bombers. A night flier in WW1 he became the father of the night bomber, so much so that it was he who advocated the development of the four-engined bomber in the late 1930s."

"These could not be made available to the RAF's squadrons in quantity until 1942 when he, now C-in-C Bomber Command, and the new aircraft, turned the tide in favour of the bomber offensive. The Stirlings, Halifaxes and Lancasters were at last able to devastate Germany's armament, industrial and economic resources with telling effect."

Above: Night bombing and bombing through overcast conditions were helped by the development of radar and navigation aids, using the experience of the first year of the bombing offensive, when many bombs missed their targets.

Left: This Avro Manchester IA flew with No 207 Squadron from RAF Waddington in 1941. Incessant problems with the Manchester's Vulture engines made operations difficult, and it was replaced by the four-engined Lancaster in 1942.

bombs, 1,833 aircraft being reported missing.

Boeing Fortress Is served with No 90 Squadron at RAF Polebrook in 1941, but the type's operational career with Bomber Command was very brief. The early Fortress could neither fly high enough or fast enough to avoid Luftwaffe fighters, and, lacking power-operated turrets or sufficient guns, they could not defend themselves well enough. Surviving aircraft were sent to Coastal Command or the Middle East.

1941 saw the gradual introduction of bigger and better bombs and in March the first 4,000lb (1,818kg) high-capacity bombs, or 'cookies' were used for the first time.

No 44 Squadron at RAF Waddington was the first unit selected to operate the Avro Lancaster. The 'Lanc' became Bomber Command's most potent heavy bomber of WW2. Altogether, Lancasters flew 156,192 operational sorties in WW2, dropped 608,612 tons of bombs and laid a substantial number of sea mines. 3,345 Lancasters were reported missing.

"Post-war, 'Bomber' Harris was pilloried for his responsibility for the so-called policy of 'area bombing' in the mistaken belief that its aim was the wholesale slaughter of civil populations. In fact, the charter for the combined British and American bomber offensive was clearly re-affirmed at the Casablanca Conference in 1943, which called for 'progressive destruction and the dislocation of the German military, industrial and economic system and the undermining of the morale of the German people to a point where their capacity for armed resistance is fatally weakened'. This accorded with his much earlier directive from the British War Cabinet."

"By the time Sir Arthur saw the massive Anglo-American bomber offensive really get underway, German aircraft production was devoted more and more to fighters at the expense of bombers. The latter dwindled from 60% in 1942 to 8% in 1944 with fighter production up to 75%. We tend to forget that their defence against

our bomber offensive put paid to the development of a counter strategic bomber force. The huge bomber formations which we saw in 1940 gave way to sporadic fighter/bomber intruders at night."

"Although not among his favoured targets, synthetic oil targets became of major importance once our forces had landed in France. Constant day and night attacks on these targets eventually starved the tanks and vehicles of the fuel they needed. By January 1945, oil production was almost at a standstill and thereafter inadequate to continue prosecuting the war."

"Suffice to say that once Arthur Harris was committed, he gave unstinted support to our armed forces, not only in preparing the way, but once they had landed. It can be claimed that they would never have overrun Germany without the massive preliminary onslaught of the bomber offensive. Arthur Harris, with our USAAF counterparts, certainly paved the way to victory!"

SHTURMOVIK

Taken in late 1944, this photograph shows Il-2M3 two-seater Shturmoviks over the Eastern Front, which by that time had been pushed beyond the borders of the Soviet Union.

The Ilyushin Il-2 Shturmovik armoured assault aircraft was one of the most formidable military aircraft of WW2, and became a real symbol of Red Air Force fighting efficiency during the war. It was produced in vast numbers, believed to have been in excess of 36,000. Designed in the late 1930s as an armoured ground–attack and anti-tank aircraft, and mainly influenced by findings from the Spanish Civil War, it featured an armoured shell, which was an integral part of the fuselage structure and protected the crew, engine, radiators and fuel tank. The first production prototype aircraft flew on 12 October 1940.

Large-scale production had just started before the German invasion of Russia in June 1941. Powered by a 1,700hp (1,282kW) Mikulin AM-38 twelve-cylinder engine, the initial versions were single-seat. It proved itself a potent weapon against German transport and armour, but during 1941/42 Russian fighter cover was then not available, and consequently losses were high. How vital the Il-2 was for the front was underlined by Joseph Stalin in his teleprint to factory workers in December 1941: 'The Red Army needs the Il-2, like air, like bread'.

In 1942 the Il-2M, the two-seat version, was introduced, answering criticisms about the Il-2's lack of defensive armament against new German aircraft. Lack of defence to the rear was condemned as a basic error – Soviet fighter units were very weak in 1941/42 and could not protect ground attack aircraft in action. The Il-2M was used in large numbers in early 1943 in the battles around Stalingrad.

From May 1943 onwards, the new automatic 37mm Il-P-37 cannon of Nudelman and Suranor were fitted to the Il-3M (with redesigned wings) and proved especially effective (even against the Tiger tank) in July 1943 during the large tank battle at Kursk. Only 30 of an original 300 tanks of the 3rd German Armoured Division were left after the battle.

The Shturmovik became an aircraft beloved by its crews and feared by opponents. From the summer of 1943, small 2.5kg bombs were carried and used against tanks, railway traffic and concentrations of weapons. The DAG-10 grenade container had provision for 200 such bombs, which were 'sown' from the air. The Il-2 also proved its worth in naval aviation units, especially against torpedo boats. The Type 3 went on to become the most important and numerous version of the Il-2. A number had a pair of 37mm NS-11 or P-37 cannon mounted in fairings outboard of the landing gear.

In the final year of WW2, Il-2s were used by Czechoslovak and Polish units flying with the Soviets, and the type served into the 1950s with the Soviet Air Force (V-VS) and other European regimes.

CHRONOLOGY

14 June 1941
The Martin Baltimore first flew, a light bomber which was delivered exclusively to the RAF.

22 June 1941
Germany launched Operation *Barbarossa*, the massive assault on Russia.

8 July 1941
First operational use of the B-17 Flying Fortress, when RAF Fortress Is made a daylight attack on Wilhelmshaven.

7 August 1941
A small force of Soviet Ilyushin Il-4 bombers, operating from Estonia, made a first attack on Berlin in reprisal for Luftwaffe raids on Moscow.

20 October 1941
The US Navy commissioned USS *Hornet*, the last carrier to join the fleet before the Japanese attack on Pearl Harbor.

PEARL HARBOR

Below: Ford Island, Pearl Harbor seen from a Japanese aircraft in the first wave of the attack.

I n April 1940 the US Fleet was moved to Pearl Harbor, in the Hawaiian Islands, from its usual base on the US West Coast, and from February 1941 it was re-christened the Pacific Fleet because of the deteriorating situation in the Far East. Ironically, this was a measure intended to deter the Japanese from aggressive action, but only served to make their surprise attack possible.

By October 1941, all signs of the peacetime US Navy at Pearl Harbor had gone – the ships no longer wore the very light grey paint, being replaced by a dark grey, with light grey top masts, camouflage scheme.

On the quiet Sunday morning of 7 December 1941, the Japanese attacked the naval base at Pearl Harbor and the United States was forced into WW2. 'AIR RAID, PEARL HARBOR, THIS IS NO DRILL!' – this famous signal was made just before 0800hr. The attackers had chosen this time because they rightly believed that the base would be at its lowest point of readiness.

The main attack came in two waves from a combined total of 376 aircraft from six aircraft carriers, escorted by 22 combat and support ships. When the Japanese aircraft arrived over Pearl, they found a large proportion of the US Pacific Fleet. In the harbour were eight

Below: At the outbreak of the Pacific War, the Nakajima B5N2 'Kate' was the most advanced carrier-borne torpedo bomber in the world. During the following twelve months, it delivered fatal blows to three separate US Navy carriers. These aircraft are replicas built for the 1960s film *Tora! Tora! Tora!*.

Day of Infamy

On the effects of Pearl Harbor, American historian Professor James L. Stokesbury wrote:
"Though it would seem every word that can be written about Pearl Harbor has been written, the argument still continues – was it a betrayal or merely a colossal bungle? Most serious authorities opt for the latter; the Americans knew the Japanese were on the move

Undoubtedly the finest Japanese aircraft of the early years of WW2, the Mitsubishi A6M 'Zero' remained a major threat until the introduction of the Grumman F6F Hellcat. This airworthy genuine 'Zero' (illustrated) is based in California.

– they had lost the Japanese carrier striking force, and had even put out what was tantamount to a war warning. Yet it was unthinkable that Japan would attack them, and throughout the Pacific they were caught asleep, wrapped in the blanket of their own complacency."

"Pearl Harbor was a massive replay of Taranto, which had convinced that a torpedo attack in a shallow harbour was in fact feasible. But instead of Britain's 20 Swordfish from one carrier, the Japanese employed six carriers and 450 planes – Mitsubishi Zero fighters, Aichi dive bombers and Nakajima torpedo planes. Japanese aircraft nomenclature was sufficiently complicated that the Americans eventually assigned nicknames to enemy planes; they were arbitrarily chosen by an officer who apparently was from the southern states. The three main types used at Pearl became known as *Zekes*, *Vals* and *Kates*; other names such as *Rufe*, *Kate*, *Hap*, *Oscar*, *Nell*, *Sally* and *Betty* were soon in common usage."

"Steaming on a circular path through the wastes of the northern Pacific, the Japanese striking force appeared undetected two hundred miles north of Oahu Island on the morning of 7 December 1941,

Left: The USS *West Virginia* and USS *Tennessee* ablaze after the devastating attack on Pearl Harbor.

launched its planes , and waited with baited breath. The results were spectacular."

" Coming in in successive waves, the Japanese found the US Fleet at anchor, and army and navy aircraft neatly lined up in rows along their airfields. Concerned over possible sabotage, the Americans had put their planes out in the open where they could be guarded. The first wave of attackers was practically unopposed. The second found a hornet's nest and took substantial casualties, but by then the damage had been done. Seven American battleships were disabled – two of them, *Arizona* and *Oklahoma*, total losses. Several other ships were near or total wrecks, almost 200 aircraft were destroyed, and there were 4,575 casualties, most of them among the fleet where hundreds of sailors were trapped in the sunken ships."

"The Japanese missed the American aircraft carriers, which were not at Pearl at the time of the strike, and they did not destroy the dock, storage and the repair facilities of the base. Nonetheless, their war of conquest got off to a smashing start."

Most of the American aircraft based at Pearl Harbor were destroyed during the Japanese onslaught. Here on Ford Island, Catalina flying boats and Kingfisher floatplanes come under attack.

battleships, nine cruisers, over 20 destroyers, five submarines and a number of other ships – a total of 86 combat and service ships, plus smaller yard craft and auxiliaries.

The Japanese aircraft were ordered to destroy any carriers and battleships which happened to be in port, together with all of the military aircraft on Oahu island. Fortunately (for the Allied cause), none of the three US Pacific Fleet carriers was in harbour. Had the Japanese waited a few more days, they might well have caught both the USS *Enterprise* and USS *Lexington*. The *Enterprise*, and her escorts, were heading back towards Hawaii after delivering fighter aircraft to Wake Island. Another carrier group, built around the *Lexington*, was on a similar mission to Midway. The other Pacific Fleet carrier, *Saratoga*, was in port at San Diego.

Both the United States and Japan were at peace with each other at the time. The Japanese broke the peace by attacking without warning and while still maintaining diplomatic relations, although they had intended to declare war shortly before the air strike reached Pearl Harbor.

The Japanese left the once peaceful base covered in smoke and fire, in apparent ruin. While this was true of some of the ships, the oil storage tanks, docks and repair facilities were virtually undamaged. Even before the smoke had cleared, the base was made operational and continued to be essential to victory in the Pacific throughout the war.

All but one of the 69 Catalina flying boats were destroyed or damaged on Ford Island – another seven were airborne and thus escaped. A total of 188 aircraft were destroyed, almost all caught on the ground. Only 30 of the attacking Japanese aircraft were shot down. The Japanese had ignored fuel oil tanks and repair facilities, and these were particularly valuable in the massive cleaning up operation that followed.

AVRO LANCASTER

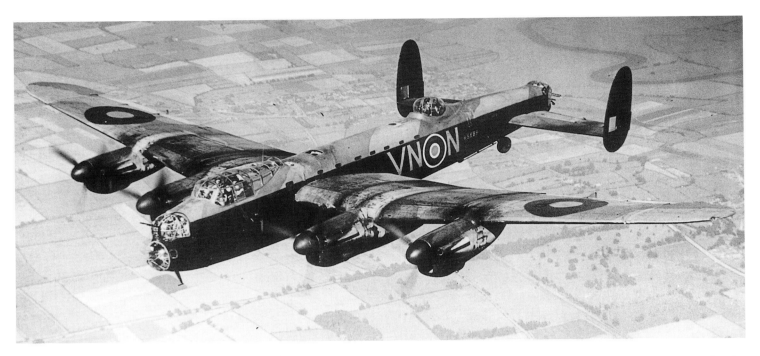

Above: Fine study of a newly delivered Lancaster of No 50 Squadron at RAF Swinderby in May 1942.

Below: A pair of Lancaster Is of No 207 Squadron over Lincolnshire in June 1942. Based at RAF Bottesford, the squadron had converted from Manchesters three months previously.

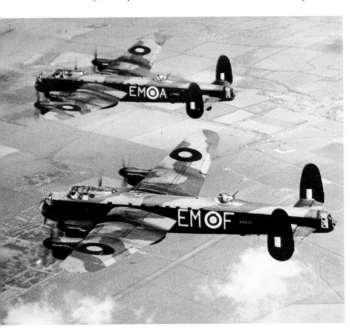

The Avro Lancaster was born out of a failure – the Manchester – yet it proved to be one of the most successful WW2 aircraft of any nation. The Manchester, powered by two Rolls-Royce Vulture engines was so beset by engine problems that it was decided to fit the aircraft with four well-proven Rolls-Royce Merlin engines. It was thus that the Lancaster (originally designated Manchester III) was born, the prototype making its first flight on 9 January 1941.

The Lancaster I would continue in production until 1946. It altered little throughout its production, a tribute to the soundness of the basic design by Roy Chadwick and its rugged construction (which incorporated a 33ft-long bomb bay). Initially there was a great danger of supply problems with Merlin engines, and the Lancaster II was produced with the Bristol Hercules VI 14-cylinder, air-cooled sleeve-valve radial engine. 300 such Lancasters were constructed, but the Merlin supply situation was eventually saved by the US Packard-built version.

As the war progressed, many detailed changes evolved – those externally visible being the deletion of fuselage side windows, enlargement of the bomb-aimer's plexiglass 'chin' and a larger astrodome. Numerous additional bumps, blisters and pimples appeared, as radar and more advanced radio aids were fitted. The ventral H2S blister became the most notable of additions. Armament continued more or less standard throughout the war, though final versions had a different rear turret housing two 0.5in machine guns.

The Lancaster I was a near-perfect flying machine – fast for its size and very smooth. Its normal crew was seven, comprising pilot, flight engineer, navigator, wireless operator, rear gunner, mid-upper gunner and bomb aimer (who also manned the front turret). The build-up of Lancaster units continued throughout 1942, and by early 1943 there were 18 squadrons using the type. By the end of the European war some 50 Lancaster squadrons were operational.

The capacious bomb bay of the Lancaster is shown to good effect in this view of the sole airworthy example in Europe, operated in the UK by the RAF's Battle of Britain Memorial Flight.

CHRONOLOGY

18 April 1942
Commanded by Gen James Doolittle, sixteen USAAF B-25 Mitchells launched from the USS *Hornet* made the first ever air attack on the Japanese mainland – a daring propaganda raid to boost morale in the US.

19 April 1942
The Italian Macchi MC205 Veltro fighter first flew.

20 April 1942
A force of 47 RAF Spitfires was flown off USS *Wasp* some 1060km (660 miles) west of Malta to reinforce the island's air defence.

7 May 1942
Start of the Battle of the Coral Sea, the strategic result being that the Japanese thrust against Australia was blunted, and that the Japanese Navy was deprived of additional carriers for the Midway operation the following month.

26 May 1942
Initial flight of the Northrop P-61 Black Widow, the USAAF's first specially-designed radar-equipped night fighter.

30 May 1942
The RAF's first '1,000-bomber' raid was launched by Bomber Command against Cologne.

3 June 1942
The first night attack on an enemy submarine was made by an RAF Coastal Command Wellington, which used a Leigh light to illuminate its target.

4 June 1942
A decisive naval engagement of WW2 was fought at Midway when four Japanese carriers were sunk.

26 June 1942
The Grumman F6F-3 Hellcat was first flown, the production aircraft becoming one of the most significant fighters in US Navy service during WW2.

4 July 1942
The USAAF's 15th Bomb Squadron, flying Douglas Bostons provided by the RAF, recorded the first USAAF offensive mission over western Europe.

18 July 1942
First flight of the Messerschmitt Me262 under jet power, though the type did not enter operational service until July 1944.

15 August 1942
The RAF formed the Pathfinder Force.

Most famous of all Lancaster users was No 617 Squadron which, following the 'Dambuster' raids of 1943, dropped the first 12,000lb (5,455kg) 'Tallboy' bombs, using specially adapted Mk Is with enlarged bomb doors, during 1944. Other specially-adapted Lancasters made attacks on the German battleship *Tirpitz* in Norway using 'Tallboys'. By early 1945, 33 Lancasters were converted to carry 22,000lb (10,000kg) 'Grand Slam' bombs – all became B1 (Specials) and were operated by No 617 Squadron.

Lancasters took part in almost every major bombing raid of the campaign in Europe from mid-1942 until the end of hostilities. Of all the bombs dropped by Bomber Command during the whole war, almost two-thirds were dropped by Lancasters in the last three years alone. The Victoria Cross was awarded to ten Lancaster crew members.

Of slightly less than 7,000 Lancasters delivered during WW2, no fewer than 3,345 were lost on operations – involving the loss of 21,751 crew members, killed or missing in action.

The First British Jet

When Britain stood on the brink of war for the second time in a quarter of a century, a decision was taken by the Air Ministry to build a jet-propelled aeroplane using an engine designed by Flt Lt Frank Whittle. By chance the design programme at Gloster Aircraft was such that a large part of the drawing office was then available to undertake the work of designing an aeroplane capable of accepting Whittle's engine.

The general layout of the aeroplane envisaged a small and compact low-wing monoplane with a single fin and rudder and having a tricycle landing gear. This landing gear configuration was necessary because of the position of the engine, which was to be mounted inside the fuselage and aft of the cockpit, and the 81gal fuel tank. Air for the engine was to be bled from a pitot-type intake in the nose of the aircraft through flat-sided ducts passing on each side of the pilot's cockpit to the engine mounted in a plenum chamber.

The E.28/39 was built at the Gloster company's own aerodrome at Brockworth. Rather than fly it from there, the jet was transported to Cranwell, which had a long prepared runway and the surrounding country was flat. It was also easier to preserve secrecy out in the bleak spaces of Lincolnshire – rather than in the populous Gloucester-Cheltenham district.

Test pilot Jerry Sayer made the maiden flight on 15 May 1941. He reported on the first flight:

Air Commodore (later Sir) Frank Whittle, the pioneer of jet engine development in Britain.

Rare colour photograph of the Gloster E.28/39 being towed out of the hangar at RAF Cranwell prior to its historic first flight on 15 May 1941.

"In the morning, the weather was entirely unfavourable, and it was not until seven o'clock in the evening that the clouds had lifted and that a light, bitterly cold wind from the west offered suitable conditions for taking off from the runway, with plenty of open fields in the line of flight towards Leadenham. There seemed a chance of getting a short test before dark and accordingly the E.28, with only 50 gal of paraffin aboard was pushed out. At 7.53pm I completed a run-up and started to taxi out to the eastern end of the runway."

"The cockpit hood was in the full-open position for the take-off and the elevator trimmer was set to give a slight forward load on the control column, as during the unsticks at Brockworth, it was felt that the nose tended to rise rather rapidly as soon as the aircraft was in the air. The flaps were set at full up for the first take-off."

"The engine was run up to the maximum take-off revolutions of 16,500 with the brakes held fully on. The brakes were then released and the acceleration appeared quite rapid. The steerable nose wheel enabled the aircraft to be held straight along the runway although there did not appear to be any tendency to swing, feet off the rudder bar".

"The aeroplane was taken-off purely on the feel of the elevators and not on the airspeed. After a run of approximately 500-600 yards it left the ground, and although the fore and aft control was very sensitive for very small movement, the flight was continued."

"The rate of climb after leaving the ground and with the undercarriage still down, is slow, and the aeroplane appeared to take some time to gain speed. The undercarriage was raised at 1,000ft after which the rate of climb and increase in climbing speed improved. The fore and aft changes of trim when raising the undercarriage did not appear to be appreciable."

"The thrust available for take-off is 860lb at 16,500rpm and as the aircraft weight is approx 400lb up on estimate, the take-off run of 500-600 yards is considered to be quite reasonable. As soon as the aeroplane was on a steady climb, engine revolutions were reduced to 16,000, which is the continuing climbing condition. The engine appeared quite smooth and the noise in the cockpit resembled a high-pitched turbine whine."

"The ailerons feel responsive and quite light at 240 ASI at small angles. The elevators were very sensitive indeed and on first impressions will require some adjustment. The rudder feels reasonably light at small angles and possibly slightly overbalanced ."

"The aeroplane feels unstable fore and aft but this may be due to the over-sensitive elevators. It is very left wing low flying level at 240 ASI and carries quite a lot of right rudder. The jet pipe is slightly out of alignment, and looking up the pipe it is offset to the left which may possibly be the cause of the turning tendency to the left."

"Gentle turns were carried out to the left and to the right and the aeroplane behaved normally. The engine ran well and the temperature appeared satisfactory up to the revolutions reached during this short flight."

"The E.28 was trimmed to glide at 90 ASI with flaps fully down and the throttle slightly open for landing. The approach was carried out in very gentle gliding turns and the controllability was very good."

"The aeroplane was landed on the runway slightly on the main wheels first, after which it went gently forward onto the nose wheel. The landing was straightforward and the landing run with the use of brakes was quite short."

WOODEN WONDER

A de Havilland Mosquito PRXVI of No 540 Squadron wearing invasion stripes, which flew photographic reconnaissance over Berlin on D-Day. Both the RAF and USAAF used the Mosquito in the PR role.

The de Havilland Mosquito was a truly successful multi-role combat aircraft of WW2. Following the scepticism which originally greeted the concept, the Mosquito was adopted as a high-speed unarmed bomber, night-fighter and reconnaissance aircraft and subsequently as a long-range interdictor/strike aircraft.

The de Havilland company's move into combat aircraft arose from its interest in air racing, especially with the DH88 Comet. Geoffrey de Havilland had to lobby the Air Ministry on behalf of his unarmed wooden bomber. Without guns, the highly efficient twin-Merlin aircraft, with a wing area twice that of a Spitfire, could outrun enemy fighters by a significant margin.

Built of bonded wood, the early plastic bakelite and the strong waterproof plywood, all of which were non-strategic materials, its construction avoided the use of aluminium, which was in short supply. The design of the aircraft was conventional apart from its remarkable cleanliness of line and relative lack of straight lines in its fuselage shape. The engine cooling system was incorporated in the leading edge of the wing, so the Merlin engine nacelles had a reduced frontal area.

The fuselage was built in two halves (which were partially equipped with internal fittings) and joined along the centre-line, greatly facilitating production. At the time of its first

121

The Mosquito was renowned for its speed and bomb load, relative to its size. This example was owned and flown by British Aerospace until the late 1990s.

flight at Hatfield on 25 November 1940, the B.1/40 prototype (as the type was then known) was very much an unknown quantity, and the merits of its radical structure far from proven.

The initial batch were completed as Mosquito PR.I photo-reconnaissance aircraft and operations began in September 1941, enabling the RAF to extend its coverage of occupied Europe beyond the range of the PR Spitfires. Most of the fighter variants were delivered either as specialised night-fighters or as fighter-bombers, the latter variant being the most versatile and widely-produced Mosquito.

A more serious problem was with the Mosquitos in the Far East, especially in the tropics, where the casein glue used in the construction of the type was a potential disaster. This presented few problems in the European theatre of operations, because the humidity was not extreme or consistent enough to affect the wood.

Originally designed to use the Rolls-Royce Merlin XX series, with a two-speed supercharger, later the two-stage Merlin 61 was fitted to Mosquito versions needing a high-altitude performance. The lack of enthusiasm for the Mosquito in Bomber Command

Pathfinders

The Pathfinder Force of No 8(PFF) Group, RAF Bomber Command – during its brief existence from August 1942 until December 1945 – became the spearhead of Bomber Command's role in the destruction of Germany during the last three years of WW2.

Its aircrew members were almost wholly volunteers. Despite the terrifying odds against any individual, or complete crew, ever completing the requisite 60-sortie tour of operations, the most feared 'punishment' for PFF members was to be 'sacked' and posted away to another unit. Such was the fierce pride and spirit of dedication to the task.

In 1942, 'Bomber' Harris, AOC-in-C of Bomber Command, began looking for new targets, and more effective ways to hit them, leading to the development of the Pathfinder force. The concept was simple – if the best pilots and navigators could be employed to find and mark targets accurately, then the average aircrew should be able to bomb that much more effectively. Although some group commanders were opposed to the idea, its results eventually proved undeniable.

The techniques of area bombing were becoming more perfected in 1943. Diversionary raids confused and scattered the defenders – the Pathfinders marked the target and the bombing stream of Lancasters and Halifaxes followed. More effective radar was being introduced – H2S was in widespread use, and radar-jamming 'Window' soon followed.

Air Vice-Marshal Donald Bennett, at the young age of 32 (but with vast and recent experience) took command of the newly-formed PFF and continued to lead the force until the end of the war in Europe. Late on in the hostilities, AVM Bennett related:

"Possibly the greatest compliment that could be paid to the PFF was the manner in which Bomber Command groups started to form their own pathfinding, using basic PFF techniques, plus *Oboe* and *Gee-H*, the main agents for precision bombing."

"It has been said that this free-for-all, do-it-yourself pathfinding justified the view that it was wrong to form a *corps d'elite* – but such a misguided view does not take into account the 'fusing' of the many experienced crews that formed and served in the force, the pooling of operational 'gen', the expertise that developed, the hard-won tactical procedures, and by no means least, the steady improvement in devices provided by the boffins."

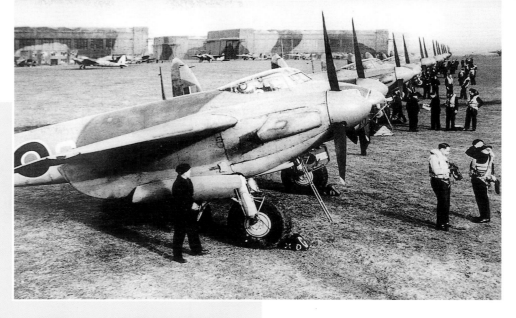

Mosquito BIVs at RAF Marham in 1942. These light bombers of No 139 (Jamaica) Squadron were used for high-speed, long-range bombing raids without the need for fighter escort.

CHRONOLOGY

24 August 1942
A specially stripped-down, but unpressurised Spitfire pursued and shot down a pressurised Luftwaffe Junkers Ju86P at 42,000ft over Egypt.

24 August 1942
The third major duel of the Pacific War occurred when the Japanese made an attempt to reinforce Guadalcanal. Aircraft carriers were heavily involved.

2 September 1942
First flight of the Hawker Tempest V, which introduced a laminar-flow thin-section wing and a longer fuselage than that of the Typhoon.

21 September 1942
The first Boeing B-29 Superfortress made its inaugural flight – the type which was to bring an end to WW2 as the delivery vehicle for the atomic bombs dropped on Hiroshima and Nagasaki in 1945.

1 October 1942
The first turbojet-powered aircraft to fly in the USA, the Bell P-59A Airacomet made its initial flight powered by two General Electric Type 1-As developed from the British Whittle engine.

3 October 1942
The first successful launch of the A-4 ballistic rocket – better known as the V2 (Vergeltungswaffen 2) at Peenemünde.

9 October 1942
The USAAF 8th Air Force's first 100-bomber sortie.

23 October 1942
The Battle of El Alamein opened in the Western Desert, when the RAF's Desert Air Force overwhelmed all opposition by the Luftwaffe and Regia Aeronautica.

accounted for the fact that the night-fighter and reconnaissance versions were deployed somewhat earlier than the bombers, and took the larger share of production in 1942/43. When Bomber Command began to appreciate its potential as a strategic weapon, it only received them in larger numbers when the Canadian-built versions came on line.

Originally designed to carry four 250lb (114kg) bombs internally, this was soon increased to a bomb load of 2,000lb (912kg), and by early 1944 4,000lb (1,824kg) bombs could be loaded. Later in the war Mosquitos formed the nucleus of No 8 Group's Light Night Striking Force (LNSF), which carried out high-speed night raids using precision bomb-aiming and navigation devices.

The vital contribution made by the Mosquito to the Allied effort in WW2 was due to its versatility. It was infinitely more flexible than the light bombers of the early part of the war, such as the Blenheim, and was capable of precision strikes well behind the battle line in the face of determined air defences. The Mosquito was one of only a handful of wartime aircraft to serve in a variety of roles other than that for which they were originally designed.

DAYLIGHT BOMBERS

From the middle of 1942, the US 8th Army Air Force was able to commence daylight bombing raids from bases in Britain, whereas the RAF continued its strategic bombing role by night operations. Aircraft losses for both were high for many months.

In the USA, the Boeing B-17 Flying Fortress had, from the late 1930s, given the Americans the chance of implementing the 'Trenchard doctrine'. They believed that their bombers, flying tight formations in daylight, would be able to defend themselves adequately against fighter attack – and the belief in their ability to penetrate Germany in daylight, unescorted, continued long after the British had for their part abandoned such ideas.

The American 'heavy' bombers were more heavily armed than the comparable RAF bombers, but the price was that the B-17 carried a mere 4,000lb (1818kg) of bombs, compared with the 14,000lb (6363kg) of the Stirling, Halifax and Lancaster. The US produced bombers in massive quantities to meet the needs of its own forces, and those of its allies in the Pacific, North Africa, the Middle East and Far East, as well as Europe.

More than 12,700 B-17s were built, of which nearly 8,700 were the B-17G model. Four 1,200hp (895kW) Wright Cyclone engines gave a speed of 287mph (462km/h) and a range of some 2,000 miles (3,220km). It carried a crew of ten and was armed with thirteen 0.50mm machine guns for self-defence. The first B-17Es arrived in Europe on 1 July 1942 and made their first sortie on 17 August.

The Consolidated B-24 Liberator was built in greater numbers than any other US aircraft – more than 18,000 were produced. Powered by four 1,200hp (895kW) Pratt & Whitney Twin Wasps, it carried a crew of twelve, and ten machine guns for self-defence.

Above: The B-17 Flying Fortress was the most famous American bomber of WW2. Day after day, despite horrendous losses, B-17s continued to attack strategic targets in Europe for three gruelling years, until victory was finally achieved in 1945.

Left: Among the most memorable missions flown by Liberators during WW2 was the attack on the Ploesti oil refineries in Romania in June 1944. Here, B-24Js of the 15th Air Force are seen under heavy anti-aircraft fire during the mission.

In Europe the problem was that the firepower of the bombers' defensive machine guns lacked the weight and concentration to defeat the Germans' cannon-armed fighters. The bombers needed long-range escort fighters to protect them, and these were not available until the end of 1943. Initially, the 8th AF Fighter Groups were equipped with the Republic P-47 Thunderbolt, but it was not until the arrival of the North American P-51 Mustang that truly long-range escort sorties were possible.

The B-24 Liberator served in many different roles and theatres, but its most important contribution to the ending of the war was as a bomber in the Pacific area. In Europe, the B-24 made its name for the spectacular attacks on the Ploesti oil refineries in Romania, whilst operating from bases in Libya. Conceived some five years after the B-17, it did not notably improve on the older bomber's performance and was more complicated. It was built

125

8 November 1942
Landings by American, British and Free French forces were made on the coast of North Africa, during Operation *Torch* when aircraft from four Allied carriers were involved.

12 November 1942
The US Ninth Air Force was formed out of the US Army Middle East Air Force to consolidate North African forces in preparation for the drive across the Mediterranean and on through Sicily, Crete and Italy.

15 November 1942
The Heinkel He219 twin-engined night fighter was flown for the first time.

27 January 1943
The US 8th Air Force made the first American bombing raid on Germany, when 53 B-17s attacked the naval base at Wilhelmshaven.

30 January 1943
RAF Mosquitos made their first daylight attack on Berlin, at precisely the time that major speeches were being made by Goering and Goebbels.

31 January 1943
The first use of H2S radar navigation by the Pathfinder Force during a heavy raid on the port of Hamburg.

1 February 1943
RAF transport aircraft dropped supplies to the first Chindit operation operating far behind enemy lines in Burma.

5 March 1943
The first flight of the Gloster Meteor twin-jet fighter – the first Allied jet fighter to see operational service during WW2.

April 1943
One of the best fighters to enter service with the Imperial Japanese Army Air Force towards the end of WW2, the Nakajima Ki-84 Hayate made its first flight.

18 April 1943
The Japanese Admiral Yamamoto was killed when his Mitsubishi G4M *Betty* was 'ambushed' and shot down by P-38 Lightnings of the 339th FS operating out of Henderson Field, Guadalcanal. Intelligence information had provided details of the aircraft's expected location.

18 April 1943
First successful anti-shipping strike by Beaufighters of the Coastal Command Strike Wing at RAF North Coates.

16 May 1943
Nineteen Lancaster B1(Special)s of No 617 Squadron, carrying special mines designed by Barnes Wallis, made an epic low-level night attack which breached the Möhne and Eder dams.

The North American B-25 Mitchell medium bomber was regarded by many as the best aircraft in its class during WW2, serving on all major fronts and establishing an unrivalled reputation. This B-25 remains airworthy in 2000 with the Confederate Air Force in Texas.

Below: The B-24J Liberator was produced in larger numbers than any other variant and featured a nose turret. The aircraft shown here is one of three B-24s airworthy in the USA.

in many versions and served on every front and flew with fifteen allied nations.

Medium bombers included the North American B-25 Mitchell, of which nearly 11,000 examples were built between 1940 and 1945 – the USAAF received 9,816. It proved to be one of the most outstanding bombers used by the American forces in WW2 and was made in larger numbers than any other twin-engined combat aircraft, also seeing RAF service with the Second Tactical Air Force in Europe, amongst others.

The Martin B-26 Marauder began its career as the chief medium bomber of the 9th Air Force in the European theatre, and by VE-Day had set a record for the lowest loss-rate of any US Army bomber in Europe. With a very high wing-loading,

optimised for high-speed efficiency rather than for landing, it was somewhat a handful for inexperienced pilots. It also served extensively in the Pacific. Total production was 5,157.

Meanwhile, the Douglas DB-7/A-20 Boston/Havoc was a fast medium bomber and was the first of the American bombers to serve in Europe, and was used for daring low-level raids over the continent. It was also in action in North Africa and the Mediterranean. Total production was 7,385, and of this total 3,125 were shipped to the Soviet Union.

Opposite page: The circular fuselage cross-section was a distinctive feature of the Martin B-26 Marauder design, which was notable for its high wing loading.

DAM BUSTERS

The breaching of the Möhne dam in Germany's Ruhr valley is depicted in this Wilfred Hardy painting of Operation *Chastise*, one of the most daring bomber raids of WW2. Carried out by the 'cream' of the RAF, the raid exacted a heavy toll on the aircrew that took part in the operation.

Barnes Wallis came up with a unique 'skip bomb' that after release would 'skip' or bounce over the water's surface and cross anti-torpedo nets on the inner side of the German dams that controlled the water vital to German industry in the Ruhr valley, and provided power for electricity generation.

Highly-experienced Wing Commander Guy Gibson (who had completed 173 operational missions) was selected, in March 1943, to form and lead a squadron of Avro Lancaster bombers to attack these targets – later allocated the now famous designation of No 617 Squadron.

In the fading light of the early summer evening of 16 May 1943, eighteen Lancasters lined up for take off at RAF Scampton. The first eight headed for the main attack on the

Guy Gibson's personal account of the Dams raid

" As we came over the hill, we saw the Möhne Lake. Then we saw the dam itself. In that light it looked quite squat and heavy and unconquerable; it looked grey and solid in the moonlight as though it was a part of the countryside itself and just as immovable."

"A structure like a battleship was showering out flak all along its length, but some came from the power house below it and nearby. There were no searchlights. It was light flak, mostly green, yellow and red, and the colours of the tracer reflected on the lake. The reflections on the dead calm of the black water made it seem there was twice as much as there was."

"We circled around stealthily, picking up the various landmarks upon which we had planned our method of attack; every time we came within range of those bloody-minded flak gunners, they let us have it. I called up each member of the formation and found that all had arrived.."

" Down below, the Möhne Lake was silent and black and deep, and I spoke to my crew and the other aircraft. 'Hello, all Cooler aircraft. I am going to attack. Stand by to come into attack in your order when I tell you.' Then to Hoppy: 'Hello, M Mother; Stand by to take over if anything happens.' Hoppy's clear and casual voice came back. 'OK Leader. Good Luck'."

"Then the boys dispersed to the pre-arranged hiding spots in the hills, so that they should not be seen either from the ground or from the air, and we began to get into position for our approach. We circled wide and came around down moon, over the hills at the eastern end of the lake. On straightening up we began to dive towards the flat, ominous water two miles away. Over the front turret was the dam silhouetted against the haze of the Ruhr Valley. We could see the towers. We could see the sluices. We could see everything. Spam, the bomb aimer, said 'Good show; this is wizard.' He had been a bit worried, as all bomb aimers are, in case they cannot see their aiming points, but as we came in over the tall fir trees his voice came up again. 'You're going to hit them. You're going to hit those trees'."

"Terry turned on the spot lights and began giving directions – 'Down - Down -Steady - Steady'. We were then at exactly 60ft. The gunners had seen us coming. They could see us coming with our spotlights on about two miles away. Now they opened up and tracers began swirling towards us. The Lancaster was really moving and I began looking through the special sight on my windscreen. Spam had his eyes glued to the bomb sight in front, his hand on his button. We skimmed along the surface of the lake and as we went my gunner was firing back with vigour, their shells whistling past us."

"Spam said, 'Left - little more left - steady - steady - steady - coming up.' Of the next few seconds I remember only a series of kaleidoscopic incidents. The tracers flashing past the windows – they all seemed the same colour now – and the inaccuracy of the gun positions near the power station; they were firing in the wrong direction. The closeness of the dam wall, Spam's exultant 'Mine gone.' Hutch's red Verey lights to blind the flak gunners. The speed of the whole thing. Someone saying over the R/T, 'Good show Leader, Nice work' Then it was all over and at last we were out of range."

"As we circled round we could see a great thousand feet column of whiteness still hanging in the air where our mine had exploded. We could see with satisfaction that Spam had been good and it had gone off in the right position."

"I had been over the Möhne for quite a long time, and all the while I had been in contact with Scampton base. We were in close contact with the AOC and the C-in-C of Bomber Command, and with the scientist Barnes Wallis. He was sitting in the Operations Room, his head in his hands, listening to the reports as one after another the aircraft attacked. On the other side of the room the C-in-C paced up and down. In a way their job of waiting was worse than mine. They did not know that the structure was shifting as I knew."

"I felt a little remote and unreal sitting there in the warm cockpit of my Lancaster, watching this mighty power which we had unleashed; then glad, because I knew that this was the heart of Germany, and the heart of her industries, the place which itself had unleashed so much misery upon the whole world."

" I circled round for three minutes, then called up all the aircraft and told Mickey and David Maltby to go home and the rest to follow me to the Eder, where we would try to repeat the performance."

Top: A reconnaissance photograph taken the morning after the raid of the breached Möhne dam. The success of the raid had tremendous propaganda value.

Möhne and Eder dams (both of which were succesfully breached), while the second formation was to attack the Sorpe dam (of different construction), and four were to be reserves. A height of 60ft (18.29m) over the water surface was critical, as was the bomb release at a specific distance from the dams, and the problem was solved by setting up two spotlights so that their beams intersected only at 60ft.

It was an epic and heroic attack which, like a number made during WW2, is difficult to assess in terms of profit and loss. It cost eight Lancasters and 55 men – only one survived as a PoW. Barnes Wallis, who made the bomb possible, regarded it as a disaster. Until the end of his days he did not forget those aircrew who had given their lives in a raid which had little long-term impact on German productive capacity.

NAVAL AIR POWER

I n September 1939, the naval situation was similar to what it had been in the First World War, with Britain attempting to prevent the main German Fleet from escaping into the North Atlantic. The Royal Navy had six front-line carriers available – *Ark Royal* and *Furious* were based at Scapa Flow with the main body of the Home Fleet to block any German movement through the Scotland-Norway Gap. The Western Approaches, important because of their mercantile traffic, were the responsibility of the Channel Fleet, to which was attached *Courageous* and *Hermes*. *Glorious* was with the Mediterranean Fleet and *Eagle* in the Far East.

Aircraft had shown themselves to be effective in anti-submarine warfare. When the German U-boats swung immediately on the offensive, it was decided to carry the war to them by means of carrier-borne aircraft operating beyond the range of available shore-based forces. HMS *Courageous* was torpedoed and sunk in the first month of the war, while it was engaged in recovering her aircraft west of Ireland – carriers were subsequently withdrawn from anti-submarine duties.

Both *Furious* and *Glorious* were involved in the Norwegian campaign in 1940, and *Glorious* was sunk by a German battlecruiser. The *Ark Royal* was then sent to the Mediterranean to help prevent the Italian Fleet breaking out into the Atlantic, and to stop the French Fleet falling under German control. During late 1940 and early 1941 the carriers *Eagle* and *Illustrious* roamed the central Mediterranean with their aircraft sinking shipping, striking airfields and mining harbours.

The effectiveness of carrier operations had been tested by the Japanese in 1940 and they had studied the results of the Fleet Air Arm raid on Taranto, with great interest. The surprise Japanese attack against Pearl Harbor in December 1941 was devastating – and was the first large attack ever mounted by a carrier strike force. The destruction of the US battle fleet meant that the deployment of aircraft carriers was the only way of taking the fight to the Japanese, and from then on the US offensive was based on the carrier task force.

Many of the early Pacific naval battles were exclusively carrier operations – the first time in history that opposing fleets had not sighted each other during an engagement. The Battles of the Coral Sea, Midway and Leyte resulted in the Japanese losing all four participating carriers, and proved a turning point in the Pacific war. Above all, it showed the carrier to be a weapon of infinite flexibility.

The US Navy organised carrier task forces, comprising one or more task groups. These were made up of a few carriers, with an escort of battleships,

Right: Seen carrying its primary weapon, a 1,620lb (735kg) torpedo, the Fairey Barracuda II saw action in most of the Fleet Air Arm's operations from 1943.

Below: A line of SBD Dauntless dive-bombers on board the carrier USS *Enterprise* taxi to the launch point for take-off at 30 second intervals.

15 June 1943
First flight of the Arado Ar234 *Blitz*, the world's first operational turbojet-powered reconnaissance bomber.

16 June 1943
Allied fighters, including RNZAF P-40 Kittyhawks, destroyed 79 Japanese aircraft out of a force of 94 which attacked shipping off Guadalcanal.

22 June 1943
The first large daylight attack on the Ruhr was made by 182 B-17s of the US 8th Air Force.

24 June 1943
The Messerschmitt Me163B rocket fighter first flew.

5 July 1943
In the last major aerial battle between Luftwaffe and Soviet air forces, 800 German bombers executed a massive attack against Kursk in Operation *Zitadels*.

9 July 1943
The first Allied airborne invasion of WW2 opened the invasion of Sicily, as paratroop and glider operations began Operation *Husky*.

24 July 1943
Over 700 Allied heavy bombers attacked Hamburg during Operation *Gomorrah*, which featured the first widespread use of metallised foil strips – known as 'Window'.

1 August 1943
In one of the USAAF's most daring operations, 177 B-24 Liberators operating from bases in North Africa attacked the oil refineries at Ploesti in Romania.

17 August 1943
The deepest penetration of German airspace to date was made when 315 USAAF B-17s launched a dual daylight strike against Schweinfurt and Regensburg.

Below: Perhaps the greatest piston-engined naval fighter of WW2, the gull-winged Vought F4U Corsair, took some time to develop its full potential. The photograph shows an FG-1D that is airworthy with the Confederate Air Force.

Right: Grumman's TBF Avenger was a strongly-built mid-wing monoplane with a weapons bay large enough to carry a torpedo or 2,000lb (908kg) of other ordnance. It made its operational debut at Midway in June 1942. This example was still airworthy in 1999.

cruisers and destroyers and this provided increased defensive power by providing a greater concentration of anti-aircraft fire. It also provided a better measure of protection against submarines.

Radar was a great scientific advance which made the task group possible and gave early warning of an air attack. It also allowed the ships to operate close together in poor visibility. In addition, the Americans' great advantage was that, having broken the enemy codes, they knew their intentions. By 1944, the US carriers had more or less destroyed the Imperial Japanese Navy.

On 18 April 1942, there was a major morale-booster and a psychological blow to the Japanese, when a force of sixteen USAAF B-25 Mitchells took off from the USS *Hornet* and made a strike on Tokyo and other cities, continuing on to land in China. Lt Col James Doolittle led this one-way mission.

In the Atlantic, Swordfish and Fulmars from HMS *Ark Royal*, together with shore-based Catalina flying boats, were involved in contacting and disabling the *Bismarck* making its way to a French port. The German battleship was subsequently sunk by gunfire. The sea war in the Atlantic was a very different matter from that in the Pacific, developing around one overriding issue – the ability of Britain to keep open her sea lanes. Escort carriers were mass-produced in the US, these being 'baby flat-tops' constructed on merchant hulls. As the escort carrier numbers increased the between U-boats and the convoys was gradually turned in the Allies' favour.

Grumman Hellcats being prepared for action aboard
USS *Yorktown* in June 1944. The F6F was the true victor
of the Battle of the Philippine Sea.

CHRONOLOGY

17 August 1943
Nearly 600 RAF bombers attacked the German research establishment at Peenemünde, which was engaged in work on rocket missiles.

25 August 1943
The first operational use of stand-off glide bombs took place when Luftwaffe Dornier Do217E-5s attacked Allied destroyers in the Bay of Biscay with Henschel Hs293A-1 missiles.

15 September 1943
The first operational use of the 5,443kg (12,000lb) high capacity Tallboy bomb when Lancasters attacked the Dortmund-Ems canal.

29 September 1943
The de Havilland Vampire single-seat turbojet fighter made its first flight, designed with an unusual twin-boom layout chosen to keep the jet-pipe as short as possible, and thereby keeping power losses to a minimum.

7 October 1943
Mosquito bombers of the Pathfinder Force employed *Gee-H* blind-bombing radar for the first time during a raid on Aachen.

ESCORT FIGHTER

The P-51 Mustang was designed in a short space of time to meet a British requirement for a fighter for service in Europe, and its outstanding qualities made it the leading US fighter in the European theatre in the latter part of WW2. Illustrated is one of the many restored P-51s still flying in 2000.

The North American P-51 Mustang was ordered by the British Purchasing Commission when visiting the USA in 1940, with a view to obtaining a fighter which would be an advance on the British Spitfire.

Mustang Is, equivalent to the USAAF's P-51A, entered RAF service in 1941. Though having many qualities, its American Allison V-1710 powerplant gave it poor performance at high altitude and its range was short. Consequently it was relegated to Army Co-operation and photographic work. It so happened that Ronald Harker, Rolls-Royce's senior liaison test pilot, was offered the opportunity to test the Mustang by the RAF. He was impressed with the aircraft's handling qualities but not by its engine, which he thought was too low-powered to exploit the aircraft's advanced aerodynamic features. He was convinced that the aircraft would be transformed if fitted with the Rolls-Royce Merlin, the powerplant of the Spitfire.

Above: Mustangs from the Eighth Air Force's 375th Fighter Squadron, 361st Fighter Group on a mission over occupied Europe from East Anglia in 1944.

Harker pressed strongly for the American engine to be replaced by the Merlin. After much official reluctance, largely from the Air Ministry, he got his way. The result was a transformation and the Mustang's top speed leapt from 390mph to 440mph. In addition, the range was extended from 450 miles to over 2,000 miles, with various configurations of drop tanks.

Thus, a great escort fighter was born and the Americans realised that the Rolls-Royce solution provided the answer to the horrific losses the USAAF's daylight bombing raids had been suffering in the early part of 1943. The fighter was put into mass production, using Packard and Continental-built versions of the Rolls-Royce engine. Soon the US Eighth Army Air Force B-17 Flying Fortresses were able to roam as far as Berlin, escorted all the way by Mustangs, which began to take a toll of the Luftwaffe's fighters. When Goering saw Mustangs escorting the American air armada over the capital of the Reich he was said to have realised that Germany had lost the war.

The British Air Ministry had wanted to put all the available Merlin 61 engines into the new Spitfire IX being developed to combat the latest Luftwaffe fighter, the Focke-Wulf Fw190, which was proving vastly superior to the Spitfire V in combat. There was, therefore, a good deal of concerted scepticism about Harker's observations.

News of the Merlin-powered Mustang's performance spread like wildfire and was greeted as 'manna from heaven' in Washington. The Americans were the chief beneficiary of Harker's initiative, since the new escort fighter enabled the 8th AF to resume daylight bombing raids which had been temporarily discontinued, since the 'invulnerable' B-17s had proved incapable of defending themselves against enemy fighters. By the end of WW2 15,582 Mustangs had been built.

CHRONOLOGY

19 November 1943
RAF Bomber Command first used FIDO (Fog Intensive Dispersal Operation) to enable its bombers to land safely in fog when returning from night operations.

1 December 1943
USAAF 9th Fighter Command began operations from England when P-51Bs flew a sweep over north west France, marking the introduction of the Merlin-powered Mustang into the USAAF.

8 January 1944
The Lockheed P-80 Shooting Star made its first flight – it would later become the first turbojet powered single-seat fighter/fighter-bomber to enter service with the USAAF.

21 January 1944
A Luftwaffe bombing offensive, known in England as the 'Little Blitz' – Operation *Steinbock* – began, with attacks by 447 German bombers.

15 February 1944
Allied aircraft dropped bombs on the mountain-top monastery at Cassino, Italy in an attempt to eliminate a powerful bastion in the German Gustav Line.

18 February 1944
RAF Mosquitos attacked the German prison at Amiens, France in Operation *Jericho*, in an attempt to allow the escape of French Resistance fighters who had been sentenced to death.

6 March 1944
The start of a major offensive by Allied bombers to destroy the communications network in Northern France, in preparation for the invasion of Normandy.

25 March 1944
A Mosquito FBVI landed aboard HMS *Indefatigable*, to become the first British twin-engined aircraft to land on a carrier.

29 May 1944
The escort carrier USS *Block Island* was torpedoed by a U-boat off the Azores – this being the first and only US Navy carrier to be lost in the Atlantic.

6 June 1944
Massive Allied air cover was provided by fighters, fighter-bombers and medium bombers in support of the Allied landings on the Normandy coast – 'D-Day'.

8 June 1944
The first 5,443kg (12,000lb) Tallboy deep penetration bomb was dropped by Lancasters attacking the Saumur railway tunnel.

ROCKET REPRISAL

The V-1 reprisal weapon was a small fixed-wing pilotless aircraft powered by a pulse-jet engine mounted above the rear fuselage. This example is preserved at the Imperial War Museum at Duxford.

CHRONOLOGY

13 June 1944
The German V-1 flying-bomb offensive against England commenced.

15 June 1944
The first B-29 Superfortress raid against Japan was made by 47 aircraft of the US 20th Air Force, operating from Chengtu in China.

19 June 1944
The first Battle of the Philippine Sea was fought by 15 US and nine Japanese aircraft carriers.

21 June 1944
Over 200 B-17 Flying Fortresses of the US 8th AF, escorted by P-51 Mustangs, began a new phase in the European air war, when they made the first UK-USSR shuttle mission – Operation *Frantic*.

18 July 1944
VHF R/T was used for the first time by ground forces to call up direct support from rocket-firing Typhoons.

18 July 1944
In support of the US 1st Army, USAAF P-38 Lightnings used for the first time a jellied explosive called napalm, carried in under-wing tanks.

German rocket research in a practical form began on 5 June 1927, with the formation of the Verein für Raumschiffarte (VfR). Demonstrations of the growing capability of the rocket motor brought state support and, in the mid-1930s, construction began at Peenemünde on the Baltic coast of a purpose-built establishment for the design, development and manufacture of military rockets.

In 1939, Fieseler had initiated design studies on a pilotless flying bomb. The Germans had decided that the bomb should be ground-launched, and they started building ramps in France and along the Dutch coast, while development work continued at Peenemünde.

Rumours of the work being undertaken began to reach the UK during the early years of the war. This led to the request that the German research site should be subjected to photo-reconnaissance sorties. By late June 1943, it emerged that long-range rockets were under development, that test firings were frequent and that increasing anti-aircraft defences in the area stressed the growing importance of the project. Peenemünde was no easy target for the RAF, being strung out for dispersal reasons along the coastline. Pin-point accuracy was essential, with moonlight needed to illuminate the target.

It was not until the night of 17 August 1943 that conditions were right. Bomber Command despatched 597 heavy bombers, preceded by Pathfinders, to mark the route and the dispersed targets, and made use of a Master Bomber for the first time. This was a distant target, and the raid cost the RAF 40 bombers (along with a further 15 destroyed on landing back at base), but it killed several key German personnel and did considerable damage to the plant. Later the Americans, in daylight operations, hit similar installations there.

On 13 June 1944, the first V-1 was fired against England. As the Allies eliminated most of the sites, the Germans built portable, prefabricated ones. The V-1 ('Doodlebug' or 'buzz bomb') was really a small, fast aeroplane, and it could be stopped by more or less conventional methods. The Germans launched some 20,000 of them before the sites were finally overrun. About a tenth of these were shot down by anti-aircraft fire, and another tenth caught and shot down by fighters.

Downing the Doodlebugs

Wing Commander Roland Beamont was asked to form the first Tempest wing to combat the V-1 flying bomb menace. In his book *'Typhoon and Tempest at War'*, Beamont recalled the start of that desperate battle:

"Aircraft from the Wing were first scrambled against V-1s at 5.30 in the morning of 16 June 1944. By the night of the same day, our score was already eight. Not that bringing down the doodlebugs was easy. Propelled by a pulse-jet engine mounted on the top of the fuselage at the rear, they sped through the skies of south east England at between 340 and 370mph."

"Their wingspan was only sixteen feet and their length twenty feet, making them a minute target for the fighter pilots against the background landscape at the height of 1,500-2,500ft which the V-1s normally flew. They were bronze on top and pale blue underneath, with the 'stove pipe' engine exhaust glowing white hot. Each carried one ton of high explosive, and were crudely manufactured by the Germans at a cost of around £120 each."

"Coming up from astern I found I had a target only three feet wide across the fuselage, and with wings only eight inches thick to aim at. Firing from 400 yards was too wasteful, but if we went close in to 200 yards, the resultant explosion of one ton of high explosive was likely to blow up the pursuer as well as the pursued. Some of my pilots returned to base with the fabric burned off the rudders of their aircraft."

"Seeing that the standard Fighter Command 'spread harmonisation' pattern for the guns was unsuitable for operations against flying bombs, I asked for official

permission to point-harmonise our guns at 300 yards. This was not forthcoming, but I went ahead anyway. On the next sortie I was able to hit the V-1s with my opening burst, and I then ordered all 150 Wing guns to be similarly treated – this resulted in sustained improvement in the Wing's scoring rate."

"All through this period our Tempests were being operated with their engines flat out – a factor which resulted in wear and tear problems later in the year when the squadrons went into mainland Europe to operate – and although the Germans continued to send V-1s over for the rest of 1944 (the last one fell on British soil as late as 29 March 1945) the menace was virtually mastered by the end of August. The final tally

The Hawker Tempest supplanted the Typhoon (from which it was developed) in many squadrons from the spring of 1944. Tempests were used mainly as fighters over Europe and on air defence duties in England to help counter the V-1 threat.

was awesome – of 6,700 bombs despatched, almost 4,000 were brought down by fighters, the guns or barrage balloons."

The part played by Tempests in this part of the defence of Great Britain was crucial. A total of fewer than 30 aircraft was available initially, building up to 114 by September 1944 – and these knocked out 632 doodlebugs.

On 8 September 1944, when the V-1 appeared largely mastered, the first V-2 hit England. This was the first of the true rockets – a long-range ballistic missile fired up into the stratosphere, travelling at incredible speed and dropping out of the sky on its target. The Allies had absolutely nothing to stop this and all they could do throughout the V-2 campaign was frantically attempt to find and bomb the launching sites. Between September 1944 and March 1945, 1,115 V-2s were launched. They and the V-1s killed nearly 9,000 people and injured a further 23,000.

General Eisenhower, in his book *'Crusade in Europe'* commented: "It seems likely that if the Germans had succeeded in perfecting and using these weapons six months earlier than they did, our invasion of mainland Europe would have proved exceedingly difficult, perhaps impossible."

With its A-4 rocket (more commonly known as the V-2), Germany produced what was really the forerunner of the cruise missile, against which there was no defence.

JET AND ROCKET FIGHTERS

The RAF was second only to the Luftwaffe in introducing jet fighters into combat service. Gloster aircraft – after the E.28/39 – embarked on the twin-jet Meteor fighter, which was designed to Specification F.9/40. This requirement called for an armament of six 20mm Hispano cannon – subsequently reduced to four, because of the lack of power expected to be available from the early Whittle engine. Eight prototypes were ordered in 1941 and an initial production requirement for 250 aircraft was notified to the company.

The first Meteor (DG202/G) with Rover-built W2B turbojets, commenced ground running tests on 29 June 1942. Because of delays with the Rover-built engine, there was accelerated development of the de Havilland-Halford H1 and Metropolitan Vickers F2 engines. First flight was on 5 March 1943, powered by H1 engines, at Cranwell.

The development and subsequent production of the W2B engine was taken over by Rolls-Royce and the name Welland bestowed. This powered the production prototype Meteor F1, which was flown on 12 January 1944. This aircraft was then shipped to the US for evaluation by the American Bell Company for its XP-59A Airacomet.

Meteors were delivered to No 616 (South Yorkshire) Squadron on 12 July 1944, and on moving to Manston were soon in action against German V-1s. The Meteor III, with Derwent engines and lengthened nacelles, appeared in January 1945, and in the final stages of WW2 the FIV, with much improved Derwent 5 turbojets, started to enter service.

With the main interest centred on the development of Britain' first jet fighter – the Meteor – another jet aircraft was taking shape on the drawing board at de Havilland – the Vampire (though originally it was known as the Spidercrab). The low power of all the early jet engines resulted in the Vampire (of balsa and plywood construction, like the Mosquito) being fairly small, with a central nacelle accommodating the cockpit and engine, the tail unit being carried on two small-section booms which terminated in the tail fins, with the tailpipe located between them.

First flight was on 29 September 1943 and 120 were ordered by the RAF in May 1944.

Right: A pair of Gloster Meteor F3s of No 263 Squadron scramble from RAF Acklington in 1945. The squadron flew Meteors as part of the fighter defences of the UK.

The first production example made its maiden flight on 20 April 1945, but it did not enter service until after the end of the war.

In addition to its Me 262 jet fighter, the German Messerschmitt company also built the Me 163 Komet, an odd-looking little creature, which made its first rocket-powered flight on 13 May 1944. This was actually a rocket fighter, armed with two cannon. It could only stay aloft for a few minutes – time for just one diving pass at enemy bombers – but as it came

Above: German engineers made giant strides with turbojets and rocket propulsion. The Messerschmitt Me163 was mildly successful as an interceptor, but suffered many accidents as a result of its lethal fuel mixture. A total of 279 Me163s was delivered to the Luftwaffe.

swooping down at more than 600mph, it was very hard to stop. But it was too little too late – it was a great aircraft in the amazing boldness of its conception and in the way it thrust into a previously unexplored realm of speed and altitudes. It also threatened to pose insoluble problems to its enemies, but in the event most of the casualties it inflicted were to its own pilots.

In the interceptor role, the twin-jet Messerschmitt Me262A Schwalbe could carry 24 R4M rockets under its wings, in addition to the four built-in 30mm cannon.

The First Jet Bomber

In the early part of WW2, the Arado Flugzeugwerke had started the design of an unarmed reconnaissance aircraft planned to fly even faster and higher than the British Mosquito. This was possible because the engines were to be turbojets, then in the early stage of development by BMW and Junkers.

The Arado Ar234 *Blitz* (Lightning) was the Luftwaffe's second jet in service and was also the world's first jet bomber. A shoulder-wing monoplane with slender double-taper wings, it had a turbojet slung under each wing. The single-seat pressurised cockpit featured an entirely glazed nose. First flown on 15 June 1943 with two Junkers Jumo 004A, the Ar234 initially had a trolley undercarriage which was jettisoned after take-off. Subsequently, the fuselage was widened to incorporate retractable landing gear.

The first operational evaluation was on 20 July 1944. Flying over England, the Ar234 soon proved that its ceiling and speed were more than adequate to avoid interception, and it was able to undertake reconnaissance missions unmolested. However, engine failures were common, and time between engine overhauls was a mere ten hours. A bomb load of 3,000lb (1,400kg) was possible by incorporation of bomb shackles under the wings, and it was able to carry a single large SC 1000 'Hermann' bomb.

By the autumn of 1944, a small number were operating photographic recce sorties over the Allied area of north-west Europe, the British Isles and the Italian front. In October 1944, Ar234B-2 bombers began flying bombing missions and joined the Ardennes counter-offensive in late 1944, but the Gruppes never attained full status. Due to a lack of fuel, Ar234 units had virtually ceased operations by March 1945.

The Ar234 had little to fear from Allied fighters, once away from the airfield circuit, but it was provided with defensive armament of two 20mm MG 151 cannon. These were mounted either side of the rear fuselage, firing aft and aimed by a periscope over the cockpit. Handling of the aircraft was excellent, and the structural strength was good, but greater engine thrust was badly needed. The only practical way, at that time, to achieve the additional power was to fit four turbojets in four separate nacelles but these were only in the experimental stage when the war ended.

A handful of Ar234Bs were fitted with cannon in a ventral tray and FuG 218 *Neptun* radar for night fighting. However effective the *Blitz* was operationally it remained something of a dodo without adequate supplies of fuel – how different this story might have been had they entered service just a year earlier.

For take-off, the Arado Ar234A (the first version of the *Blitz*) sat on a large trolley, which could be steered by the pilot and was released on reaching flying speed. A retractable skid and outriggers were used for landing.

ONE SUPERFORTRESS, ONE BOMB

CHRONOLOGY

14 October 1944
The largest single night bombing effort was made by the RAF, when 1,294 aircraft attacked numerous targets in Germany.

24 October 1944
The Battle of Leyte Gulf marked the fifth and last aircraft carrier engagement of the war.

25 October 1944
Japanese suicide (kamikaze) attacks from the Shikishima unit of Japan's Special Air Corps began against US warships in the Pacific, with specially prepared Mitsubishi A6M-5 fighter bombers.

12 November 1944
The German battleship *Tirpitz* was attacked by Lancasters carrying Tallboy bombs, and capsized in Tromso Fjord, Norway.

24 November 1944
B-29 Superfortresses of the USAAF's 21st Bomb Group flew their first mission against Japan from the Marianas, after being transferred from China.

6 December 1944
The Heinkel He162 Salamander – designed as the Volksjagen (People's fighter) – and powered by a turbojet mounted on top of the fuselage behind the cockpit, made its first flight.

1 January 1945
Operation *Bodenplatte*, a last major attack by the Luftwaffe to destroy Allied airfields in Holland and Belgium when over 800 aircraft were used.

13 February 1945
Hitherto untouched by Allied bombers, the city of Dresden received a controversial heavy raid. It was alleged to be a key German communications centre behind the Eastern Front.

9 March 1945
Over 300 B-29s, operating at low-level at night, made a massive incendiary attack on Tokyo.

By the late 1930s, world scientists had come to the conclusion that in theory it should be possible to generate energy by nuclear fission – then referred to as 'splitting the atom'. Such a small mass of fissionable material would produce immense energy, and that from such material might be contrived a devastating weapon.

In December 1944, the USAAF's 509th Composite Bomb Group – its only operational squadron being the 393rd Bombardment Squadron (Very Heavy) – formed at Wendover Field, Utah equipped with the new Boeing B-29 Superfortress for training in the deployment of the atomic bomb. Components of the 509th CBG transferred to North Field, Tinian, in the Marianas Islands on 29 May 1945 and were joined by the 393rd Bombardment Squadron shortly afterwards.

By June 1945, the first test bombs had been detonated successfully at Alamogardo in New Mexico, and the B-29s began a process of familiarisation by making conventional attacks on Japanese targets. On 26 July 1945 the Allies issued an ultimatum to Japan that called for unconditional surrender – its immediate rejection brought the decision to use atomic weapons if reason did not prevail after further heavy conventional attacks.

At 08.15hr (local time) on 6 August 1945, Major Thomas W. Ferebee – bombardier of the B-29A *Enola Gay* – with Lt Col Paul W. Tibbets in command, dropped the world's first

Top: Groundcrew from the 73rd Bomb Wing at Saipan in the Mariana Islands prepare a B-29 Superfortress with ammunition and 2,000lb bombs.

Above: No other aircraft has ever combined as many technological advances as Boeing's B-29 Superfortress, which entered combat service in the Pacific in mid-1944. *Fifi* is the sole airworthy example of the type, operated by the Confederate Air Force at Midland, Texas.

Col Paul Tibbets (centre), the pilot of *Enola Gay*, with his grouncrew, in front of the aircraft that dropped the atomic bomb on Hiroshima on 6 August 1945.

atomic bomb from a height of 31,600ft over Hiroshima. In a millisecond, the Japanese city was nearly obliterated. One Superfortress, one mission and one bomb had changed the course of warfare for ever. Lt Col Paul Tibbets recalled:

"We took off from Tinian in B-29 *Enola Gay* (named after my mother) at 02.45hr on 6 August 1945. Two more B-29s carrying instruments and observers accompanied us and it seemed another routine mission. We hauled up our landing gear and headed into history."

"Tucked in the bomb bay was *Little Boy*, nearly five tons of bomb with a 137lb (62.3kg) heart of uranium 235. *Enola Gay* headed for Hiroshima – Kyóto had been the original choice, but was decided against because of its religious and cultural significance. Hiroshima was chosen because it was an embarkation point and an industrial city, and because it had not been bombed before. We wanted a clear demonstration of what the bomb alone would do."

"We reached the target at 09.15hr. On the ground the Japanese paid little attention, as by now they were used to small flights of B-29s making reconnaissance runs. Dropped from an altitude of nearly 32,000ft *Little Boy* detonated at 800ft. Its force was that of 29,000 tons of TNT. Forty-three seconds later, Hiroshima ceased to exist as a city It swept almost five square miles of the city and killed almost 70,000 people. As the mushroom cloud rose into the sky, we stared in awe. On the ground there was chaos. It was if the world was ending."

Three days later, the Americans repeated this strike against the city of Nagasaki, this time bombing through cloud by radar. Damage was not as bad as at Hiroshima, being contained partly by surrounding hills, but the general effects were the same and about 35,000 people were killed. The Japanese were defeated, and on 15 August 1945 they surrendered.

Nuclear Attack

Group Captain Leonard Cheshire VC was invited, with Dr William Penney, to witness the dropping of the Allies' newest weapon on Japan, from B-29 *Bock's Car*, with Major Charles W. Sweeney in command. It changed the life of the experienced bomber pilot, who witnessed the second explosion, over the city of Nagasaki on 9 August 1945. Cheshire wrote of his epic mission:

"We reached Japan, comfortably and in accustomed silence, in short sleeves, without oxygen mask, at 39,000ft and 400mph and in conditions that in terms of speed, height, aircraft and crew discipline, were all utterly foreign to me."

"It was a summer's day, hot and cloudless. I put on my welder's glasses and looked out at the unsuspecting city that seemed to drowse unwarily in the sun's fresh warmth. I looked out and wondered what would happen below there."

"As our aircraft droned lazily towards Nagasaki, the not very efficient Japanese Air Raid Service issued an alert and later, almost immediately, relaxed it. In the two valleys that forked into the heart of the city about 100,000 people lived poorly, and worked stolidly, in their national fashion. On the other side of the city about 160,000 dwelt and worked."

" Then suddenly the faint rhythmic droning of American engines, so different from the erratic harshness of their own aircraft, was heard....and three parachutes dropped lazily....and men and women looked upwards curiously."

"There came a bright flash in the sky and many shut their eyes at its brilliance. Others kept them opened....and in a few seconds the bright flash built up within itself a heat so incredibly radiant and vicious that their eyeballs were seared into blindness."

"Then the ball of fire above them belched out a haze of white smoke which roared downwards at them and the summer day darkened un-naturally. There was a sense of wind and heat."

"Trams and buses for a few miles around were destroyed, and the people in them. Wooden houses burst into flames. Screaming citizens fled from a horror that no ordinary bombing had inspired in them. Injured Japanese, trapped in buildings that had been crushed by blast from above, then squeezed inwards by pressure at the sides and finally torn apart by a blast of suction as the heat waves cooled off....these injured lay helpless and unable to move whilst slow-growing fires incinerated them."

"All the crops and vegetation for 2,000 yards vanished, leaving only blackened earth....Almost all of the wooden-housed factories of the Mitsibushi clan, in the valley, caught fire or collapsed. Workers were crushed, burned or blasted to death...."

"Everywhere steel-work buckled, walls blew outwards, roofs were dented downwards, woodwork ignited as if by magic and the town rocked as though in the grip of a vast cyclone. All this happened in one ten-millionth of a second, then passed, leaving a ghastly silence. A silence broken by the crackle of flames, the moaning of the injured and the faint, rhythmic droning of two American Superfortresses."

Post-war, Japan's Kantaro Suzuki commented: "It seemed to me unavoidable that in the long run Japan would be almost destroyed by air attack, so I was convinced that Japan should sue for peace. Unfortunately, this did not come until after the second atomic bomb had been dropped. In retrospect one must believe that this enormous loss of life saved the even greater Allied and Japanese losses that would have occurred had Japan been invaded."

The enormous devastation caused by the dropping of atomic bombs on Hiroshima and Nagasaki forced the Japanese into surrender within days.

CHRONOLOGY

13/14 March 1945
An RAF Lancaster dropped the first 9,979kg (22,000lb) Grand Slam bomb on the Bielefeld railway viaduct.

21 March 1945
Initial use of the Japanese Yokosuka MXY7 *Ohka* (Cherry Blossom) rocket-powered suicide aircraft.

21 March 1945
RAF Mosquitos destroyed the Gestapo HQ in Copenhagen in a low-level daylight raid.

23 March 1945
Operation *Varsity*, the Allied crossing of the Rhine, when over 2,000 transport aircraft and gliders were deployed.

7 April 1945
P-51D Mustangs, with a much longer range than earlier variants of the fighter, were used for the first time to escort USAAF B-29 Superfortresses on attacks over Japan.

15 April 1945
The US 15th Air Force in Italy launched its largest raids of WW2 when 830 bombers, with P-38 Lightnings as escorts, attacked German strongpoints leading northwards from Bologna.

25 April 1945
The last heavy bomber mission of WW2, when B-17s of the US 8th AF attacked the Pilzen-Skoda works in Czechoslovakia.

8 May 1945
VE-Day – the end of the war in Europe.

23 May 1945
Some 565 B-29s were despatched from the Marianas to attack Tokyo, the largest WW2 mission involving the Superfortress.

6 August 1945
B-29 Superfortress *Enola Gay* of the 509th Bombardment Group, 20th AF dropped the first nuclear bomb (codenamed *Little Boy*) on Hiroshima, destroying 80% of the city's buildings.

7 August 1945
The Nakajima Kikka, Japan's first jet fighter (based on the Me262) made its first flight.

9 August 1945
The second, and last, nuclear weapon (codenamed *Fat Man*) was dropped by B-29 *Bock's Car* on Nagasaki.

15 August 1945
VJ-Day – Japan finally surrenders.

2 September 1945
WW2 was formally ended when the Japanese surrender was signed by delegates aboard USS *Missouri* anchored in Tokyo Bay.

THE COLD WAR YEARS
1945–1989

McDonnell Douglas F-4E Phantom

HIGH SPEED TESTING

During 1944, tests had been carried out by the Aerodynamic Section of the Royal Aircraft Establishment at Farnborough to establish whether or not the high speed characteristics of the Gloster Meteor could be improved. These resulted in various modifications being suggested, among which was an increase in engine nacelle length to change the airflow pattern around the centre section. These modifications – and the availability of the greatly improved Rolls-Royce Derwent engine – formed the basis of the Mk.4, and they were incorporated in the two production F3 airframes (EE454 and EE455) taken from the assembly line to be used for a record attempt. EE454 was finished in a special high speed RAF day fighter camouflage finish and named *Britannia*, whilst EE455 was painted yellow overall – which led to it gaining the unofficial nickname of *Yellow Peril*. The pilots selected to fly the aircraft were Group Captain H. J. Wilson, CO of the Empire Test Pilots' School and Gloster test pilot Eric Greenwood.

The RAF Speed Record Flight moved to Kent for trials over the record course in Herne Bay towards the end of 1945. A further attempt using the Meteor was made in 1946 by the RAF's High Speed Flight. Although the same mark of aircraft was used, the pilots and course differed, with the measured three kilometres running part of the way between Littlehampton and Worthing on the Sussex coast. The Flight's Meteors were ready for trials in the middle of August, but a typically English summer and technical problems resulted in three weeks of frustrating delays and few promising flights. Finally, on 7 September, Group Captain E. M. Donaldson was able to establish a new speed record of 615.78mph, and when the Air Ministry decided that no further attempts were to be made, it was left to the Americans to pursue the speed challenge.

With endurance, speed and height records to its credit, the Meteor continued to make headlines throughout the world, all of which helped to establish its reputation and support the overseas sales campaign mounted by Gloster.

Above: Gloster Meteor F4 EE454 (named *Britannia*) of the RAF High Speed Flight at Tangmere, flown here by Group Captain H. J. Wilson on 7 November 1945, when he achieved a speed of 606mph.

Jet Records

Group Captain H. J. Wilson, one of the pilots with the RAF's Speed Record Flight in 1945, reported on the Meteor flights that were flown on 7 November that year:

"Conditions were just about right, for although it was cold and overcast and visibility varied between seven and twelve miles, the wind component was about 12mph from the direction of East Anglia."

"Ideally, a wind from the north-east, which would have travelled over the North Sea and consequently would have been

Gloster Meteor EE455, brought up to F4 standard (less VHF mast and armament), had an overall yellow finish applied for the 1945 World Speed Record attempt.

very smooth, would have been perfect. But time was against waiting for such a situation. In EE455, I made my runs first and recorded 604, 608, 602 and 611mph, giving an average of 606mph (975.67km/h) – which was a new record. Later in the day Eric Greenwood recorded 599, 608, 598 and 607 – an average of 603mph. The target we had aimed for had been 610mph and the slightly lower speeds were mainly a result of the prevailing north-westerly wind."

On 7 September 1946, on a grey and wet evening, the Officer Commanding of the High Speed Flight, Group Captain E. M. 'Teddy' Donaldson was able to make another record attempt. He wrote of this flight: "Well in the afternoon I decided that a stretch of better weather forecast for the early evening made an attempt possible. I took off in EE549 at 17.58hr. There was ten-tenths cloud broken only by a very small patch of blue sky well inland, the temperature was 14° C and the wind component was 10mph from the south-west, that therefore slightly favoured the west-east runs."

"I made five runs and conditions were markedly bumpy, spending seventeen minutes in the air – with an average speed for four runs of 615.78mph – setting another record for the Meteor. Squadron Leader Waterton followed me, but conditions deteriorated and he could only manage an average of 614mph. This is possibly the fastest that a Meteor can go in these conditions of temperatures and bumps. At 30° C , another 16mph could possibly be added to this speed."

The emphasis on temperature during these flights is because the speed of sound decreases as temperature rises, so that the ratio between air speed and Mach number is better in higher temperatures.

SUPERSONIC FLIGHT

The de Havilland DH.108 was a single-seat research aircraft with no horizontal tail surfaces, built to investigate the behaviour of swept wings – and to provide basic data for the DH.106 Comet airliner and DH.110 fighter. Three examples were built around standard Vampire fuselages – VW120 was the third prototype, with improved cockpit streamlining.

I n the closing stages of WW2, pilots of high-performance fighters began to encounter strange and sometimes frightening characteristics in the performance of their aircraft. Travelling fast in a steep dive, the wings would shudder violently and tail surfaces vibrate unaccountably. Many aircraft did not survive such behaviour and, losing part of their structure, were destroyed as they crashed to the ground. Eventually the problem was found to be caused by shock waves as the airflow over aerofoil surfaces neared supersonic speed.

Early research aircraft to explore supersonic flight evolved in the USA, Great Britain and France in the immediate post-war era. In Britain the de Havilland DH.108 Swallow was flown on 15 May 1946 – a single seater intended to investigate the behaviour of swept-wings. The third DH.108, piloted by John Derry, set a closed-circuit speed record of 605.23mph (974.02km/h) on 12 April 1948 and on 6 September exceeded Mach 1 in a dive – the first British aircraft to do so.

Above: The second Bell X-1 on final approach. Its shape was based on the .50 calibre bullet, and it featured a conventional straight wing with ailerons and flaps. The tailplane incidence was adjustable in flight.

Above: A Bell-built B-29B Superfortress was modified to carry the X-1 to its required altitude for air launch.

One of the earliest French projects, the VG 70, built by the Arsenal de l'Aéronautique was first flown on 23 June 1948. Intended to explore the problems of high-speed fighters, it demonstrated good performance on a low-power Junkers Jumo 004B-2 turbojet, but was abandoned when fuselage redesign was needed to install a more powerful Rolls-Royce Derwent.

These credible performances in Europe were accomplished with turbojet-powered aircraft. However, in the United States the USAAF and NACA (predecessor of NASA) wanted to investigate, with minimum delay, the problems of supersonic flight and contracted the Bell Company to build a series of prototypes.

The bullet-shaped XS-1 (later X-1) had a thin straight wing, and was powered by a bi-propellant rocket engine. First flown in unpowered flight on 19 January 1946 after release from a B-29 Superfortress 'motherplane', it was piloted by Captain Charles 'Chuck' Yeager on 14 October 1947 to a speed of 670mph (1078km/h), or Mach 1.05 – so becoming the first aircraft in the world to exceed the speed of sound in level flight.

In the UK, Miles Aircraft was commissioned in 1943 to design to Specification E.24/43 an ultra high-speed research aircraft to fly at speeds of up to 1,000mph (1609km/h). Good progress was being made with the Miles M.52, when suddenly in 1946, the Ministry of Supply cancelled the entire project. The almost inexplicable (to all those working on this exciting project) reason given, was that it was considered to be 'too dangerous'.

CHRONOLOGY

24 July 1946
First recorded manned ejection from an aircraft on the ground was made by Bernard Lynch by means of a Martin-Baker ejection seat installed in a specially modified Gloster Meteor F3.

8 August 1946
In the USA, the giant six-engined Convair XB-36 bomber prototype was flown for the first time. It was the biggest US bomber of all time.

7 September 1946
A new world speed record was set by the RAF High Speed Flight when Group Captain E .M. Donaldson flew at 616.81mph over Littlehampton, England in a Gloster Meteor F4.

1 October 1946
Adopting the title Force Aérienne Belge or Belgische Luchtmacht, the Belgian Air Force was re-established.

9 December 1946
The Bell XS-1 rocket-engined research aircraft, dropped from a converted B-29, was flown for the first time in powered flight. An unpowered descent had previously been made on 19 January.

10 March 1947
The first Swedish jet fighter – the Saab 21R, made its first flight, and 60 were built for service from 1950.

17 March 1947
First flight of the four-engined North American XB-45 – later named Tornado. It was the first US all-jet bomber to become operational.

27 June 1947
Designed from the outset for turbojet power, the Tupolev Tu-12 Soviet jet-engined bomber made its first flight. It used a Soviet copy of the Rolls-Royce Nene engine.

27 July 1947
First British designed production helicopter, the Bristol Sycamore, made its first flight from Filton.

18 September 1947
The United States Air Force (USAF) was established under General Carl A. Spaatz.

1 October 1947
First flight of the North American XP-86 Sabre – the world's first swept-wing jet fighter to enter operational service.

14 October 1947
USAF Major Charles E. 'Chuck' Yeager became the first person to break the sound barrier after his Bell X-1 was dropped from a B-29 at 20,000ft.

17 December 1947
The first B-47 Stratojet strategic bomber made its first flight on the 40th anniversary of the Wright brothers' historic first powered flight.

First through the sound barrier

'Chuck' Yeager described his experiences in the Bell XS-1, leading to the first flight through the sound barrier on 14 October 1947:

"During the first three powered flights a shock wave was forming at the thickest part of the wing and was starting to move back, and behind the shock wave, you have turbulent air. This shock wave also killed off a little more lift on one wing than it did on the other, so you would get a slight wing drop due to the non-perfect contours. It is almost impossible to make one wing a perfect replica of the other."

"On the fourth flight we took the aeroplane up to 0.94 Mach number — 94% of the speed of sound. At this speed I laid the aeroplane over and pulled back on the control column and the aeroplane did not turn, it went the way it was headed so I shut everything off and came down and had a heart to heart talk with the engineers. We looked at all our data and it showed that the shock wave that had formed on the horizontal stabilisers the same as on the wing, had moved back and attached itself to the trailing edge of the stabiliser, just in front of where the elevator was hinged. So all the 'long hairs' got together and talked and talked and talked and

finally they came out with the next programme. We would go up. Instead of turning with the elevator – the flippers on the aeroplane – we would change the angle of incidence on the horizontal stabiliser, or change the whole tailplane and make the aeroplane turn, starting at Mach 0.86 where our elevators were very effective."

"After that it was just a matter of a couple of flights, the buffeting got very heavy and we did get a little bit of pitch up. On trim change we changed the angle of incidence on the horizontal stabiliser to keep the nose down and we kicked it on up on the sixth flight to about Mach 1.04. Came down and looked all over the data. Actually we got a jump on the Mach meter from about 0.96 to about 1.04."

"We made a total of some 80 flights on the X-1. We had a lot of fires in the rear end of it but fortunately it did not blow up on us, and we lost a lot of pieces off it – but fortunately they made some new ones...."

Fueling the Orange Beast by Henry Godines shows the rocket-powered Bell XS-1 at Muroc AFB, California, being refuelled before its record-breaking first supersonic flight.

THE BERLIN AIRLIFT

The Berlin Airlift was the first time that transport aircraft were used to sustain a city under seige. The tonnage carried by US, British and French aircraft remains unsurpassed among humanitarian airlift missions. It broke new ground in the logistics of airpower and taught technical lessons that guided future air policy.

On 26 June 1948, the world's biggest mercy mission got underway with the landing of 80 tons of food and fuel carried by US Air Force C-47s and RAF Dakotas. Decisive action by the Western Allies not only saved millions from starvation, but almost certainly prevented a third world war.

The intensity of Operation *Vittles* telescoped a decade of air transport experience into a one-year period. The airlift marked the transition to the instrument flying age, with radar and GCA (Ground Controlled Approach) making possible round-the-clock operations in nearly all weather conditions. It demonstrated the value of large aircraft, as success would not have been possible with C-47s alone. Just as the larger USAF C-54 Skymasters and RAF Yorks and Hastings were able to deliver greatly increased tonnage (with the same number of aircraft, crews and landing times), so even larger transports would have been more efficient still.

Moscow may have counted on the people of Berlin losing heart or for the weather to

USAF C-47 Skytrains being unloaded at Tempelhof after flying down the narrow air corridor to Berlin. Each C-47 could carry a three-ton load of supplies.

Above: A line of Avro Yorks await their turn to be unloaded on the ramp at Gatow.

Right: German children gather to watch as a USAF C-54 Skymaster flies in with vital supplies to the airport at Tempelhof, in the American controlled sector of Berlin.

CHRONOLOGY

23 March 1948
A new world altitude record of 59,000ft was achieved by Group Captain John Cunningham flying a specially modified De Havilland Vampire.

28 March 1948
First air-to-air refuelling tests between two B-29s were completed. This proved the feasibility of extending the range of the USAF's Strategic Air Command fleet.

26 April 1948
The sound barrier was broken for the first time by a turbo-powered jet fighter, when an XP-86 Sabre exceeded Mach 1 in a shallow dive.

1 June 1948
The beginning of Operation *Firedog* – RAF operations against terrorists in Malaya, in support of security forces.

3 June 1948
First air victory by an Israeli Air Force pilot when an Avia S-99 shot down an Egyptian Air Force C-47.

ground the airlift – but neither happened. On 12 May 1949, the Russians gave up and reopened surface routes to the city. The airlift continued until 30 September, stockpiling supplies against a possible new blockade. By then the Allies had flown some 2,325,510 tons of supplies to Berlin in 277,569 flights. Not only had the Soviet leader failed to force the West out of Berlin, his pressure tactics had backfired. The Western Powers went ahead with plans to create the Federal Republic of Germany, which became a strong barrier against Soviet expansion. It also laid the foundations for the establishment of the North Atlantic Treaty Organisation (NATO), which has helped to keep the peace in Europe ever since.

152

Down the Berlin Corridor

This personal description of a flight into Berlin was written by Paul Fisher, a reporter for the US aero-engine manufacturer Pratt & Whitney:

Lieutenant Victor Wiebeck, a native of Adrian, MI was piloting 609. He had flown both B-17s and B-24s on missions over Germany during the war. Five times his destination for today, Berlin, had been a bomb target.

At 1:55, as the thirty-ninth C-54 in the noon block, he began taxiing his plane north. His was the second ship in line. His co-pilot, Lt George Jones, had the check list ready and shortly Wiebeck's staccato voice was demanding of him, "Cowl flaps open?" "Open", he responded. "Tank selectors on main?" "On main". "Cross feeds off?" "Off"...and so on down checks.

Exactly at 2:15, Wiebeck opened the throttles, the big Skymaster surged forward, and the instant it broke away from the ground, Wiebeck reduced his engine speed and manifold pressure. For the next few minutes he followed the prescribed climb and course procedure to reach his assigned altitude of 6,000ft. He had picked up the Darmstadt beacon almost at once. As he climbed,

the last pockets of the morning storm vanished; ahead the sunlight was sucked into huge cumulous formations. The hand of the air speed indicator held at 170mph.

"We're by Aschaffenburg," the co-pilot said. Motioning downward with his thumb he added "Fulda" (Fulda was the radio range beacon marking the entrance to the southern corridor).

"In about eight minutes start looking down and to the right," said Wiebeck. "We'll be over Russian territory. See if you see what I always see on good days."

The C-54 plunged into an enormous white cloud. After a time, Wiebeck said, "Off to the right". There lay an airfield. Scattered around the edges were scores of Russian fighters. "Probably all Yaks," Wiebeck observed. "Look like Yaks to me anyhow. I guess the Stalin boys aren't flying today."

"Tempelhof in sight. I don't know what Goering and Hitler were thinking of at Tempelhof. Got a damned seven-storey apartment block just where you let down to hit the Tempelhof strip. If I'd known what I was going through on the airlift, I would have managed to drop some eggs on that building, believe me."

Shortly afterwards Wiebeck began his left-hand

turn in the pattern of let-down for the Tempelhof landing. He swung over the Wedding beacon, cut right and circled toward the apartment building. Below, the city lay broken and mottled, walls leaning drunkenly, unroofed buildings gaping, the most shattered capital in the world. Far to his left stood a 400ft chimney, untouched by the devastation. The sweeping pattern of Tempelhof's field was spread below, its mile-long administration and hangar building curving along the ramp. Dropping down, he touched on the power, straightened out, and smoothed out for the landing.

As he started his taxi run, a jeep, with a big board painted in diagonal maroon and yellow stripes, whipped out in front of him. It bore the sign 'Follow Me'. Wiebeck's C-54 clocked along behind the small guide, pulled up at its assigned stand, and almost at once a tractor backed a trailer against 609 and 17 Germans, many of them middle-aged, began the job of unloading the Skymaster.

Berlin Airlift by Robert G. Smith illustrates a typical winter's scene at Tempelhof with USAF Douglas C-54 Skymasters being unloaded on the apron.

RECORD-BREAKING BOMBER

W. E. W. Petter became the chief engineer of the English Electric Company's Aircraft Division at Preston, Lancs after leaving Westlands in 1944. There he began work on a three-seat high-altitude bomber to meet the requirements of AM Spec B3/45. He did not follow the 'fashionable' swept wing theme, but adopted one with a broad chord centre-section and tapered outer panels. This gave the aircraft – later named Canberra – features that included excellent low-speed flight characteristics, good fuel economy and superb manouverability at very high altitude.

On 13 May 1949, Wing Commander Roland 'Bee' Beamont flew the first all-blue prototype on its maiden flight from Warton airfield. He was later to comment in his book *Testing Years*:

"The overriding impressions were of a straightforward and simple aeroplane with exceptional smoothness and lack of high noise level from engine or aerodynamic sources. It had that indefinable impression of engineering and aerodynamic integrity that all pilots recognise in the description 'a pilot's aeroplane'."

How right he was – this remarkable aircraft, built in large numbers by English Electric and licence-manufacturers in numerous variants, entered RAF service in 1951 and is still operational – although reduced to just a handful of PR9 reconnaissance versions – into the year 2000 and beyond.

Canberras have set 22 world records, and many of those point-to-point speeds still stand. Notably, on 21 February 1951, a Canberra B2, flown by Sqn Ldr A. E. Callard with a crew of two became the first jet bomber to make a non-stop transatlantic flight between Aldergrove, Northern Ireland and Gander, Newfoundland. The time of 4hr 37min was bettered by 'Bee' Beamont on 31 August 1951, flying a Canberra B2 intended as a pattern aircraft for the US Martin company, over the same route in 4hr 18min. A year later, on 26 August 1952, the Canberra became the first aircraft to complete a two-way crossing of the Atlantic within 24 hours, again piloted over the same route by Beamont.

In addition to far-ranging point-to-point flights of this nature, Canberras set world absolute height records in 1953, 1955 and 1957 – the last, when fitted with a Double Scorpion rocket engine, to an altitude of 70,308ft.

When prototype Canberra VN799 made its maiden flight from Warton on 13 May 1949, the small group of company personnel present were probably unaware that they had witnessed the birth of a thoroughbred.

CHRONOLOGY

26 June 1948
The USAF and RAF commenced the first deliveries of food into Berlin – Operation *Vittles*. The Berlin Airlift continued until 30 September 1949.

5 July 1948
First crossing of the North Atlantic by jet fighters. Six RAF Vampire F4s, from RAF Stornoway via Iceland and Greenland to Goose Bay, Labrador.

8 July 1948
The Ilyushin Il-28, the Soviet Union's first successful turbo-jet powered bomber, made its maiden flight.

16 August 1948
First flight of the Northrop XF-89 Scorpion – the first two-seat all-weather turbojet interceptor.

23 August 1948
The McDonnell XF-85 Goblin 'parasite' fighter, intended to be air-launched and recovered from a Convair B-36, made its first free flight. It was developed as a radical solution to the problem of escort fighters for intercontinental range bombers.

1 September 1948
First flight of the Swedish Saab-29, which incorporated design changes resulting from examination of German swept-wing research.

26 October 1948
First Gloster Meteor T7 two-seat jet fighter made its maiden flight and in December became the first jet trainer to enter service with the RAF.

26 February 1949
A USAF B-50A Superfortress completed the first non-stop round the world flight, relying on in-flight refuelling.

28 February 1949
The swept-wing Dassault MD450 Ouragan made its first flight. A total of 350 were built and the type was also purchased by the Israeli Air Force.

9 March 1949
First flight of the Avro Shackleton MR1 maritime reconnaissance aircraft.

26 March 1949
First flight was made by the Convair B-36D powered by four turbojets, mounted in pairs under the outer wing sections, in addition to the six pusher engines.

1 May 1949
The Grumman F9F Panther entered service with the US Navy. It became the Navy's principal jet fighter during the Korean War.

13 May 1949
The prototype of the English Electric Canberra twin-jet bomber made its first flight.

SWING-WING PIONEER

The Messerschmitt P1011 was the prototype of an advanced jet fighter design, with a single jet engine and variable-sweep wings. It was captured at the Messerschmitt test facility at Oberammergau in southern Bavaria and taken to the US, but after suffering damage during ground handling, no attempt was made to fly the aircraft.

In the late 1930s German aerodynamicists were researching the advantages of wing sweep to reduce the effects of compressibility. Dr Alex Lippisch, the well-known German scientist, appreciated the benefits of swept wings but was concerned that the sharply swept wing would give unsatisfactory low-speed flight characteristics. So, in 1942, he patented his proposals for a variable-geometry wing.

During WW2, Dr Waldemar Voight of the Messerschmitt company began the design of a small single-seat research aircraft designated P1101 (Projek 1101). This was finalised with 40deg wing sweep, all-swept tail surfaces and retractable tricycle undercarriage, initially to be powered by a 2,866lb st Heinkel-Hirth 011 turbojet, but later to have a 1,984lb st Junkers Jumo 004B.

Subsequently, the design was revised to allow the wings to be set on the ground at three alternative angles of wing sweep (35, 40 and 45deg), this allowed evaluation at any one of the three settings.

The P1101 had not flown before the US forces overran the factory in the closing stages of WW2. The unfinished aircraft was crated and shipped to Wright Field in the USA. Robert J. Woods, Chief Designer of the Bell Aircraft Corporation had seen the P1101 in Germany, along with the Combined Advanced Field Team (CAFT). It was not put to any good use until it was declared surplus and borrowed by Bell in late 1948 and Woods subsequently gained support for the construction of two variable-geometry research aircraft, based on the P1101. Designated Bell X-5, work began in 1948 and developed the mechanism that would allow the wing sweep to be varied in flight, from a minimum of 20deg to a maximum of 60deg. The wing was conventional, incorporating ailerons and full-span leading-edge and

large trailing-edge flaps. Special attention was given ensure that all angles of sweepback the wing-root fairing provided a smooth aerofoil surface.

The first Bell X-5, powered by a single 4,900lb st Allison J53-A-17, took almost two years to complete, making its maiden flight on 20 June 1951. During the flight – and the following three in July – the wings were kept at maximum span. From the fifth flight, on 27 July 1951, sweep-back angle was progressively augmented and max sweep-back angle was attained on the ninth flight. The USAF accepted the X-5 on 7 November 1951, and turned it over to NACA which set up an extensive fight-test programme.

Commenting on the project, Bell's test pilot Jean 'Skip' Ziegler said: "Various test pilots encountered numerous problems – some of them serious. In fact the X-5 was a difficult aircraft to fly, being quite unstable under certain circumstances and showed nasty stall characteristics. But it provided us with excellent data concerning variable geometry."

The second prototype flew at Edwards AFB on 9 December 1951, but was lost in a spin recovery test on 14 October 1953. Further tests were made with the surviving example until the autumn of 1955, when the aircraft was withdrawn from use after its 153rd flight, flown by Neil Armstrong. It is now in the USAF Museum.

This small but important aircraft provided the US aircraft industry with a great deal of information on variable-geometry configuration.

The Bell X-5 with wings at the maximum sweep angle. The X-5 was essentially similar to the P1011, but its structure and systems were much more sophisticated.

CHRONOLOGY

24 June 1949
The Douglas D-558-II Skyrocket exceeded Mach 1 for the first time.

10 September 1949
The Sikorsky S-55 helicopter prototype made its maiden flight. It featured an engine mounted in the nose, becoming the first helicopter with a cabin that was unrestricted by an engine installation.

19 September 1949
First flight of the Fairey Gannet – the first aircraft to be powered by a double-propeller turbine engine.

13 January 1950
The MiG-17 jet fighter first flew. With better all-round performance than the MiG-15, it remained in Soviet service until 1960.

3 June 1950
First flight of the YF-96A Thunderstreak. This was Republic's first swept-wing aircraft, a fighter-bomber based on the F-84 Thunderjet. The designation was changed to YF-84F in September 1950.

26 June 1950
F-82 Twin Mustangs had the USAF's first encounter with a Communist aircraft whilst providing air cover for evacuation ships in the harbour at Inchon.

22 September 1950
First non-stop crossing of the North Atlantic by a turbojet powered aircraft, a Republic F-84E Thunderjet. The flight, from the UK to Limestone, ME, lasted ten hours, with three in-flight refuellings.

8 November 1950
The first all-jet battle took place when F-80 Shooting Stars attacked Chinese MiG-15s – the first occasion that one jet was destroyed by another in combat.

SABRE AGAINST MIG

Powered by a General Electric J47-GE-9 turbojet engine, the early F-86A Sabre had some deficiencies when compared to the MiG-15, but thanks to superior piloting skills, it usually prevailed in battle. The F-86A shown here is a restored example based in the UK.

The North American F-86 Sabre is remembered for its air superiority role in the Korean War when, high over the Yalu River, it tangled with Russia's MiG-15 in the world's first jet-versus-jet combats close to the speed of sound. It was in the cut-and-thrust of high-speed air battles over Korea that the Sabre captured the initial imagination of the Western world. The new swept-wing North American design represented a major step forward from the then current front-line F-80 Shooting Stars and F-84 Thunderjets.

The advances made by UN forces came to a halt in November 1950, as they began encountering Chinese troops who had now become openly involved in the conflict. A new danger also developed overhead, as the first Chinese MiG-15 jet fighters appeared over North Korea in the same month. One was shot down by a USAF F-80C Shooting Star in the first jet-to-jet combat in history, but the faster Soviet type provided the first serious opposition to United Nations air superiority. However, the situation was rectified by the deployment of the F-86A Sabre to the theatre in December, which proved more than a match for the MiGs in spite of some early teething troubles. Though the arrival of the F-86A in the theatre of operations had already greatly enhanced the Allied air combat capability, the ever-increasing numbers of Chinese MiG-15s in early 1951 resulted in the Far East Air Force's air superiority gradually being diminished.

CHRONOLOGY

21 February 1951
An RAF Canberra B2 was flown from Aldergrove, Northern Ireland to Gander, Newfoundland covering the 2,072mile(3,335km/h) distance in four hours 37 min – this being the first turbojet aircraft to make a non-stop unrefuelled transatlantic crossing.

23 February 1951
The French Dassault MD452.01 Mystère prototype first flew – the air force's first indigenous jet fighter.

18 May 1951
First flight of the Vickers Valiant four-jet bomber – the first of three V-bomber types for the RAF.

18 May 1951
The Douglas D-558-II became the world's fastest aircraft when it achieved a speed of Mach 1.72 at 62,000ft – the first time a human being had travelled at over 1,000mph (1,613km/h).

20 June 1951
A Martin B-61 Matador missile, later the TM-61, was launched for the first time – the USAF's first tactical guided missile.

20 June 1951
First flight of the Bell X-5 research aircraft, based on the unflown Messerschmitt P1101 – the first aircraft with a variable wing sweep, adjustable in flight.

The Mikoyan-Gurevich MiG-15 was designed using captured German research data, and powered by an unlicensed copy of the Rolls-Royce Nene turbojet. This restored example is airworthy in the US.

MiG Killer

Lt-Col Bruce H. Hinton, an experienced WW2 pilot, recalled his first MiG kill:

"We entered the combat area at a leisurely, fuel-conserving speed as we wanted to extend our patrol time. When the flight sighted a battle formation of four MiG-15s our F-86s were flying too slowly to achieve maximum effectiveness."

"Fortunately, the MiGs were below and climbing – their pilots doubtless believed that the American planes were F-80s, otherwise they would almost certainly have climbed for altitude on their own side of the Yalu."

"They realised their mistake only when we came diving on them, rapidly gaining speed, whereupon the MiGs broke away and dived for the safety of the river. They were too late."

"I clung to the tail of the number two MiG and I fired three four-second bursts from my six 0.50in machine guns. The enemy aircraft burst into flames and went into a slow spin."

These were the first of 792 MiG-15s which were to be claimed as destroyed by Sabre pilots during the two and a half years of air combat that followed.

The F-86 Sabre's main drawback was its lack of endurance. Patrolling at speeds of Mach 0.85 and higher the Sabre pilots could afford to spend only 20

minutes in the vicinity of the Yalu, before being forced to head for home with a safe margin of fuel. The MiG pilots quickly realised this limitation and exploited it to the fullest advantage. They climbed to altitude north of the Yalu and then diving at high speed to make their attacks as the Sabres were withdrawing towards the end of their patrol.

From July 1951, the USAF undertook to replace FEAF's F-86As with F-86Bs on a one-for- exchange basis, but this process was to continue for many months.

'Gabby' Scores Again by Bob Cunningham, shows the top-scoring Korean War ace Col Frances Gabreski claiming another kill against a MiG-15.

LAST OF THE PISTON FIGHTERS

As the jets were coming in, the last generation of piston-engined fighters were being phased out – although many of these were still very capable aircraft. In the US, the Grumman F8F Bearcat – a pure interceptor fighter, designed as the smallest aircraft that could be built around a 2,000hp (1,491kW) 18-cylinder Pratt & Whitney engine – together with the F4U Corsair and F7F Tigercat, were all excellent machines that flew in US Navy service. In the USAF, the North American P-51 Mustang and P-47 Thunderbolt were at their peak. The Hawker Sea Fury – a variation on the Typhoon/Tempest line – served in

Though designed as a dedicated shipborne air-defence fighter, the F8F Bearcat found its niche as a land-based fighter-bomber. Powered by a big R-2800 Double Wasp, Grumman designed the smallest and lightest airframe possible that would be able to accommodate the specified armament, armour and fuel.

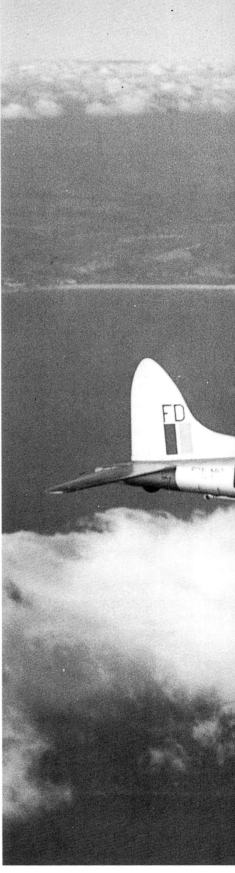

CHRONOLOGY

20 July 1951
The Hawker P1067 – the Hunter prototype – was first flown. The Supermarine Swift fighter prototype made its maiden flight a few weeks later, and the Supermarine Scimitar naval fighter first flew in the same month.

5 September 1951
A contract was awarded to modify a B-36 Peacemaker to carry a nuclear reactor for tests on airframe, instruments and electronics. This provided vital research to ascertain whether an atomic-powered bomber was feasible.

1 April 1952
First Piasecki H-21 Workhorse helicopter made its maiden flight – it was the US forces' first tandem-rotor helicopter.

15 April 1952
Boeing YB-52 eight-jet strategic bomber was flown for the first time. Designed to carry nuclear weapons to any target in the world, the first deliveries of RB-52B Stratofortresses were made to Strategic Air Command in June 1955.

26 April 1952
The Japanese Maritime Self-Defence Force was formed as an anti-submarine and maritime patrol force for home defence purposes only.

29 July 1952
An RB-45C Tornado was flown from Elmendorf AFB, Alaska to Yokota AB, Japan – the first non-stop transpacific flight by a turbojet aircraft, which involved two in-flight refuellings from KB-29s.

Above: The Hawker Sea Fury was the Fleet Air Arm's last piston-engined fighter in first-line squadrons, where it served from 1947 until 1954. As the FAA's leading single-seat fighter, the Sea Fury fought with distinction during the Korean War. It was powered by a 2,480hp Bristol Centaurus radial engine, giving it a maximum speed of 460mph.

Right: The de Havilland Sea Hornet was the Fleet Air Arm's version of the RAF's long-range fighter, and it became the first twin-engined single-seat fighter type to be operated from the Royal Navy's aircraft carriers.

front-line service with the Royal Navy from 1947-1954 and was also an excellent fighter. The twin-engined de Havilland Hornet in RAF service (and flown by the Royal Navy, as the Sea Hornet) was one of the fastest operational fighters.

In other categories, propeller-driven aircraft survived – for transport, maritime reconnaissance, artillery observation, and for other uses where endurance was more important than speed. For first-line operations, the propeller fighters and bombers went to smaller air forces, where they soldiered on for many years. American-built B-25 Mitchells, A-26 Invaders, P-47 Thunderbolts and P-51 Mustangs; British-built Spitfires, Tempests, Mosquitos and Lancasters; Russian MiGs and Tupolevs – all entered the service of lesser powers.

MAXIMUM ALTITUDE

The flight for maximum altitude is part of the routine tests for any modern aircraft; but on 15 August 1951, routine meant discovery as the Douglas D-558-II Skyrocket, released from a B-29 Superfortress, carried William Bridgeman much higher than man had ever been. His altitude was confirmed at 79,000ft.

He describes the flight in his book *The Lonely Sky* (Cassell 1956):

"Today I am going to let her go as far as she will. It is up to her. Time! It will be in ten seconds. The chase plane at this end checks in and stands by."

"Four...three...two...one. I hold the cold wheel in my bare hands and lean forward...Drop!"

"Four buttons down. One, two, three, four, and four gigantic blow-torches rumble into life. Going up. The numbers on the dials, 0.85 on the Machmeter."

"The needles slide up and down and around – 0.85 becomes Mach 1, she bumps into the quiet area and the high-drag rise of the shock waves. The larger altimeter hand winds up to 42,000, 43,000, reeling off the altitude. No pushover. Straight up. All the way, bending back a

Opposite page and below: As a result of research into captured German aerodynamic reports, the Douglas D-558-II Skyrocket was designed around swept wings. To supplement the insufficient thrust of the available turbojets, a rocket engine was installed with fuel for two minutes operation at 4,000lb (1814kg) thrust.

CHRONOLOGY

31 July 1952
First transatlantic flight by helicopters, when two Sikorsky H-19s flew from Westover AFB to Prestwick, Scotland. Landings were made en route in Labrador, Greenland, Iceland and the Hebrides.

30 August 1952
The delta-wing bomber prototype Avro 698 Vulcan four-jet V-bomber made its first flight.

16 October 1952
The prototype French Sud-Ouest 4050 Vautour made its maiden flight – developed as a two-seat all-weather fighter, single-seat ground attack aircraft and a two-seat bomber.

28 October 1952
The heaviest aircraft to operate from an aircraft carrier – the Douglas XA3D-1 Skywarrior nuclear-capable bomber – made its first flight.

3 November 1952
The prototype Swedish Saab 32 Lansen all-weather fighter made its first flight.

24 December 1952
The prototype HP80 Victor crescent-wing four-jet bomber made its first flight – the third and last of the aircraft for the RAF's V-bomber programme.

30 January 1953
First flight of the B-47E Stratojet. This version was the major production type, of which 1,341 were eventually delivered, together with 255 RB-47Es.

2 March 1953
A mixed-powered research aircraft – the Sud-Ouest SO.9000 Trident – was first flown on turbojet power. It featured wing-tip mounted turbojets and a rocket motor in the rear fuselage and was flown in excess of Mach 1.5.

25 May 1953
The prototype North American YF-100A Super Sabre, the first of the Century fighters, made its first flight. It was the first Western combat aircraft able to sustain supersonic performance in level flight.

20 July 1953
First flight of the Martin B-57A – the American-built version of the English Electric Canberra bomber.

7 August 1953
The Leduc 0.21 ramjet research prototype made a successful powered flight, following launch from a Sud-Est SE161 Languedoc 'motherplane'. The inner shell of its double-skinned tubular fuselage incorporated the pilot's cockpit – the outer shell formed the duct for the ramjet.

1 September 1953
First jet-to-jet in-flight refuelling, when a YB-47F was refuelled by a KB-47G, using the British hose and drogue system.

little more, a little, a little more. The only world I am aware of is the world of dial eyes in front of me. The perpendicular light on the newly installed angle-of-attack instrument creeps up steadily as I move the stabiliser trim switch. Zut...zut...zut, pointing her nose higher, a little bit higher."

"In the thin air, actually she does not want to fly but miraculously she does; she is held by a fantastic power that takes over. She is going up at such a speed that in reality she is close to stall. We are buoyed on a pivot that keeps us in balance. Although I am acutely aware of this circumstance, I am not alarmed by it. I am reluctant to believe she will not continue to fly."

"With this adrenalin-inflicted state floats a feeling of detachment. It is an incompatible set of emotions I experience. Fear seems to be independent, a ghost sitting on my shoulder. And although it is most surely there, I am anaesthetized to its warnings. I am without

The second Skyrocket, in all-rocket configuration, at the moment of release from its 'motherplane' – a modified US Navy Boeing P2B-1S (ex-USAAF B-29).

CHRONOLOGY

18 September 1953
The prototype of the MiG-19 was flown for the first time in the Soviet Union.

24 October 1953
The prototype Convair YF-102 made its first flight. It was designed as a scaled-up version of the delta-wing Convair XP-92A.

20 November 1953
A Douglas D-558-II Skyrocket became the first aircraft to reach Mach 2, this being achieved in a shallow dive at 62,000ft.

12 December 1953
'Chuck' Yeager, in the Bell X-1A supersonic research aircraft attained a speed of Mach 2.44. The flight confirmed that a more formidable challenge lay ahead in the form of a 'thermal' barrier.

anxiety. I am powerless to anticipate what will happen next moment. Time is now. I have complete faith that wraps me like a warm blanket now, that she will not be interrupted in this freedom."

"The instruments stand out brighter – 64,000ft on the altimeter, reeling away...the Mach number...the rocket-seconds left to spend. Seventy-six thousand feet registers on the dial and the rockets sputter off. The altimeter stops its steady reeling and swings sickly around 80,000ft. The altitude is too extreme for the instrument to function."

"Eighty thousand feet. It is intensely bright outside; the contrast of the dark shadows of the cockpit is extreme and strange. It is so dark lower in the cockpit that I cannot read the instruments sunk low on the panel. The dials on top, in the light, are vividly apparent. There seems to be no reflection; it is all black or white, apparent or non-apparent. No half-tones. It is a pure, immaculate world here."

"It is as if I am the only living thing connected to this totally strange, uninhabited planet 15 miles below me. The plane that carries me and I are one alone."

"I am on my descent and slowly I return to what I knew before. Again I hear myself labouring for oxygen inside the helmet, and the world under me comes gradually into focus as something identifiable with life. At 15,000ft it is comfortingly familiar. I take the face-plate out of the helmet and breath air again, deeply, and I am back, fully returned to time and dimension and the brief span that is allowed me."

A New Generation

The pattern of Soviet policy, coupled with the Communist victory in China in 1949, led the West to put off any thoughts of reducing their forces to normal peacetime level – and consequently air forces were much enlarged and equipped with much more powerful aircraft.

The Convair B-36, which entered service in 1947, was a monster hybrid that bridged the gap between the last of the conventionally-powered bombers and the first of the real jets. It was powered by six twenty-eight cylinder pusher radial engines and four turbojets. Its wingspan was almost 100ft greater than the B-29. Though maximum speed was only 410mph, it had a commendable range of some 7,000 miles.

The first generation of jet bombers, which began appearing in the 1950s, were designed to outfly rather than outfight the latest jet fighters. In the US, the six-engined Boeing B-47

The Boeing B-47 Stratojet became an important element in US nuclear deterrence and foreign policy. On 12 January 1954, Secretary of State John Foster Dulles declared that the United States would rely on 'massive nuclear retaliation to counter a Soviet conventional or nuclear attack against Europe or a nuclear strike against the North American continent'.

167

Above: The Convair B-36 Peacemaker's primary mission was intercontinental nuclear strike against targets deep within the Soviet Union. The first B-36As were delivered to the USAF in the summer of 1948. A host of improvements were fitted to the B-36 during its time in production, including underwing pods that housed four J47 turbojets, as seen in this RB-36E example.

Stratojet – followed by the eight-engined B-52 Stratofortress – were designed to replace the Convair B-36 Peacemaker. In Britain the four-engined V-bombers - initially the Vickers Valiant, followed by the delta-winged Avro Vulcan and the crescent winged Handley Page Victor, entered front-line service.

In due course these bombers would carry the thermo-nuclear (hydrogen) bomb that was first tested by the Americans in 1952, and first dropped by a B-52 in 1956.

Russia, who neglected the development of strategic heavy bombers during WW2, copied a B-29 Superfortress that had forced-landed in Mongolia after a raid on Japan. This was put into production as the Tupolev Tu-4 'Bull'. The Tu-20 and Tu-22 soon followed.

Left: The Soviets had no doubts that they would get their hands on a B-29, but this happened sooner than expected when three USAAF B-29s force-landed in the Soviet Far East and were instantly appropriated on 29 July 1944. The first example of the Soviet copy, the Tupolev Tu-4 'Bull', was flown on 19 May 1947, and about 900 were eventually built.

CHRONOLOGY

15 January 1954
The French Nord Gerfaut 1A delta-wing research aircraft was flown, and later in the year it became the first aircraft in Europe to be flown at Mach 1 in level flight, without the use of afterburner.

28 February 1954
First Lockheed XF-104 Starfighter made its first flight at Edwards AFB.

1 May 1954
The Myasishchyev M-4 'Bison' swept-wing bomber made a dramatic appearance over the May Day parade at Red Square, Moscow.

22 June 1954
First flight of the Douglas XA4D-1, which became the A4D Skyhawk – an outstanding carrier-based attack bomber used extensively in the Vietnam War.

28 June 1954
USAF's first Douglas RB-66A Destroyer (evolved from the US Navy A3D Skywarrior) made its maiden flight.

3 August 1954
The Rolls-Royce Thrust Measuring Rig (TMR) – dubbed the 'flying bedstead' – was first tested in 'free' flight. It had made a tethered flight on 9 July 1953. It represented the UK's first essay into VTOL (Vertical Take-Off and Landing) jet aircraft.

4 August 1954
The English Electric P1 was first flown. It was developed as the Lightning, the RAF's first combat aircraft capable of supersonic level flight.

29 September 1954
First flight of the McDonnell YF-101 Voodoo. It accomplished the unprecedented feat of going supersonic on its first flight.

5 May 1955
The US and Canada reached agreement on the construction of the Defence Early Warning (DEW) radar line, to protect the North American continent from unexpected Soviet air attacks.

4 August 1955
The first Lockheed U-2 spyplane had its 'official' maiden flight in the Nevada Desert.

22 October 1955
First flight of the Republic YF-105A Thunderchief. It exceeded the speed of sound on this flight.

25 October 1955
The Swedish Saab-35 Draken supersonic all-weather interceptor made its first flight.

10 December 1955
First vertical take-off and conversion to horizontal flight of the Ryan X-13 VTOL research aircraft.

The announced intention of these bomber forces was the application of a deterrent to war, but faced by the prospect of the unthinkable, and unacceptable mass destruction, each side merely implemented more subtle and limiting ways of furthering their political aims, short of global atomic war.

These aircraft carried the manned strategic bomber concept probably as far as it could, or was likely to go, and these types – products of the 1950s – were in service in one role or another throughout the Cold War era. Even with the advent of intercontinental missiles, they remained a potent element of their countries' arsenals, their power increased enormously over the years by the ever-growing lethality of the weapons they carried.

VERTICAL FLIGHT

The Bachem Ba 349 Natter. The crude airframe of the Natter is shown with the nosecone removed to reveal its unguided rocket armament. The first vertical launch, without a pilot, took place on 23 February 1945, but the concept was never tested in actual combat.

Conceived as a research platform for the evaluation of jet-deflection for VTOL applications, Bell's X-14 was intended only for low-speed trials. It first flew in February 1957, and the X-14 undertook a long series of experimental test flights with the USAF before being transferred to NASA.

Though the V/STOL (Vertical/Short Take-Off and Landing) concept had its origins in Germany during WW2 – the rocket-powered Bachem BA349 Natter (Adder) had made its first piloted flight in February 1945 – practical progress had to wait until the 1950s, when the real demands of V/STOL were better appreciated, jet engines were far more advanced, and there was a stronger operational motivation.

One of the driving forces behind V/STOL development was the US Navy, who had funded the Lockheed XFV-1 and Convair XFY-1 turboprop 'tailsitters' – but these tests ceased in 1956. The other tailsitter was the single-seat Ryan X-13, powered by a 10,000lb (44.5kN) Rolls-Royce Avon turbojet. It was the world's first jet-powered VTOL research aircraft and was first flown on 10 December 1955. It featured a hook mounted beneath the forward fuselage from which it was suspended for take-off thrust, and was launched from (and recovered to) a tilting platform.

Of high-set delta-wing configuration, the X-13 had no landing gear and was designed to take off vertically. Two prototypes were built, and the first complete transition from vertical take-off to horizontal flight, and the reverse procedure to a vertical landing, was accomplished on 11 April 1957. The Vertijet proved highly successful, and was thought to have formed the basis for the proposed XF-109 VTOL fighter for the USAF. However, the tailsitter had its limitations, and attention increasingly turned to the flat-riser, which required less mental gymnastics from the pilot.

What made possible a comparatively simple V/STOL combat aircraft was the invention of a new type of powerplant, in which the thrust could be turned through more than 90deg, rotating about a point very close to the engine CofG. This led to the Bell X-14, which made its first flight and hovers in 1957 and completed transition on 24 May 1958. The X-14 is acknowledged as the world's first successful vectored-thrust V/STOL demonstrator.

Seen hovering next to its specially designed platform, the Ryan X-13 Vertijet was one of the first VTOL research aircraft. Once clear of the hydraulic platform, the Vertijet would transition to wing-borne flight like a conventional aircraft.

BEYOND THE WALL

The Illyushin Il-28 'Beagle' became the Soviet Air Force's standard bomber in the early 1950s.

In the early post-WW2 period the first long-range Russian heavy bombers were largely represented by piston-engined aircraft. The Tupolev Tu-4 'Bull', the Soviet equivalent of the Boeing B-29 Superfortress (from which it was copied) served for many years in considerable numbers.

One of the first heavy jets was the Tu-14 'Bosun' bomber/torpedo carrier and in 1948 the Ilyushin Il-28 'Beagle' entered service. By the early 1950s the Tu-16 'Badger' was entering service – the 16A a nuclear carrier and the 16KS a missile carrier. With a crew of six or seven it was powered by two RD-3M engines, armed with seven 23mm guns and could carry a load of 9,000kg. Overall some 50 modified versions of the Tu-16 appeared.

In 1955, the Tu-95 'Bear' very long-range heavy bomber – fitted with four NK-12 turboprops, driving contra-rotating propellers, commenced production. It could cover 15,000km without air-to-air refuelling. Defensive armament consisted of six NR-23 guns

172

The Soviet Naval Aviation Tupolev Tu-16 'Badger-D', seen here on exercise in 1975, was equipped with two remote controlled missiles for attacks on ships.

CHRONOLOGY

10 March 1956
The world air speed record was advanced beyond 1,000mph (1,609km/h) for the first time, achieved in a Fairey FD.2 research aircraft.

21 May 1956
A USAF B-52B, flying at 50,000ft over Bikini Atoll in the Pacific Ocean, dropped the first air-transportable hydrogen bomb.

7 July 1956
The de Havilland Comet C2 entered RAF service, creating the world's first jet transport squadron.

19 July 1956
A Northrop F-89J Scorpion fired a Douglas MB-1 Genie – the first nuclear-armed air-to-air missile to be launched.

24 July 1956
The Dassault Etendard II prototype was first flown. Developed as the Etendard IVM, the type entered French naval service with the Aéronavale aboard the carriers *Clemenceau* and *Foch* in 1962.

9 August 1956
The prototype of the Fiat G91, which had been designed as a light strike fighter to equip NATO forces, was flown for the first time.

31 August 1956
First flight of the Boeing KC-135A Stratotanker – of which 731 more examples would follow before production ended in 1965.

11 October 1956
First British nuclear weapon to be dropped by an RAF aircraft – a Vickers Valiant over Maralinga, South Australia.

1 November 1956
The first operational tactical reconnaissance flights by U-2s were made over Britain, France and Israel, monitoring activity there as the Suez conflict developed.

11 November 1956
Initial flight of the Convair XB-58 Hustler four-jet delta wing bomber. Weapons and a large amount of fuel were carried in a disposable under-fuselage pod.

17 November 1956
The French Dassault Mirage III supersonic delta-wing fighter made its first flight.

26 December 1956
First flight of the Convair F-106 Delta Dart all-weather supersonic interceptor.

16 January 1957
Three B-52 Stratofortesses made the first non-stop round the world flight by turbojet-powered aircraft. The 24,325-mile flight lasted 45hr 19min.

and the bomb bay could accommodate a load of 12,000kg. The 'Bear' had a number of modified versions over the years – the Tu-95MS, Tu-95K and Tu-95K22 – armed with various guided missiles – and could carry from six-eight free-falling nuclear bombs. The Tu-95MS was intended to destroy stationary targets by using their stand-off winged missiles fitted with nuclear warheads.

Another intercontinental strategic bomber was the Myasishchev 3M and M4 'Bison', powered by four AM-3A turbojets. A re-designed version of the 3M, dubbed 'Atlant' is still in service to carry large components of the *Energiya* carrier missile and the Buran spacecraft to the Baykonur cosmodrome.

The first Soviet-made supersonic bomber was the Yak-28 'Brewer', which appeared in 1959. The Tu-22 'Blinder' of the early 1960s had an unusual (for the time) configuration. Its wing had an increased sweep, while the engines were installed in the tail portion of its elongated fuselage. It was used as the basic development of a modern supersonic bomber – which became the Tu-22M.

Above: The Tupolev Tu-22 'Blinder' (originally called 'Beauty') caused considerable concern to the Americans when it appeared unexpectedly at the Soviet Air Force show at Tushino on 9 July 1961.

Below: The first (and only) production turboprop bomber was the Tupolev Tu-95 'Bear', a huge aircraft with contra-rotating propellers.

The Sukhoi Su-24 'Fencer' was put into production in 1972 – the first Soviet strike-aircraft capable of conducting combat operations in all-weathers, night and day. It was also the first aircraft to carry an integrated computer-based fire control and navigation system, that combined various radar and optromic target detection means with modern navigational aids. By 1983 the modernised Su-24M was adopted by the Soviet Air Force.

In the mid-1970s the long-range aviation received a supersonic missile carrier – with variable geometry wings – the Tu-22M 'Backfire'. The Tu-95 was modified into the Tu-95 'Kama' missile carrier – intended to carry out combat missions in the oceanic and marine theatres. By the late 1970s the Tu-22M3 missile carrier-bomber, with a maximum speed of Mach 1.7 was entering service – followed, in the early 1980s, by the Tu-95MS armed with X-55 missiles.

Finally in the Cold War era, the Tu-160 'Blackjack' – a multi-role strategic intercontinental missile-carrier with a variable geometry wing, and a maximum speed of Mach 2. This was designed to penetrate the enemy air defences by using low altitude and stealth, as well as an advanced ECM system.

SUPERSONIC DELTA

The Fairey Delta 2 shows off the clean lines of its delta shape. The 'bullet' above the jet nozzle contained the three braking parachutes.

I n the early 1950s, the British came to the reluctant conclusion that, however costly, it would have to go ahead with the design and development of a manned supersonic aircraft. Specification E.R.103 was issued – to which English Electric offered its P.1, later to gain fame as the Lightning.

The other contender was Fairey Aviation, whose FD.2 was intended only as a research aircraft to investigate flight and control characteristics in transonic and supersonic flight. It was of clean delta-wing configuration, powered by a 10,000lb (44.5kN) Rolls-Royce Avon RA.28 turbojet.

The choice of a delta wing gave the desired leading edge sweepback, together with structural integrity and good fuel consumption, but had the disadvantage of a steep angle of attack in the landing phase. However, this was overcome by introducing a 'droop-snoot' – the entire cockpit hinging downwards to give the pilot the best possible view. This feature was subsequently adopted for the Anglo-French Concorde programme.

Two FD.2s were built – the first flying on 6 October 1954 and the second on 15 February 1956, both deltas making effortless transitions from subsonic to supersonic flight.

1,000mph+ World Speed Record

Test pilot Lieutenant Commander Peter Twiss recalls his experience in the FD.2:

"Despite opposition from the Air Ministry, it was decided to make an attempt, in 1956, on the world absolute speed record with the Fairey FD.2."

"With preparations completed I took-off in WG774 from Boscombe Down at 11.22 on 10 March 1956 to make two passes over the selected course off the Sussex coast between Chichester and Ford. The attempt was flown at 38,000ft without incident and when I landed back at Boscombe 23 minutes later I had tucked a new record under my belt."

"It had raised the previous speed record by an unprecedented 310mph (499km/h) to the FAI accredited figure of 1,131.76mph (1821.39km/h). Lack of fuel capacity had forced each attempt to be started at well below the maximum speed of Mach 2, reached only at the end of each run."

This was the last absolute speed record to be held by the UK, but the amount of speed increase over the previous record remains a record in itself.

Undoubtedly the greatest loss to Britain was the neglect of the potential inherent in the record-breaking Fairey design. The French immediately started work on the Mach 2 Dassault Mirage III series, doubtless inspired by the success of the British design. The delta-wing, and the so-called double delta, eventually led to other Mach 2 designs , and these entered service during the early 1960s. Prominent amongst these were the Swedish Saab J-35 Draken and the Russian MiG-21. A development of the Delta Dagger saw USAF service as the F-106 Delta Dart.

BOEING'S BIG STRATOFORTRESS

CHRONOLOGY

16 May 1957
The Saunders Roe SR53 first flew – the first hybrid-propulsion aircraft, fitted with a de Havilland Spectre rocket motor and a Viper turbojet.

12 August 1957
An F3D Skyknight, using an experimental automatic landing system for the first time, made a landing on the USS *Antietam*.

4 October 1957
The world's first artificial satellite, the Soviet Union's *Sputnik* was put into earth orbit. This resulted in a US decision to deploy Thor intermediate-range ballistic missiles to European NATO forces. Britain reached an agreement to station a number of these in the UK.

31 January 1958
The first US satellite, *Explorer I*, was launched into orbit from Cape Canaveral, using a Jupiter C rocket.

The Boeing B-52 Stratofortress is one of the century's truly great aircraft, acting as a major deterrent to communist aggression during the critical days of the Cold War. Few aircraft will be able to rival the long-range bomber's longevity, being designed as a strategic bomber in the middle of the 20th century and scheduled to remain in service with the USAF until the fourth decade of the 21st century. Today's B-52 aircrew are flying an aircraft that is older than many of them are themselves, the current fleet having been built in 1961-62.

The first B-52 flew on 15 April 1952 and entered service in mid-1955. Subsequently 744 'Buffs' (Big Ugly Fat Fellows) were built through to 1962, in eight major types – all of which have now been withdrawn except the B-52H (of which 102 were built). During the Vietnam War, the B-52D was used for high-density bombing with conventional bombs - a role that was never considered in the original design specification, which called for for a strategic nuclear bomber.

The B-52G, that was at the heart of USAF Strategic Command until the early 1990s, introduced a shorter vertical tail, remote control tail guns and a 'wet' wing. It saw action during the Gulf War of 1991, with some of the bombers being converted to carry 12

AGM-86 cruise missiles fitted with conventional warheads. The ultimate version, the B-52H, was introduced in 1962 to carry the Skybolt ballistic missile and was powered by more economical 17,000lb st (75.7kN) Pratt & Whitney TF33-P-3 turbofans, which increased the bomber's range by a third.

With the cancellation of the Skybolt, the B-52Hs were progressively upgraded to adapt to new roles, mission profiles and technologies. Equipment such as terrain-following radar, comprehensive ECM protection and EVS (Electro-Optical Viewing System) were all improved and they were adapted to deliver cruise missiles, iron bombs or sea mines. Plans to re-engine 60 of Air Combat Command's 75 surviving 'Buffs' for their continued service on the USAF's front-line until 2035, include replacement with four Rolls-Royce RB211-535 turbofans.

Above: The B-52H shown here carrying a pair of *Hound Dog* missiles has the short tail of the 'G' model, but is distinguishable from the earlier version by the larger inlets of the TF33 turbofan engines.

Opposite page: A B-52H modified as a launch aircraft carrying two D-21B Tagboard Mach 3 reconnaissance drones for trials over the Nellis range in the late 1960s.

Stratofortress at war

Writing late in the 1970s, a pilot recalls the B-52's enormous contribution to the Vietnam War.

"In Vietnam, B-52Ds, 'Es and 'Fs were used extensively in a basically tactical role and we flew our first mission on 18 June 1965. In the *Big Belly* programme of 1965 our B-52Ds were modified to carry forty-two 750lb or eighty-four 500lb 'iron bombs' internally, plus up to twenty-four bombs of the same size in clusters of twelve under each wing."

"We flew *Arc Light* strikes from Guam against the Viet Cong in South Vietnam and Cambodia, and later in North Vietnam and Laos. From mid-1967 we were also operating from U-Tapao in Thailand and the total B-52 effort reached a peak of 3,150 sorties a month early in 1972."

A B-52D taking off from U-Tapao, Thailand during the Operation Linebacker *offensive in the spring of 1972.*

"Many modifications and updating programmes have been applied to the B-52 to improve its operational capabilities. Under the USAF *Pacer Plan* programme 80 of our B-52Ds underwent extensive structural rebuilding during 1975-76 to extend their service life. Under the USAF *Rivet Ace* programme of 1974 about 270 B-52Gs and Hs were fitted with 'Phase VI' ECM equipment. New avionics, ECM and electronics devices are being installed, such as the AFSATCOM kit permitting worldwide communication by satellite. The size and scope of this updating is probably unrivalled for any combat aircraft, and reflects the USAF's expectation that B-52s will remain in active service for the rest of this century."

Above: A camouflaged 'Big Belly' B-52D over Vietnam drops a train of 500lb iron bombs from the bomb bay and wing pylons.

Left: A total of 744 B-52s was built between 1952 and 1961. Few could have foreseen that the last of these would still be flying in front-line service nearly half a century later.

HAWKER HUNTER

The Hawker Hunter was Britain's most successful post-war fighter – and in its heyday was regarded as 'the finest fighter in the world'. Combining tremendous aesthetic appeal with outstanding handling characteristics, the Hunter became widely accepted overseas.

The RAF requirement F.3/48 was for a swept-wing fighter to supersede the Gloster Meteor and called for some improvement on the F-86A Sabre for the high-altitude clear-weather interceptor role. Some work had been done by Hawkers (who had produced the Sea Hawk for the Royal Navy) on the development of the swept-wing, and the company produced a series of stepping stones between the P.1040 and the P.1067 that became the Hunter.

The requirements included an armament of four 20mm Hispano cannon, radar ranging for the guns, a level speed capability of Mach 0.94 and an endurance of one hour. The engine was to be either the Rolls-Royce Avon or Armstrong Siddeley Sapphire – both axial flow designs, and at that stage completely unproven.

The first flight of the prototype took place on 20 July 1951. The second Avon-powered aircraft flew on 5 May 1952 and the Sapphire-powered Hunter on 30 November 1952.

The Hunter F1's service introduction was delayed through problems with engine surging when the guns were fired and an inadequate airbrake. As with most of the early RAF jet fighters, the Hunter was found to be chronically short of internal fuel, being designed for a quick climb to the intercept point and no patrol time.

The early F1 and F2s were soon phased out in favour of the F4 (Avon powered) and F5 (Sapphire powered). The F6 was a major step forward and first flew on 22 January 1954 and went on to serve with 19 RAF squadrons. Other major users were the Indian and Swiss air forces. The RAF employed the T7 two-seat derivative of the F4 for weapons training, while the 'hooked' T8 series was used by the Royal Navy, which also used the single-seat GA11 and PR11 derivative of the F4. For ground-attack duties the Hunter FGA9 was selected to replace the de Havilland Venom.

Left: This Wilfred Hardy painting shows a formation of Hawker Hunter F1s of No 43(F) Squadron – the first RAF Hunter squadron, based at RAF Leuchars in 1954.

CHRONOLOGY

10 April 1959
The Northrop YT-38 Talon made its first flight. It was to serve as the USAF's first supersonic fighter trainer.

14 April 1959
The Grumman OV-1 Mohawk made its first flight – the only fixed-wing aircraft ever to be specially designed for the US Army.

8 June 1959
The North American X-15 high-speed research aircraft, which relied heavily on rocket propulsion, made its first gliding flight and reached a speed of Mach 0.79.

17 June 1959
First flight of the Dassault Mirage IVA two-seat supersonic strategic bomber. This gave France the capability to deploy a fee-fall nuclear weapon of indigenous design and manufacture.

3 July 1959
The Hawker Hunter FGA9, the first ground attack version of the type, made its first flight.

9 September 1959
USAF Strategic Air Command test launched its first Atlas ICBM.

17 September 1959
The X-15A research aircraft made its first powered drop from a B-52 and attained a speed of Mach 2.11 (1,393mph).

19 April 1960
US Navy close-air support and interdiction aircraft, the Grumman A-6 Intruder, made its first flight.

24 May 1960
The first early warning satellite, MIDAS II, was placed in orbit.

21 October 1960
Prototype of the Hawker P1127 vertical/short take-off experimental aircraft made its first tethered hovering flight over a special grid at the company's airfield at Dunsfold. The first untethered flight took place the following month.

Above: The final fighter variant, the Hunter F6, was built in larger numbers than any other version, with a total of 383 being supplied to the RAF.

The Hunter was popular amongst pilots from the outset, because it proved to be very strong and had no real vices – whereas many other fighters of the period displayed dangerous handling characteristics in high-speed and low-level flight. Its moderate wing-loading and good thrust/weight ratio resulted in an aircraft that was exhilarating to fly. With their long fatigue life and versatile performance, Hunters remained in military service into the 1990s.

Neville Duke describes the Hunter's first supersonic flight

Hawker Chief Test Pilot Neville Duke, who made the Hunter's maiden flight, gave this account of his first supersonic flight in the new fighter:

"I needed a rapid acceleration whilst I was at high altitude in thin air. To achieve this I must put the Hunter into a much steeper dive than she had ever done previously."

"I had a trial run first with another shallow dive reaching Mach 0.95 and staying there with all the usual buffet, vibration and control difficulties. I throttled back, waited until she recovered and climbed back to 45,000ft. For a moment I paused, as I had once paused many years before when I was sent up to do my first solo spins in a Tiger Moth. You know the drill by heart, you know by now

instinctively how to recover, but still there is that pause as you look around the sky – a pause which you dare not leave too long – before you pull up the nose to the stall, kick over the rudder and thrust the machine in a spin towards the earth. I had known, however, that the Moth was used to being spun; but nobody knew the Hunter's handling properties in a steep dive near the speed of sound."

"I looked around the sky. It was empty of other aircraft. Below I could see the Surrey hills and in the far distance ahead the coastline curving into the point of Selsey Bill. I opened up the throttle, accelerating quickly at full power to maximum level speed, and did a partial roll into a dive about forty degrees from the horizontal. Speed built up quickly.

The Mach meter needle swung round to 0.95, the buffet and vibration seemed to strike with extra violence, but they were sharp and short-lived."

"At 0.96 the Mach number effects decreased, and by the time the needle reached 0.97, the aircraft was free of all vibration. I thought then that this might mean we were actually flying faster than sound, and on landing I was told of reports of a loud explosion in the Petworth area. In the pilots' room we looked at one another. Could it be a sonic bang?"

"The next day I repeated the run and this time aimed the dive at Dunsfold aerodrome. In the cockpit I could see or hear nothing myself, but over the r/t came the message; 'Two bangs received, loud and clear'. The Hunter was definitely supersonic."

SPYPLANES

The Lockheed U-2 is probably the most famous spyplane in history and at the turn of the century it remains an important part of US intelligence gathering capabilities. In the early 1950s, the US initiated development of a purpose-built spyplane which could fly at extreme altitude – where it was hoped it would be immune to interception – with its main purpose to make clandestine unarmed reconnaissance flights at the greatest possible height over Communist-controlled territory.

Developed by Lockheed's Skunk Works, it was given the U-2 designation (U for utility)

First seeing USAF service in 1968 over Vietnam, the Lockheed SR-71 was the world's fastest air-breathing aircraft, combining this performance with an even greater operational altitude than that of the U-2.

The Lockheed TR-1A entered service in 1981 and was subsequently re-designated U-2R. Sensors and other mission equipment are housed in interchangeable packs fitted in the nose or mounted above the fuselage.

CHRONOLOGY

21 October 1960
The Grumman E-2A Hawkeye maritime airborne early warning aircraft made its first flight.

1 February 1961
Launch of the first LGM-130 Minuteman ICBM, which would eventually provide half the total weaponry supporting the US nuclear war plan.

3 February 1961
Operation *Looking Glass* – the constant operation of SAC's airborne command post – began with specially-equipped KC-135B ACP aircraft to provide continuous cover. Each was airborne for eight hours at a time.

6 March 1961
First flight of the B-52H Stratofortress – the final version, developed to carry the Douglas GAM-87A Skybolt air-to-surface missile.

6 April 1961
The X-15 became the first aircraft to travel faster than 3,000mph (Mach 4.62/3,074mph). It achieved Mach 5 on 23 June and Mach 6 on 9 November, and was the first manned aircraft to reach 200,000ft (on 11 October).

17 June 1961
First flight of India's Hindustan Aircraft Ltd (HAL) HF-24 Marut – a supersonic single-seat fighter for the Indian Air Force.

16 August 1961
The Bell UH-1D made its first flight and was purchased by the US Army as an infantry support helicopter.

21 October 1961
First flight of the Breguet 1150 Atlantic maritime patrol aircraft.

14 April 1962
The first Bristol Type 188, designed to meet a demanding requirement for a research aircraft to fly at speeds in excess of Mach 2 over lengthy periods, made its first flight. Intended to explore the effects of prolonged kinetic heating, the airframe was constructed of stainless steel.

26 April 1962
First flight of the top-secret Lockheed A-12 single-seat spyplane, which was subsequently developed as the SR-71 Blackbird.

14 October 1962
A USAF Lockheed U-2 reconnaissance flight over Cuba confirmed that launch sites for Soviet medium-range ballistic missiles were being installed there. This sparked the Cuban missile crisis.

to hide the aircraft's true role. First flown in August 1955 it had an outstanding high-altitude performance and good endurance – despite payload restrictions – and has been used by the USAF and CIA for many years. The U-2 played a crucial role during the Cuban crisis in 1962 and helped prevent the possible outbreak of WW3 during this critical part of the Cold War period.

Initially 43 were built, but the line was re-opened in 1979 to build a further 37 (these were originally designated TR-1, but since re-designated U-2R). Sensors are carried in detachable noses, in the forward fuselage and in underwing pods. These carried the Precision Location Strike System (PLSS) – an advanced sensing system to locate hostile radar sites and to direct strike aircraft or ground-based missiles against them.

Some aircraft now carry *Senior Span* satellite communications equipment for real-time global data transmission in a tear-drop shaped dorsal-mounted pod. Since the early 1990s Lockheed have been re-engining the surviving U-2R fleet with a more powerful and yet more efficient GE F101 turbofan.

The Lockheed SR-71 programme began in 1959 as a CIA-sponsored programme to develop a high-speed high-flying reconnaissance platform to supplement the U-2. Thirty-one SR-71s were built and served with the 9th Strategic Reconnaissance Wing at Beale AFB, CA until the early 1990s. Known as the Blackbird, it flew faster and higher than any other production aircraft, being able to cruise at a sustained Mach 3.0 on the edge of space. Its high

Cuban Missile Crisis

Major Rudolph Anderson, flying a U-2 from McCoy AFB, FL during the Cuban crisis, recalls the importance of his reconnaissance mission:

"Bad weather prevented the consummation of the first overflight for several days but finally, on 14 October 1962, I took off at 7.00am and headed for Isla de Pinos and then flew north toward the Cuban mainland. The run from San Cristobel, perhaps the most critical part of the mission, lasted no more than five minutes. When it was over, I set course for McCoy, and as it turned out, a memorable page in US history. The film I shot contained the first images verifying beyond any doubt the arrival of Soviet IRBMs on Cuban soil."

"U-2 overflight activity was accelerated to a rate of six or seven a day. The 4080th logged some twenty sorties between 14 October and 22 October – each mission being followed by transportation of the film to Washington."

Below: A U-2D high-altitude research version with a second crew capsule within the fuselage bay normally occupied by sensors, in company with a U-2A. On the fin is the insignia of the Air Research and Development Center (now the Air Force Flight Test Center).

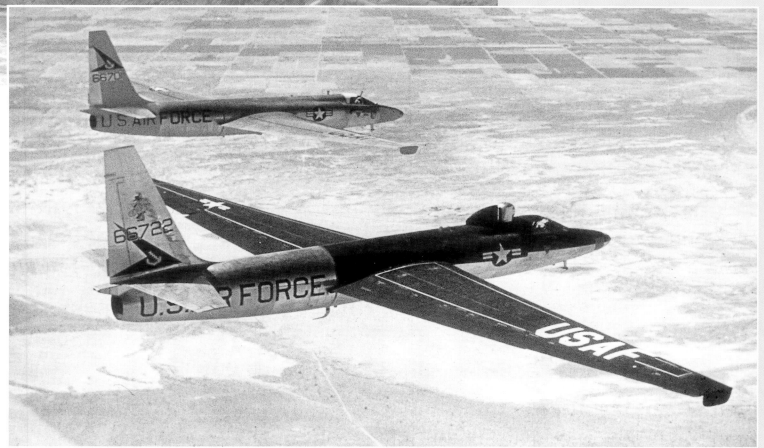

Above: The SR-71 was restricted in normal operations to Mach 3.2, but the aircraft could go faster. The shape of the Blackbird was tailored to reduce its radar cross-section, while the structure incorporated large wedges of radar-attenuating material.

CHRONOLOGY

7 December 1962
The Süd-Aviation SA 3210 Super Frelon three-engined heavy-duty helicopter made its first flight.

14 February 1963
First of three RAF Vulcan squadrons became operational with the Blue Steel stand-off bomb.

25 February 1963
First flight of the Franco-German Transall C160 twin-turboprop military transport.

8 February 1963
The first Hawker P1127 prototype carried out the first V/STOL operation from an aircraft carrier.

18 March 1963
The French Dassault Balzac V-001 VTOL research aircraft made its first transition from vertical to horizontal flight and vice versa.

18 April 1963
The Northrop X-21A (a converted Douglas WB-66D) commenced a research programme aimed at the evaluation of boundary layer control techniques.

11 June 1963
Republic F-105F two-seat mission trainer version of the Thunderchief was flown for the first time.

performance was achieved by its aerodynamic design, titanium construction and the Pratt & Whitney J58 continuous bleed turbojets. At speed, more thrust was produced by the suction at the intakes and from the ejection nozzles than from the engines themselves.

In 1974 Kelly Johnson, the aircraft's designer, wrote in his diary: 'The SR-71s played a vital role in the Yom Kippur War flying missions out of the east coast of the US over the Mediterranean battle lines. Based on SR-71 photographic evidence, the Israelis were advised where to strike. Made many missions using several refuelling sessions. Aircraft and crews operated well.'

The Vietnam War had successfully justified the SR-71's existence from the time of its operational début during 1968 through to 1973. Some 600 missions were logged during the course of these operations, as the aircraft gained an enviable record of dependability and mission successes.

Temporary deployment to Forward Operating Locations (FOLs) worldwide were undertaken with considerable alacrity and during the course of its service career the Blackbird overflew almost every major political and militarily significant hot spots in the world... gathering intelligence data of inestimable political and military value. At least one mission in excess of 14,000 miles was flown, and though unrefuelled range continued to be a limiting tactical factor, the availability of the special KC–135Q fleet allowed the aircraft to overfly targets anywhere on the globe.

Head-on view of the futuristic SR-71, showing the curvature of the chines. Note the canted fins and rudders, large intake cones and triple-wheeled main undercarriage units.

HELICOPTERS
IN ACTION

Left: Westland Dragonflies were used extensively on Royal Navy carriers for both communications flying and 'plane guard' duties, to provide rapid rescue facilities in case of accidents during flying operations.

The first helicopters to see operational service were those of the German armed forces during the latter part of WW2 – in particular the Flettner Fl265 and Fl282 'Kolibri' with the German Navy. The first Allied operational use was made during May 1950 in Malaya when Westland-Sikorsky Dragonflies were involved in casualty evacuation duties from jungle clearings. Dragonflies were also used for defoliant spraying for anti-terrorist purposes. The helicopter needed no roads and could supply forward units with men, weapons and food in places where no land transport could reach.

In the early post-war years, helicopters were increasingly being used with US Air Observation Post squadrons – who were among the first to replace their light aircraft with the helicopter. By the time of the Korean War in the early 1950s, helicopters were used for liaison, artillery spotting and casevac roles – these included the Bell H-13, Hiller 360 and Sikorsky H-5 and H-19. By 1952 the H-19, powered by a 600hp Pratt & Whitney R-1340-57 Wasp was becoming the main helicopter as it had an increased operating range and a larger cabin which could accommodate up to ten people. Although the US Army did not use its helicopters as weapons of war until much later, some US Army and Marines H-19s were used in the battle zone with a rudimentary standard issue bazooka strapped on to the side.

In the Malayan emergency, which continued until 1960, the difficulties of jungle warfare

Left: The Westland Whirlwind HAR10 differed from all earlier versions that served with the RAF in that it was powered by a turbine engine. In November 1963, RAF HAR10s joined the Far East Air Force and operated in Borneo during the confrontation with Indonesia.

CHRONOLOGY

29 June 1963
The Swedish Saab 105 military trainer/light attack aircraft was flown for the first time.

31 July 1963
The first single-seat Northrop YF-5A was flown. The aircraft was selected by the Defense Department as the 'Freedom Fighter' for participating countries in the Military Assistance Program.

20 September 1963
Prototype of the German EWR VJ101C VTOL research aircraft made its first vertical to horizontal flight transition, powered by six Rolls-Royce RB.145 turbojets – two in each wingtip swivelling pods and two mounted vertically in the fuselage.

17 December 1963
The Lockheed C-141A StarLifter was flown for the first time – designed specifically for the strategic transport elements of the US Air Force.

5 January 1964
The Short Belfast, the first military transport aircraft with a fully-automated landing system, made its first flight. It was the first British aircraft to be designed from the outset as a military transport.

7 March 1964
The first Hawker Siddeley Kestrel V/STOL aircraft, developed from the P1127, made its initial flight.

9 April 1964
The de Havilland Canada DHC-5 Buffalo first flew – a larger and turboprop-powered version of the DHC-4 Caribou.

Right: No 84 Squadron, the last Whirlwind squadron in the RAF, flew from Akrotiri, Cyprus from January 1972 until March 1982, combining air-sea rescue duties with United Nations support flights.

CHRONOLOGY

1 May 1964

The BAC 221 (a re-worked Fairey FD.2) delta-wing aircraft made its first flight. It was fitted with an ogive wing to test aerodynamic flight characteristics with a prototype Concorde-shape wing.

25 May 1964

The Ryan XV-5A 'fan-in-wing' Vertijet first flew. Two large down-flow fans in the wing could be powered in addition to conventional thrust for forward flight. It made a vertical take off, hovering flight and vertical landing on 16 July.

21 September 1964

The first of two North American XB-70A Valkyrie six-engined supersonic bombers made its maiden flight. The most powerful aircraft ever built, an unusual feature of its design was that the wingtips folded down in cruising flight.

27 September 1964

First flight of the BAC TSR.2, designed as a supersonic replacement for the English Electric Canberra. The TSR.2 enjoyed a phenomenal performance and had a sophisticated navigation and attack system.

29 September 1964

First conventional take-off of the LTV XC-142A VTOL transport. The four turboprops were mounted on a wing that could pivot upwards through 90 degrees.

21 December 1964

With its wings locked at 26 deg sweep-back, the General Dynamics F-111A variable-geometry multi-purpose tactical fighter-bomber was flown for the first time.

22 December 1964

The first prototype Lockheed SR-71 Mach 3+ strategic reconnaissance aircraft was flown.

meant that the value of the helicopter was quickly appreciated. Though the RAF had no suitable helicopters for this type of work, the Royal Navy loaned some of its Westland-built S-51 Dragonflies, and a Far East Air Force Casualty Evacuation Flight was formed. Later 848 NAS, equipped with Whirlwind HAS21s from the carrier HMS *Perseus* was diverted for use in Malaya. The first all-British helicopter to serve in theatre was the Bristol 171 Sycamore, which entered operational service in 1954.

In 1953, the French expeditionary force was engaged in bitter fighting with the Viet Minh in Indo-China (now Vietnam) and a few S-55 helicopters were used in the casevac role. By the mid-1950s the French were using S-55s, S-58s and Vertol H-21 Shawnees in Algeria in the assault role, because the mountainous terrain was considered too risky for paratroopers.

On 5 November 1956, the Anglo-French Task Force was engaged in the disputed Suez Canal Zone. Royal Marines were ferried ashore in a mix of Whirlwinds and Sycamores from RN carriers HMS *Theseus* and *Ocean* – the first example of a helicopter-borne assault in history. The RN was impressed with the helicopters' role during the operations and went on to form specialised commando assault squadrons, equipped them with helicopters and embarked them on commando carriers.

In 1957 the Army Air Corps (AAC) was formed to control its own light aircraft and small helicopters – initially the Saunders-Roe Skeeter. It was not until the early 1960s that Westland Scouts and Alouette 2s entered AAC service.

The Bristol Sycamore was the first British-designed helicopter to enter service with the RAF at home and overseas. Sycamores operated in the 1963 campaign in Borneo.

V-BOMBER FORCE

T he first of Britain's V-bomber force, the Vickers Valiant, arrived at RAF Gaydon in
early 1955 to mark the beginning of the third phase of Bomber Command's post-
war expansion – and to give it a strategic nuclear bombing capability. The Valiant's
gestation process had been long – eight years since the British Government's decision in
January 1947 to develop a nuclear weapon. It was a period of intensive and highly secret
research that resulted in three types of bomber coming into production – together with the
Blue Danube plutonium bomb.

A specification issued in December 1946 sought a turbojet-powered bomber capable of a
speed of 600mph (966km/h) and a height above the target of 45,000ft. It was to have a five-
man crew, but no defensive armament. By the end of 1947 a large-scale procurement
programme was underway, with Handley Page contracted to proceed with what was to

Below: An early Avro Vulcan B1 in the original anti-flash white applied to all the V-bomber fleets. A large delta-wing aircraft, the Vulcan was easily the most impressive of the RAF's bombers.

The third V-bomber type was the Handley Page Victor, ordered into production as an insurance policy against failure of the revolutionary Vulcan design. Although fewer were produced, it proved faster than the Vulcan and could carry a larger bombload.

CHRONOLOGY

12 February 1965
The first prototype of the Dassault Mirage III-V single-seat VTOL strike aircraft began hovering trials.

27 February 1965
The Soviet Antonov An-22 long-range strategic military heavy transport made its maiden flight.

16 July 1965
The North American YOV-10A prototype made its maiden flight. Designed as a counter-insurgency aircraft for the US Marine Corps, the Bronco later saw USAF and US Navy service.

7 September 1965
The prototype of the Bell Model 209 Huey Cobra, the armed helicopter development of the Bell UH-1B Iroquois, was first flown.

27 September 1965
The LTV A-7A Corsair II attack bomber made its first flight. It remained in service with the US Navy and Marine Corps for more than 30 years.

1 January 1966
The first Minuteman II ICBM was placed on alert.

3 May 1966
First air-snatch of a man on the ground by an aircraft in flight using the Fulton Recovery System was successfully completed by an HC-130H Hercules.

12 July 1966
A first unpowered flight, following release from a B-52 'motherplane' at 45,000ft was completed successfully by the Northrop/NASA M2-F2 lifting body research aircraft.

31 August 1966
Initial hovering flight was made by the first of six development examples of the Hawker Siddeley Harrier V/STOL tactical support aircraft.

14 November 1966
First landing of a jet aircraft in Antarctica was made by a USAF C-141A StarLifter at McMurdo Sound.

23 December 1966
The Dassault Mirage F1 multi-mission fighter made its maiden flight.

27 December 1966
The Fiat G91Y single-seat tactical reconnaissance and support fighter made its first flight in Italy.

become the Victor, and Avro with the future Vulcan.

As an insurance against undue development and production delays with these very advanced types, two prototypes of a more conventional aircraft – the Short Sperrin – were ordered, but in the event the type was not needed for production. A fourth bomber was ordered in 1948 – at a time of mounting international tension – from Vickers, which became the Valiant, the 'interim V-bomber' which was the last to be ordered but the first to enter squadron service.

In the course of development only one technical problem caused prolonged anxiety – the manner of emergency escape at low-level of the three crew members, only the pilot and co-pilot having ejector seats. Improvements were adopted, but the situation was never radically altered.

The first Vulcan squadron was formed at RAF Waddington in May 1957 and the Victor entered service the following April. The bomb which the V-force originally carried was the Blue Danube – a free-fall plutonium bomb developed for the RAF and tested in October 1952 in the Monte Bello Islands. The priority was to turn this first generation of V-bombers into an efficient fighting force, first and foremost as a deterrent to Soviet aggression, but capable of delivering bombloads in high-level operations with pinpoint accuracy. Dispersal airfields were developed to ensure that aircraft would not be destroyed at their home bases by a hostile pre-emptive strike.

With the British hydrogen bomb in production, the second generation of V-bombers (the Victor B2 and Vulcan B2), with greatly improved performance, entered service in 1961. At this time, 60 US Thor ground-launched intermediate-range ballistic missiles (IRBM) were deployed to RAF bases in eastern England.

The Fylingdales early warning station became operational in 1963. At this time the Quick Reaction Alert (QRA) procedure was introduced, in which one aircraft from each

Operation Black Buck

The only V-bomber operational mission in anger took place in the twilight of the Vulcan's career, during the Falklands conflict of 1982 – Operation *Black Buck*. Flt Lt Martin Withers recalls the Vulcan attack on Port Stanley airfield:

"In May 1982 I captained the reserve Vulcan B2 (XM607) and was tasked to carry out the attack on Port Stanley airfield. With such an enormous distance to cover, the tankers as well as my solitary bomber had to be refuelled in flight."

"For one and a three quarter hours after take-off from Wideawake on Ascension Island the gaggle of large aircraft headed south. Then, about 840 miles out from Ascension, four Victors refilled the tanks of the others and then turned back. A fifth Victor topped up the Vulcan's tanks, but continued with the formation for a little longer. The bomb-laden Vulcan, with the sole remaining Victor, continued south making for the next refuelling point 400 miles short of Port Stanley. We then continued southwards alone. The operation had been flown with minimum radio traffic, to avoid alerting the Argentine garrison on the Falklands."

"When we were 290 miles from Port Stanley, I eased back the throttles and put the Vulcan into a steady descent to keep it below the horizon of the early warning radars on the Falklands. We switched on our radar briefly and observed returns from the top of Mount Usborne, the highest point on East Falkland. That confirmed that we were almost exactly on track."

"Shortly after 00.04am Port Stanley time, the Vulcan was 46 miles from the target and I pushed forward the throttles to bring the four Olympus engines to maximum thrust. I pulled into a steep climb to bring it to its attack altitude of 10,000ft. Once there I levelled out and let the speed build up to 400mph, while the radar operator turned on his equipment once more and commenced the bombing run."

"It was a smooth night, everything was steady, the steering signals from the radar operator were steady and the range was coming down nicely. All of the switching had been made and ten miles from the target we opened the bomb doors. I was expecting flak and missiles to come up, but nothing happened."

"On reaching the release point a computer set in motion the bomb release mechanism, and the entire load of twenty-one bombs was released in five seconds. As briefed, the bombs were released in one long stick as the Vulcan flew across the runway at an angle of 30 degrees. That gave the greatest chance of at least one hit on the runway."

"Our task complete, I pushed the throttles wide open and hauled the bomber into a steep turn to get out of the defended area as quickly as possible. After a fall lasting 20 seconds, the bombs exploded in a line across the airfield. One of them impacted almost exactly in the middle of the runway and blew out a large crater."

"After taking on fuel once more during our return flight we landed back at Wideawake, very tired after just over 16 hours airborne. So ended the first *Black Buck* mission."

Vulcan B2 XM607 of No 44 Squadron at RAF Waddington was the first of its type to drop bombs in anger.

The unexpected grounding of the Valiant tanker fleet left the RAF with a serious shortage of tankers, and many Victors were converted to fill the gap. Victor K2 tankers served from July 1975 until the last examples (with No 55 Squadron at RAF Marham) were finally retired in 1993.

bomber squadron was permanently at fifteen minutes readiness – and Britain's nuclear deterrent force was deployed on fifteen squadrons.

The Blue Steel had limited range and the British Government cancelled the Blue Streak, deciding instead to order the American Skybolt. When this was also cancelled, Britain was offered the submarine-launched Polaris missile in compensation. The V-force was left with Blue Steel Mk1 as its only stand-off weapon. To maintain its credibility as a deterrent, the V-force modified its tactics from high- to low-level operations and the whole force was dedicated to NATO. Many surplus Valiants and Victors were converted into tanker aircraft.

COLD WAR 'ENEMY'

Above: The Yak-17, first flown in 1947, was the tricycle undercarriage development of the single-seat Yak-15 – the first successful Soviet jet-propelled fighter, that had been converted from the piston-engined Yak-3.

CHRONOLOGY

8 February 1967
First flight of the Saab 37 Viggen all-weather fighter. It confirmed Sweden's position as one of Europe's leading aircraft manufacturers.

10 February 1967
The first of two experimental V/STOL transport aircraft, the Dornier Do 31E1 made its maiden flight. In addition to vectored thrust turbofans it featured eight wingtip lifting jets. First transition from vertical to horizontal flight was made on 16 December.

3 March 1967
The Beriev Be-30 twin-turboprop STOL transport made its first flight in Russia.

12 March 1967
The first of a new family of air-to-ground missiles was used in Vietnam. US Navy A-4D Skyhawks fired optical-guided AGM-62 Walleye missiles.

15 March 1967
The Sikorsky HH-53B 'Super Jolly' heavy-lift helicopter was flown for the first time, which became operational with the USAF's Aerospace Rescue and Recovery Service.

Immediately after WW2 Russia began intensive work on re-arming the country's combat aviation with jet aircraft. The first was the MiG-9 'Fargo', with two fuselage-mounted jet engines which first flew on 24 April 1946, The single-engine Yak-15, Lavochkin La-150 and La-160 (the Soviet's first swept-wing fighter) also flew in 1946.

The MiG-9 was in use for a few years, but was soon succeeded by the MiG-15 'Fagot'. The Yak-15 'Feather' was developed into the Yak-17. Both the MiG-9 and Yak-15 were fitted with 'trophy' German engines, under the respective Russian designation RD-10 and RD-20.

The MiG-15 commenced production in 1947 and entered service in 1949, being mass-produced to become the main fighter aircraft of the Soviet Air Force. By then the Russians had perfected a copy of the Rolls-Royce Nene jet engine. It had a maximum speed of 1,050km/h (652mph) and featured a swept wing and empennage, pressurised cockpit and ejector seat – and carried an armament of one 37mm and two 23mm guns. The MiG-17 'Fresco' followed in the early 1950s and became the world's first series produced aircraft to repeatedly exceed the sonic speed in level flight. It was also the first

Soviet aircraft to be fitted with a brake parachute to reduce landing distance.

The MiG-19 'Farmer' followed in 1958 – featuring a thin and steeply swept wing powered by two fuselage-mounted engines, and armed with air-to-air (AA) guided missiles.

During this period, Yakolev developed and launched the Yak-17 'Feather' (developed from the Yak-15) and the Yak-23 'Flora' into production. In 1952 the Yak-25 'Flashlight' appeared, a two-seat night-mission interceptor with two AM-5 engines and was the first Russian aircraft to be equipped with a powerful radar.

The Sukhoi Su-7 'Fitter' was put into large-scale production in 1957 and remained in service until 1989. This aircraft was the predecessor of an entire family of fighter bombers. The delta-wing Su-9 'Fishpot' appeared in 1957. Sukhoi developed the first national all-weather supersonic interceptor Su-15 'Flagon', which made its maiden flight in 1966. By the late 1960s the Su-17 'Fitter' variable-sweep wing fighter became operational.

In 1959, Mikoyan – often regarded as being abreast, or sometimes ahead of its time – produced a new multi-function front-line delta-wing fighter, designated MiG-21 'Fishbed'. Over a period of some 28 years, the MiG-21 was in series production, had over 20 configurations and set up 17 world records. Delivered to many countries, the MiG-21 was equipped with one gun, AA missiles, bombs and rockets. This aircraft attained a speed in

The Sukhoi Su-7, seen for the first time at Tushino in 1961, was more successful in the ground attack role than as a pure fighter. This is an Su-7B variant, which was widely exported. Take-off could be made with the aid of the auxiliary rocket engines seen mounted beneath the fuselage.

CHRONOLOGY

1 June 1967
First non-stop helicopter flight across the North Atlantic was made by two Sikorsky HH-53Es.

30 June 1967
The first F-4E Phantom II, equipped for the first time with a 20mm M-61A1 cannon, made its initial flight.

28 August 1967
The Lockheed U-2R, for which Lockheed had received a production contract in 1966, was flown for the first time. It was designed in the light of operational experience to offer improved performance, better payload and less demanding flight characteristics.

3 October 1967
The X-15A-2, with greatly increased fuel tankage and engine burn increased from 86 to 145 seconds, achieved a speed of Mach 6.72.

5 October 1967
The Japanese Shin Meiwa PX-S, a four-turboprop STOL anti-submarine flying boat, first flew.

18 November 1967
The Dassault Mirage G variable-geometry experimental aircraft made its first flight in France.

27 February 1968
The first Lockheed AC-130A Gunship II went into action in Vietnam, armed with four 7.62mm Miniguns and four 20mm Vulcan cannon and illuminating equipment for night operations.

25 May 1968
First flight of the Grumman EA-6B Prowler, developed for the US Navy as a four-seat electronic countermeasures (ECM) aircraft.

28 June 1968
The first production Hawker Siddeley Nimrod MR1 maritime reconnaissance aircraft first flew.

Above: For over three decades, the Mach 2 Mikoyan-Gurevich MiG-21 has been one of the best known Soviet aircraft in the world. This example served with the East German Air Force during the Cold War.

Right: The Sukhoi Su-15 'Flagon' was the standard Soviet single-seat interceptor from the 1960s through to the 1980s, but had relatively short range.

excess of Mach 2 and was ready for an extended war of attrition.

The early 1970s saw the advent of the MiG-23 'Flogger' lightweight-fighter generation and saw action against Israeli F-15s in air battles over the Bekka Valley. The MiG-25 'Foxbat' and MiG-31 'Foxhound' were long-range two-seat interceptors and carried long-range guided missile weapons.

In the mid-1970s the front-line air arm of the Soviet Air Force acquired supersonic jets of the third generation – Sukhoi Su-17 'Fitter', MiG-27 'Flogger' and Su-24 'Fencer' – which were in production until the late 1980s, and underwent many modifications.

By the early 1980s, the first MiG-29 'Fulcrum' and the Su-27 'Flanker' entered limited service with the front-line fighter force. These were the new generation complexes, which represented a new tactical aviation system consisting of lightweight (Su-27) and heavyweight (MiG-29) aircraft that were jointly intended to secure air superiority. These were intended to solve all the tasks of the front-line aviation – including delivering effective strikes at ground targets with the use of a wide range of both guided and unguided weapons.

The Mikoyan MiG-25 'Foxbat' is the world's fastest fighter. Developed in the 1960s to counter the threat posed by the supersonic B-70 Valkyrie, production continued despite the cancellation of the American bomber. The 'Foxbat' is capable of reaching Mach 3 (2,000mph/3200km/h) for short periods.

CENTURY FIGHTERS

Much emphasis was placed during the late 1950s and early 1960s on all-weather interceptors, the bomber threat being perceived as the main danger to continental USA. During this period, the US aviation industry was embarking on a new and promising period of aircraft development – the 'Century' series fighters.

In the Korean War era, the F-94 was introduced into service. Numerically this was followed by some variations on aircraft in service – F-95, F-96 and F-97 – together with two anti-aircraft missiles, F-98 and F-99.

Therefore, the next major aircraft was the F-100, and this was to be followed by five

Left: Developed as one component of an all-embracing air defence system, the delta-winged Convair F-102A Delta Dagger entered USAF service in 1956. It was the first all-missile fighter, with armament consisting of AIM-4 and AIM-26 Falcon missiles.

Below: The first of the USAF's Century-series fighters and the world's first operational fighter capable of level supersonic performance, the North American F-100 Super Sabre was evolved from the earlier F-86 and first flew on 14 October 1953. It saw extensive service during the Vietnam conflict.

Lockheed convinced the USAF of the need to proceed with a lightweight and relatively unsophisticated air superiority day fighter. This resulted in the productiuon of the F-104 Starfighter, which made its first flight on 4 March 1954. The type saw limited USAF service and only realised its full potential as a fighter-bomber with a number of European air arms.

aircraft in the '100' series that would be the basis of US Air Force fighters in the 1960s. They became known as the 'Century' fighters, attaining a mystique and glamour that matched their exciting attributes.

The F-100 was the North American Super Sabre. Fitted with sharply swept wings and an afterburner this gave the 'Hun' supersonic performance – taking the USAF into a new era. Though still armed with guns (but later given Sidewinder missile capability), it became the standard air defence day fighter. Later in life it was used more as a fighter-bomber, and in the Vietnam War period it became a 'bread and butter' attack aircraft.

The McDonnell F-101A Voodoo was conceived as a SAC escort fighter and bomber destroyer and entered USAF service in May 1957. It was able to carry internal stores in addition to unguided rockets and Falcon missiles. The F-101B was the tandem two-seat all-weather interceptor version of the Voodoo for Air Defense Command and was equipped with the most fearsome air-to-air weapon ever – the nuclear-tipped Douglas AIR-2A Genie missile. The F-101C was a single-seat tactical fighter with the capability to carry a US tactical nuclear weapon. Most successful was the RF-101 reconnaissance version.

Above: Designed to serve with Strategic Air Command as a long-range escort and 'penetration' fighter, the McDonnell F-101 Voodoo was subsequently developed for both tactical and air defence roles.

Convair's F-102 Delta Dart was another interceptor, with high-performance to catch Soviet bombers before they could penetrate US air space and deliver the weapon. It relied, in the main, on the newly-developed Hughes Falcon missile. Its prowess in the air superiority role was unchallenged for many years.

The Lockheed F-104 Starfighter was produced as a direct result of the Korean War, but it failed to find full US service as a fighter. Only when it was developed as a fighter-bomber for export did the Starfighter achieve phenomenal success.

The Republic F-105 Thunderchief – in addressing the disadvantages of the F-84 – became a rugged, no-nonsense all-weather attack bomber that was also no slouch at air-to-air fighting.

Convair's F-106 Delta Dart was the final successful 'Century' fighter. It replaced the F-102 as the prime USAF interceptor, in which role it served for some thirty years.

This 'Century' series represented a dramatic advance in fighter technology, firmly placing the genre in the supersonic arena in the early Cold War period, but most were to see combat in the steamy jungles of southeast Asia in the 1970s.

Below: Declared operational in January 1959, the Republic F-105 Thunderchief was the first supersonic tactical fighter-bomber designed from scratch. It was to become one of the USAF's most important assets during the Vietnam War.

CHRONOLOGY

30 June 1968
The Lockheed C-5A Galaxy heavy logistics transport made its maiden flight.

4 November 1968
The Czechoslovak Aero L-39 two-seat turbofan-powered basic and advanced trainer first flew.

30 June 1969
The first example of the Sikorsky CH-54B – an advanced version of the S-64 Skycrane heavy lift helicopter – was flown for the first time.

16 July 1969
NASA's Apollo 11 was launched towards the Moon and on 21 July Neil Armstrong became the first man to stand on its surface. The successful Moon-landing operation ended with splashdown on 24 July.

20 August 1969
First flight of the Argentinean IA58 Pucarà twin-turboprop counter-insurgency combat aircraft.

12 October 1969
The first SEPECAT Jaguar to be completed in Britain made its first flight at Warton.

19 February 1970
The first of three Canadair CL-84-1 tilt-wing V/STOL aircraft for evaluation by the Canadian Armed Forces was first flown.

19 March 1970
Following launch from a B-52 'mother plane', the Martin Marietta X-24A lifting-body wingless research aircraft made its first powered flight powered by a turbo-rocket engine.

18 July 1970
The prototype of the Fiat/Aeritalia G222TCM twin-turboprop military transport made its first flight. It was designed to a NATO requirement of 1962.

19 August 1970
The first LGM-30G Minuteman III ICBM was placed on alert at Minot AFB, ND. 550 of these missiles were eventually to be deployed at four bases.

20 August 1970
Two Sikorsky HH-53Cs completed the first non-stop Pacific crossing by helicopter, from Eglin AFB, FL to Da Nang, South Vietnam. They were refuelled en route by HC-130 Hercules tankers.

19 September 1970
General Dynamics F-111Es began arriving at RAF Upper Heyford. Forward-basing of F-111s was viewed as vital to the success of any mission which may have involved penetrations of hostile European airspace.

12 November 1970
The prototype of the Nihon XC-1 twin-turbofan tactical military transport was first flown. Thirty of these aircraft entered service with the JASDF.

MIGHTY HERCULES

An un-camouflaged USAF C-130B taking-off from Da Nang Air Base, South Vietnam in 1966.

On 23 August 1954, a new turboprop transport aircraft made its maiden flight at Burbank, California. In the 46 years since that auspicious occasion, the Lockheed C-130 has become a legend. The Hercules, as it was soon to be named, presents no problems in attempting to sum up its achievements other than to run out of superlatives and space before running out of exploits to describe.

The Lockheed C-130, and its L-100 civil counterpart, has been almost everywhere from the Arctic to the Antarctic. It has landed on dirt strips, on snow and ice, on roads and even on an aircraft carrier. The Hercules has carried all sorts of cargo, from bombs and bullets in military conflicts around the world, to food and medicine on humanitarian relief operations. It has undertaken a greater variety of missions than almost any other type of aircraft, ranging from pure cargo-hauling through photo-mapping to in-flight refuelling and search-and-rescue. Perhaps most remarkable of all, the C-130 has been in continuous production at Marietta, Georgia for longer than any other type of aircraft in the western world.

That longevity provides testament to the 'rightness' of the design in the first instance. Nevertheless, Lockheed has not been reluctant to incorporate changes at appropriate moments and this evolutionary process has undoubtedly helped to ensure a long production run. Today, the company and its Marietta work force are building the C-130J version, which is radically different from its predecessors and may fairly be called a Hercules for the new millennium.

In the early 1980s, 29 of the RAF's Hercules fleet had their fuselages 'stretched' to accommodate up to 36 more troops than the 92 that could be carried by the standard C1. The new version was designated C3.

The Versatile Hercules

Wing Commander Tony Webb AFC RAF (Retd), a former RAF Hercules pilot, describes his encounter with 'Fat Albert', as the C-130K is affectionately known.

So you've been chosen to fly the Hercules. When you first look at the machine, what exactly do you see? It's big; with a wing that spans 133ft; an enormous fin, the top of which sits nearly 100ft off the ground; and four paddle-shaped blades on each of the four propellers. It's also rugged, workmanlike, practical, but strangely seductive too. Perhaps you sense this because you could hardly have avoided knowing something of the C-130's considerable reputation, and because that knowledge persuades you to look beyond the familiar shape.

Having moved to the Hercules from much smaller aircraft, size was the first thing that struck me; it was a longish climb from the ground up to the flight deck, via two sets of stairs. The flight deck itself was spacious and the seats looked more like armchairs than the cramped

ejector seats fitted to fighters and trainers. There were two bunks at the back of the area, making me feel this was no cockpit, but something altogether different. It also had the feel of a greenhouse, with glass above and below eye level, as well as a very wide wrap-around main window. Every other surface that was visible appeared to be jammed with hundreds of instruments, switches and circuit breaker panels. There was clearly no way that one person would be able to understand, or even remember, what they were all for.

In front of each pilots' seat there stood a large control column, with spectacle-style handlebars fitted on the top. There was no clue that, one day, it would be possible to control the aircraft precisely with just a finger and thumb on the spectacles and to extract whatever information was relevant by taking a quick glance at the right instrument. However, that skill would take time to acquire and several years of experience would have to be under the belt, before such a level of handling could be attained – and the matching confidence assured.

The cargo compartment seemed enormous. When

Right: The RAF's Hercules fleet has played a key role in operations around the world throughout its service career – from troop withdrawals in Aden in 1967 and the airlift of Harriers to Belize in 1977 – to tactical use in the Falklands and Gulf conflicts, and on-going relief efforts in the Balkans.

empty, a long, dark cavern stretched out from `Station 245', the wall at the rear of the flight deck. This cavern was capable of seating nearly 100 passengers, or of holding up to 45,000lb of freight, or of housing several large vehicles. It was also capable of providing the means to air-drop a very wide range of freight as well as 60-plus paratroops. On the other hand, the cargo compartment could not be called pretty – the only gesture towards appearance was coincidentally provided by the sound-proofing material; other than that, the guts of the aeroplane were hanging out for all to see: control runs, flap motors, hydraulic reservoirs; equipment stowage racks, and much more besides.

When the engines were running, the area was also disturbingly noisy; conversation was out of the question, and some form of ear protection was essential. Long distance travel in a C-130 was clearly not likely to be a relaxing experience – unless one happened to be stone deaf and adept at sleeping on a vibrating bench.

The Hercules has always been the subject of fierce loyalty from its crews, and perhaps especially so from its pilots. What is it about the C-130 that commands this respect? Is it just a simple reflection of the affinity that all aircrew feel for the aircraft that they fly? Or is there something unique and special about the Herky Bird, Fat Albert or Charlie One-Thirty, as it is variously known?

Resoundingly, I would have to say yes – and not just one thing, but many. The word that springs most frequently to mind is 'versatility' but there is a particular versatility of handling, of piloting, of operating that all Hercules possess. The same aircraft, without modification, can operate effectively between the climatic extremes of the poles and the tropics, can haul up to 17 tons of cargo over a distance of 4,000 miles, can land on an unprepared 2,500ft strip at night, can provide an accurate and stable

An RAF Hercules brings aid to the children of Serkhet as part of the World Food Programme. The C-130 has performed this kind of humanitarian role many times over.

platform for high level and low-level aerial delivery, and can out-manoeuvre many smaller and faster aircraft.

It also offers a dependability and reliability that is seldom found in its rivals (though few Hercules aviators would even accept that rivals exist), and an impressive degree of redundancy in its systems; in other words, a lot of things have to go wrong at the same time before a mission must be cancelled.

The Hercules also handles easily and is possessed of low-level manoeuvrability that is quite astonishing for its size. On the minus side, it is not the most stable aircraft to fly by reference to flight instruments, especially in the pitching plane, and close attention is necessary to maintain accurate speed or height, while it is also a handful (or, more accurately, a footful) with two engines out on the same side. Fortunately, the aforementioned reliability means that this is a situation that is encountered almost exclusively in training and most often in the safety of a flight simulator.

It is, above all, a forgiving aeroplane and that is possibly its greatest virtue. All pilots are prone to error and some

Special delivery – using the Low Altitude Parachute Extraction System (LAPES), the Hercules can pinpoint aerial drops of heavy duty equipment, demonstrated here by a USAF C-130.

aircraft will bite back at the slightest provocation – not so the Hercules. A generous flight operating envelope can be breached without experiencing unexpected or fatal consequences. Control response is good throughout the speed range, and the 'feel' of the aircraft is both consistent and sensitive; a pilot gets plenty of warning when the edge of the envelope is being approached.

These are just some of the reasons why the Hercules

appeals so strongly to those lucky enough to fly it. The combination of reliability, flexibility, ease of operation, and, above all else, its unmatched versatility, continue to convince aircrews and everyone else connected with it, that the C-130 is the exceptional workhorse of military transport operations. It is the only contender for the title – the only undisputed successor to the world-famed Dakota; and the backbone of tactical mobility.

SUPERSONIC INTERCEPTOR

English Electric Lightning F1s of No 74 Squadron, RAF in 1960. The Lightning established its place in history as the first RAF single-seat fighter to achieve supersonic speed in level flight.

First flown on 4 April 1957 (as the P.1B) the English Electric Lightning was the first highly-supersonic all-weather interceptor designed and built in Britain, and entered service in 1960. Setting different and higher standards that heralded a new era for the RAF with its rate of climb and interception speed – and still in many ways, unsurpassed – its excellent handling qualities earned it the affection of a generation of pilots.

But for Government vacillation, the Lightning, with its overseas sales potential, could have revitalised the British military aircraft industry. It evolved at a time when British aviation still led the world and it suffered at the hands of politicians in the same way as the industry that created it.

CHRONOLOGY

26 July 1971
Start of the Apollo 15 mission to the moon.
It had an all-USAF crew and saw the first use of
the Lunar Roving Vehicle.

10 September 1971
First of three prototypes of the VFW-Fokker
VAK 191B experimental V/STOL strike/reconnaissance
fighter made its first non-tethered flight.

1 December 1971
The US Navy made the first operational use of
laser-guided bombs (LGBs). These were from aircraft
based on USS *Constellation* attacking strategic
targets in North Vietnam.

21 January 1972
First flight of the Lockheed S-3A Viking twin-jet
carrier-based ASW aircraft. A total of 187 was
built for the USN.

9 February 1972
The first of two Boeing EC-137D AWACS prototypes
was flown. They were converted B707-320B civil
airliners equipped with a Westinghouse AN/APY-1
radar system, with a large external radome.

4 March 1972
USAF's SAC received its first operational examples
of the Boeing SRAM (short-range attack missile).
This was a supersonic air-to-surface missile,
powered by a solid-propellant motor.

29 April 1972
The prototype YRF-4C Phantom, subsequently
modified with some F-4E features, became the first
aircraft to be flown in the US with a fly-by-wire
control system.

1 May 1972
First flight of the de Havilland Canada C-8A Buffalo
augmentor wing turbofan-powered STOL research
aircraft. This incorporated boundary layer control
and an augmentor flap system.

10 May 1972
The first of two Fairchild Republic YA-10A
prototypes, eventually to be called Thunderbolt II,
made its maiden flight. This was designed to meet
the requirements of the USAF's A-X close-support
aircraft programme. The other contender (which
proved to be the unsuccessful submission) was the
Northrop YA-9A, which flew on 30 May.

27 July 1972
The McDonnell Douglas YF-15A prototype made its
first flight. Following an intensive development
programme, the production go-ahead for the F-15A
Eagle air-superiority fighter was given in March 1973.

11 August 1972
Northrop flew the first example of the F-15E Tiger II
light tactical fighter, which had been developed from
the earlier F-5.

With its outstanding performance and the roar of its after-burners, the 'Frightening', as it was nicknamed, thrilled thousands at air shows all over the world. Despite its great size, the Lightning handled beautifully. It was the first truly supersonic British aircraft and went on to become the first to achieve twice the speed of sound. On entry into service with the RAF not only did it double the performance of the fighter defence of Britain, but it also soon began to show other exceptional qualities.

The fighter pilots found that, despite this quantum jump in performance and in the complexity of their all-weather, radar-interception task, their new fighter was no more difficult to fly than their previous equipment and was in fact more precise, accurate and

A Lightning pilot's view

"One is conscious, when walking out to the aircraft, of just how big a machine it is for one pilot. The pre-flight walk-around confirms this view – up on tiptoe to peer down the intake and walking under the wing without lowering one's head, perhaps to comment 'look at those narrow high-pressure tyres – no wonder they only last a few landings'. The thin high-speed aerofoil wings dictated the use of a long spindly undercarriage with thin cross-section wheels and tyres. Now comes the tricky bit – climbing up with all your flying kit on and squeezing past the refuelling probe. This 20ft-long black 'drain pipe', which is semi-permanently bolted on under the port wing, has given generations of Lightning pilots more than a few sore heads and has provided endless amusement for ground crews."

"Once airborne, even in cold power, the aircraft accelerates very quickly and one has to be quick to raise the nose at 430kt to peg the climb speed at 450kt. Similarly, it takes concentration to ensure that one converts to Mach 0.90 during the climb, otherwise it is easy to get supersonic in the ascent."

"The Lightning, although it was designed as a tropospheric interceptor, has an abundance of power throughout its flight envelope and this, coupled with the nicely balanced and harmonised controls, makes it a delight to fly."

Three Lightning F6s in formation in December 1992 whilst engaged in trials, following their withdrawal from interceptor duties with RAF Strike Command in 1988, when they were replaced by the Tornado F3.

delightful than anything before it. The quality, which was no surprise to the makers, who had deliberately aimed a totally new standard of controllability to ensure that this potent new defence weapon would be an entirely practical operating proposition, was to become one of the hallmarks of the Lightning over a quarter of a century of successful service. A 'tour' on Lightnings was still as much sought after by enthusiastic young fighter pilots as it had been by their fathers.

ENTER THE PHANTOM

The McDonnell F-4 Phantom II was the most important western fighter of the Cold War period, and more than 5,000 were built between 1957 and 1981, equipping many air arms. Although designed as a fleet fighter to operate from aircraft carriers, the US Department of Defence took the unprecedented step in 1965 of ordering the F-4C for the USAF. When the type first flew on 27 May 1958, it demonstrated performance levels far above anything then flying. Navy Phantoms set a series of speed, altitude and time to height records in the late 1950s and early 1960s. It was subsequently purchased by Egypt, Iran, Israel, Japan, South Korea, Spain, Turkey and West Germany. Re-engined with Rolls-Royce Speys, the F-4K and F-4M were flown by the Royal Navy and RAF respectively.

This USAF F-4E Phantom is seen dropping bombs with extended 'daisy cutter' fuses, designed to detonate before they dug themselves into the ground and thus maximising the blast effect.

13 June 1973
The maiden flight was made by the first of four Boeing E-4A advanced airborne national command posts (AABNCPs). They were designed and equipped to provide a communication link at all times between the US National Command Authority and the front-line forces of all three services.

12 September 1973
Westland Helicopters flew the prototype of the Commando helicopter, a modified version of the Sea King, providing accommodation for the airlift of up to 27 troops.

26 October 1973
The first prototype of the Franco-German Dassault-Breguet Dornier Alpha Jet basic/advanced trainer and close-support aircraft made its maiden flight.

1 November 1973
The first flight was made by an F-111A fitted with a supercritical wing to evaluate the benefits of this concept for military aircraft design – known as TACT (transonic aircraft technology). The new wing generated twice the lift of a conventional F-111A wing at transonic speed.

23 November 1973
The Aeronautical Industrial Development Centre of the Chinese National Air Force in Taiwan flew the first prototype of the XH-C-1A turboprop secondary trainer. This was AIDC's first indigenous aircraft.

2 February 1974
The prototype General Dynamics YF-16 was officially flown for the first time – though it had been airborne the previous day during a fast taxy test.

22 March 1974
Grumman flew the first A-6E TRAM version of the Intruder. It incorporated a turreted electro-optical sensor package for delivery of laser-guided weapons.

27 June 1974
Aérospatiale flew the first prototype AS350 Ecureuil (Squirrel) light general-purpose helicopter.

Above: A mix of F-4D and F-4E Phantoms heading for a refuelling rendezvous over Vietnam in October 1972. These F-4s were assigned to the 432nd Tactical Fighter Reconnaissance Wing at Udorn, Thailand.

Right: The tactical reconnaissance RF-4C Phantom (the replacement for the RF-101) carried forward, oblique and high- and low-altitude panoramic cameras in the nose. Sideways-looking radar and an infra-red line scanner were fitted in the fuselage.

Unusual features of the F-4 included the sharp dihedral on the folding outer wings and even sharper anhedral on the slab tailplane. These outstanding aircraft out-performed and out-numbered all other US combat aircraft in the 1960s and 1970s. They also provided the backbone of the tactical air offensive in Vietnam from 1966 to 1973.

The definitive Phantom variant was the F-4E equipped with APQ-120 radar and guns. It first flew on 7 August 1965 and some 1,500 examples were delivered. Its speed, range and availability also made the Phantom suitable for conversion as a reconnaissance platform, and the RF-4C was ordered in 1965 to replace the Voodoo. This version introduced a lengthened nose containing an APQ-99

forward looking radar, together with APQ-102 side-looking radar and various optical cameras. A *Wild Weasel* derivative of the F-4E airframe, the F-4G was the final version of the Phantom delivered to the USAF. The fighter's last operational service with the USAF came during the Gulf War in 1991. Though no longer active in USAF service the F-4 is still operated by Germany, Spain, Israel, Greece and Turkey.

Left: Carrier-based Royal Navy F-4K Phantoms of 892 Naval Air Squadron, (note the 'omega' insignia on the fin) being refuelled by a Royal Navy Buccaneer.

Combat over Vietnam

Colonel Robin Olds, an F-4 pilot with the USAF's 8th TFW, describes a combat mission over Vietnam:
"D-Day was set for 2 January 1967. The only way to destroy MiGs was in air-to-air combat. The mission hinged on a method to get a sizeable number of MiGs airborne."

"The QRC-160 ECM pod – a barrage-type noise jammer – had been used by some American warplanes to partially neutralise Hanoi's defences. But the F-4C Phantom had never used QRC-160, which arrived at Ubon in December 1966. For Operation *Bolo*, our Phantoms were configured asymmetrically with a fuel tank under one wing and a QRC-160 under the other, a centreline fuel tank, four Sidewinders and four Sparrows."

"The weather was not quite as good as I'd felt was the minimum for a successful first combat outing by the F-4s. Over the battle area there was undercast up to 8,000ft. Into the imperfect weather came our entire armada – F-4s, F-104s, F-105s and EB-66s, supported by KC-135s and RC-121s. As the attack force got into North Vietnam, MiG-21s taxied out, guided by GCI operators who were directing the MiG pilots, they thought, towards easy pickings."

"I led the flight on past Phuc Yen airfield and MiGs were popping up through the clouds. After 90deg of turn in a modified break, I sighted an aircraft at my 11 o'clock in a left turn, slightly low, about a mile away. I closed on this target for positive identification. The target was positively identified as a MiG-21, silver in colour, too distant for markings to be seen."

"It was hairy. I pulled sharp left, turned inside him, pulled my nose up about 30deg above the horizon, rechecked my missiles and ready panel, switched fuel to internal wing transfer, barrel-rolled to the right, held my position upside down and behind the MiG until the proper angular deflection and range parameters were satisfied, completed the rolling manoeuvre, and fell in behind and below the MiG-21 at his seven o'clock position at about Mach 0.95."

"My first Sidewinder leapt in front and within a split-second turned left in a definite and beautiful collision course direction. Suddenly the MiG-21 erupted in a brilliant flash of orange flame. A complete wing separated and flew back in the airstream, together with a mass of smaller debris. It then fell, twisting, corkscrewing, tumbling lazily toward the top of the clouds."

"Our guys shot down no fewer than seven MiG-21s that day."

Above: This F-4C in Vietnam carries two MiG 'kill' symbols ahead of the engine intake – achieved by downing a MiG-21 on 2 January 1967 and a MiG-17 on 13 May the same year.

Left: One of several air arms still flying the Phantom, the Luftwaffe's F-4Fs took over the air defence role from the 2nd Allied Tactical Air Force (ATAF) in 1990.

HELICOPTER GUNSHIP

A US Marines Bell AH-1W in three-tone Marine Corps camouflage, armed with AGM-114 Hellfire missiles and Zuni rocket launchers. Chaff dispensers are mounted on top of each stub wing.

Right: This Bell AH-1S Cobra is quipped with the TOW launcher as well as a 19-tube FFAR rocket pod, and has a dorsal mount for the AN/ALQ-144 infra-red jammer.

When US Forces went into action in South Vietnam the helicopter, especially the UH-1 Huey, was well established as a battlefield delivery and air support 'vehicle', particularly for such tasks as flying troops directly to the area of battle. But with the hostile air over the battle zone, the unarmed Hueys were increasingly vulnerable to ground fire.

In the 1960s it was decided to deploy armed helicopters to escort troop-carrying and casevac aircraft. This was to enable casualties to be cut by keeping the enemy's head down with suppressive fire while heli-borne troops were disembarking. Accordingly the Bell UH-1B, powered by a 1,100shp T53-L-11 turbine, was fitted with machine guns and grenade launchers and this went on to achieve widespread combat use – and was the first to be named 'Cobra'. These were able to cruise at 90-100mph and soon proved their worth in escorting the larger troop-carrying helicopters, such as the CH-34 Choctaw.

A better-armed helicopter than the Huey was needed and Bell developed the AH-1G HueyCobra, which first flew on 7 September 1965. This employed the rotor system and transmission of the UH-1C Huey. With a very thin fuselage, only 36in wide, tandem seating – both under a fighter-like canopy – the HueyCobra was a much more difficult target in the air. The Cobra could reach its target in half the time taken by the Huey, deliver twice the firepower and loiter in the combat zone twice as long.

A wealth of equipment and armament fits was eventually produced for the Cobra – the first being Emerson's TAT-102A turret fixed under the nose and fitted with two 7.62mm machine guns or six-barrel miniguns. The more common installation became the M28 armament system comprising either two Miniguns, two M129 40mm grenade launchers each with 300 projectiles – or one of each. On its stub wings could be hung four launchers for 76 rockets, or pods of larger rockets, or Miniguns or 30mm cannon. In later years it was fitted with the quadruple TOW missile installation and with the Hughes stabilised sight in the nose.

Over the years in Vietnam, the HueyCobra became more commonly known as the Snake, working in a hunter/killer partnership with the Loach (OH-6A Cayuse) to form a deadly front-line team, that for the first time used the helicopter as a true front-line weapon.

Deliveries of the original AH-1G reached 1,126 by late 1971. The US Marine Corps bought the AH-1J SeaCobra, which was powered by the 1,800shp (1,343kW) PT6T (T400) coupled twin-turbine.

The Vietnam War, the longest war in American history, was for the Americans the most traumatic event since the Civil War. Its possible or potential lessons were legion, but hardly anybody agreed what they were, except that, as in Korea before, the political constraints upon the forces were such as to make wars both difficult to win and frustrating to wage.

SWING-WING OPERATIONS

Below: General Dynamics F-111Fs were assigned to the 48th TFW in the UK, based at RAF Lakenheath. The 'F' model differed from the 'D' in having Mk II avionics and the uprated TF-30-P-100 engines.

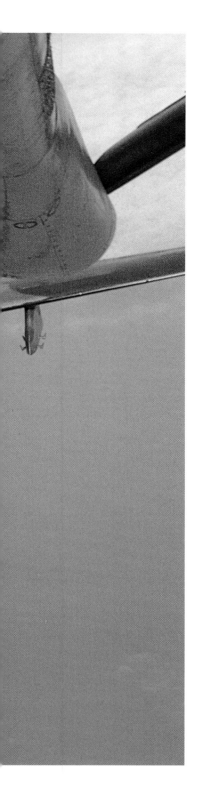

Upper Heyford-based F-111Es demonstrate the three different angles of wing sweep. Incorporated for the first time in an operational aircraft, this feature made it possible to achieve the low speeds necessary for take-off and landing, and (at full sweep) the high speeds required for combat operations.

CHRONOLOGY

3 June 1975
The first Mitsubishi FS-T-2 Kai – later designated F-1 – single-seat close-support fighter prototype was flown.

26 August 1975
The McDonnell Douglas YC-15, an advanced military STOL transport, made its first flight. It featured an externally-blown flap system that depended on the slipstream from the four turbofan engines.

16 September 1975
The prototype MiG-31 'Foxhound' made its first flight, as a derivative of the MiG-25 design.

30 September 1975
Hughes helicopters flew the prototype YAH-64 anti-tank helicopter – later to become the Apache, the winner of the US Army's AAH (Advanced Attack Helicopter) requirement.

1 November 1975
The first USAF 'Red Flag' air-to-air combat manoeuvring exercise took place at Nellis AFB, NV – a highly realistic combat exercise.

15 December 1975
First flight of the Grumman EF-111A – later known as the Raven – an advanced ECM aircraft equipped with an AN/ALQ-99E tactical jamming system.

1 February 1976
The USAF received its first Fairchild A-10A Thunderbolt IIs. These heavily armed and armoured single-seat close-support aircraft were regarded as the 'ultimate' tank-busters.

5 March 1976
The Boeing AGM-86A air-launched cruise missile (ALCM) made its first flight after being dropped from a B-52 at a height of 35,000ft.

5 June 1976
A US Navy Grumman A-6 Intruder launched the first fully-guided Tomahawk cruise missile.

9 August 1976
First flight of the twin-turbofan Boeing YC-14 contender for the AMST programme. The engines were positioned so as to blow their efflux over the inboard portion of the wing and trailing edge flaps in an upper surface blowing (USB) concept.

The General Dynamics F-111 supersonic strike fighter was the world's first production aircraft to feature a variable-sweep wing, and epitomised the USA's technological leadership in aviation by the 1960s – and paved the way for later swing-wing aircraft.

In the late 1950s, the USAF initiated plans for the replacement of the Republic F-105 Thunderchief nuclear strike fighter. The replacement would have to operate at low-level in all weather conditions by day and night, fly from bomb-damaged runways, or small dispersed airfields. It also had to fly further – in terms of continental deployment – with minimum reliance on flight refuelling.

A possible solution to the problem of combining long ferry range, short-field performance and high-speed dash was the swing-wing – although this concept was still in its infancy at that time. However, a breakthrough was achieved by NASA in the early 1960s, using computers to predict

Of the F-111Fs that took part in Operation *El Dorado Canyon*, eight attacked the Libyan leader's HQ at Al Azziziyah and the barracks at Sidi Bilal, with five making attacks on military targets at Tripoli airport.

Eleven Minutes over Tripoli

Colonel Robert Venkus was USAF Deputy Commander of the Lakenheath, England-based 48th Tactical Fighter Wing at the time of Operation *El Dorado Canyon*. In his book '*Raid on Gadafi*'(St Martin's Press, New York 1992) he gives this first-hand account of the strike on Libya.

"The Lakenheath strike force was split into six three-aircraft groups or cells, each with its own callsign. However, aborts due to equipment malfunctions reduced the size of the force that was actually able to make the final attacks. Strict rules of engagement required that all the complex and delicate targeting systems on the F-111Fs be fully functional so that no bombs would go astray and cause politically embarrassing collateral damage."

"Of the eighteen aircraft that should have attacked targets, two aborted due to equipment problems before crossing the Libya coast and four aborted as they made their final bomb runs. First over the city was *Remit* cell that was heading for the Azziziyah complex and the very first aircraft delivered its bombs in the face of radar guided anti-aircraft fire."

"The first bombs landed 50 metres from Gadafi's headquarters and the next aircraft suffered a systems failure on its navigation system so it had to abort. Other equipment problems dogged the third aircraft but it

wing and tail geometries. Ironically, although the variable-geometry configuration was the really major challenge in the development of the F-111, the swing-wing worked very well from the outset – but the aircraft suffered a series of teething troubles in other areas.

Deliveries to the USAF began in early 1968 and a detachment was sent to Vietnam, but three aircraft were lost in mysterious circumstances. A total of twenty-four F-111s were delivered to the RAAF in 1973, but the intended fifty F-111Ks for the RAF (to replace the ill-fated BAC TSR.2) were cancelled.

The F-111 was deployed to Europe (USAFE) in April 1970 and some eighty-eight aircraft saw operational service in the UK based at Lakenheath and Upper Heyford, together got its four 2,000lb laser-guided bombs on target. The tapes of their bomb aiming system showed two Libyan surface-to-air missile (SAM) in the air near the aircraft."

"Next over was *Karma* cell, who were now facing even more alert defences. *Karma 51*, the lead aircraft, put its bombs some one and a half miles off target, causing the only major incident of collateral damage of the raid, the four 2,000lb bombs falling in the area near the French Embassy. The aircraft's Pave Tack possibly malfunctioned releasing bombs off mark, but the crew only realised something was wrong when the weapons had left the aircraft. The weapon system operator was unable to visually identify his target before activating the laser-guidance devices. This was possibly due to navigational problems during the long flight to Libya which resulted in errors being entered into the system."

"Almost at the same time as *Karma 51* was getting into trouble, its sister aircraft was about to suffer a fatal mishap. To this day, the official version is that *Karma 52*'s loss is still unexplained, although most accounts say it 'flew into the sea'. However, I believe the aircraft was shot down by the now fully alerted Libyan SAM defences, causing the death of the crew."

"A report from one of the crew of the following F-111Fs said he saw a fireball in the sky ahead, and US Navy aviators reported the fireball dropping to the sea. The subsequent autopsy of the pilot, when his body was returned by the Libyans four years later recorded 'death by drowning' as the cause of death, which I consider is consistent with the crew jettisoning their escape capsule, and then drowning after it hit the sea."

"If their aircraft had flown into the sea, the crew would have shown major fractures and internal injuries from the impact. None of these tell tail signs were found on the body. The heavy SAM and AAA fire added to the

Photographs taken during the night raid on Tripoli Airport from the Pave Tack system fitted to the attacking F-111Fs, showing several Libyan Il-76 transports being targeted with pinpoint accuracy.

likelihood that *Karma 52* was hit."

"Next over Tripoli was the *Jewel* cell, that was heading for Sidi Balal. The three aircraft that made it to the target area all delivered their bombs, but one aircraft's ordnance was wide by a few dozen yards, after smoke from previous aircraft's weapons obscured the target, interfering with its laser guidance system. At Tripoli airport five-aircraft *Puffy* and *Lijac* cells, were to attack at low level with 500lb 'Snakeye' retarded bombs. Only one of the aircraft put its bombs bang on target, but the remaining five got their ordnance close to the target causing damage to Libyan Ilyushin transport aircraft, helicopters and airport facilities."

"After debriefing pilots, viewing video footage from Pave Tack systems, and post-strike reconnaissance photographs obtained by USAF Lockheed SR-71 Blackbird aircraft, it is likely that only four of the Tripoli raiders actually hit their intended targets. Two missed due to the intensity of enemy defences and six others missed for a variety of reasons, although it is suspected that navigational errors introduced into the F-111F's computer systems during the long flight to Libya were the main culprit, rather than 'battle shock' among crews facing battle for the first time."

"The raid was major feat of airmanship – on a par with the Doolittle raid on Japan in WW2. Nothing like it had been attempted before or since. After flying for almost seven hours, the 48th Wing still managed to hit and badly damage all three of its targets."

"Libyan sponsored acts of violence subsided after the raid and the faults identified in the F-111F's systems were identified in time for Operation *Desert Storm*, where the aircraft performed with outstanding distinction."

with around twelve EF-111 Ravens (the electronic countermeasures variant) with the Electronic Combat Squadrons, until 1993.

Aircraft from the 48th TFW got their first taste of combat in mid-1986, when eighteen were sent to bomb Libya during Operation *El Dorado Canyon* – and about seventy went to Taif, Saudi Arabia for the 1990-91 crisis. In Operation *Desert Storm*, they accumulated an impressive record, logging almost 2,500 sorties and delivering over 4,500 precision munitions against targets such as armoured fighting vehicles, command bunkers and hardened aircraft shelters. Combat in the Gulf provided a fitting finale to the Aardvark's European service career, for the process of winding down began soon after.

THE VERTICAL REALITY

Throughout the latter part of the 20th century, the British Aerospace/McDonnell Douglas Harrier family represented the world's only high-performance V/STOL combat aircraft to see service on a significant scale – just as its Rolls-Royce Pegasus vectored-thrust turbofan remains the only series-built V/STOL engine. It must be admitted, however, that the Harrier/Pegasus monopoly of the V/STOL business is also partly attributable to what turned out to be a fluctuating but very restricted demand for this class of specialised aircraft.

The concept of a combat aircraft that could be dispersed away from main-bases arose in the early days of the Cold War, as Western fears grew that the Soviet Union would soon possess literally thousands of tactical nuclear weapons, which could be delivered accurately against large fixed targets by manned aircraft and ballistic missiles.

An RAF Harrier GR1 of No 1 Squadron flying from Akrotiri, Cyprus during an armament practice camp.

222

A US Marines Corps AV-8A when operational with VMA-513 based at Yuma, Arizona.

CHRONOLOGY

27 June 1977
Designed by CASA in Spain, with collaboration from MBB in Germany and Northrop in the US, the prototype C-101 Aviojet made its maiden flight – a tandem two-seat basic and advanced trainer with light attack capability.

30 June 1977
US President Jimmy Carter announced cancellation of the Rockwell B-1 strategic bomber programme – funding was to go instead to the development of cruise missiles.

4 November 1977
The first production Saab JA37 Viggen made its initial flight fitted with cannon, BAe Sky Flash missiles and I/J band pulse-Doppler radar.

26 February 1978
The McDonnell Douglas F-15C made its maiden flight.

10 March 1978
The first of five prototypes of the Dassault Mirage 2000 single-seat air-superiority fighter made the type's first flight. The 2000 had been selected as the primary combat aircraft for the French Air Force from the mid-1980s.

7 August 1978
Production example of the General Dynamics F-16A single-seat lightweight air combat fighter was flown at Fort Worth.

12 August 1978
Pilatus, in Switzerland, flew the first PC-7 Turbo Trainer for the first time.

20 August 1978
The first example of the BAe Sea Harrier was flown – the maritime version of the RAF's Harrier.

9 November 1978
The first McDonnell Douglas YAV-8B Advanced Harrier prototype was flown for the first time.

19 November 1978
McDonnell Douglas flew the first of eleven pre-production F-18 Hornet carrier-based naval strike aircraft.

1 December 1978
HMS *Ark Royal* was paid off at Devonport and its Buccaneer S2s transferred to the RAF.

By the mid-1960s, the concept of a V/STOL combat aircraft was rendered largely obsolete by NATO's switch in planning from an all-out nuclear war from Day One to a 'graduated' response. It took several years for the RAF to accept fully that the Harrier really did provide unique survivability when operating from dispersed sites in Germany. Fortunately the US Marines Corps came to the realisation in the late 1960s that the Harrier was ideally suited to fulfilling its aircraft requirement to get fixed-wing air power immediately after an amphibious assault.

The demand for V/STOL implied a technological advance of a completely different order of magnitude. It was to prove comparable to the mid-1940s transition from propeller-driven to jet-powered fighters.

On 15 July 1960, the first P.1127 prototype was transported from the Hawker factory at Kingston to Dunsfold and the first tethered hover was undertaken on 21 October 1960. Untethered hovering followed on 19 November and the first conventional take-off and landing was recorded on 13 March 1961.

In May 1962, the governments of the UK, the US and West Germany agreed to fund an improved version of the P.1127, as a means of evaluating the service potential of V/STOL fighters – and the go ahead was given for the development and production of nine Kestrel aircraft, the first making its maiden flight on 7 March 1964.

Renamed Harrier in 1967, it was designed to provide a serious warload-radius performance, although the single-engine concept suffered as a result of being overpowered for low-level cruise.

The primary role of the Harrier GR1A, introduced in 1971, was to attack second-echelon armoured units in the face of relatively advanced air defences. It operated at high subsonic speed and mainly at extremely low level, although its Hunting BL755 cluster weapons and 68mm SNEB rockets required more height in the attack phase. The improved Harrier GR3 followed in 1976.

Early Harrier trials

Former Hawker Siddeley Aviation Chief Test Pilot Duncan Simpson recalls his involvement with the development flying on the first Harriers.

"The Harrier had been designed to be operated world-wide, and the sixth development aircraft was set aside for an early look at its performance in hot weather conditions. Originally it was intended to operate from Wheelus Air Base in North Africa under the auspices of the United States Air Force. But due to political trouble in Libya we had to search for an alternative which afforded suitable conditions. Fortunately the Italian Navy were showing interest in the Harrier and offered us the use of its airfield at Sigonella in Sicily, which was a joint NATO base."

"The trial had to start no later than the last week in July 1967 in order to take advantage of the highest temperatures at Sigonella. I took off for Rome and the flight across France went well and, as usual, we were intercepted by the French Air Force. I had kept a precise log of the fuel state in the cruise and this compared precisely with the predictions. Corsica came and went and I let down towards Rome in excellent weather. My main concern was the air temperature at Pratica, which was passed to me as +30deg C. I stood off clear of the circuit and made my calculations for a vertical landing.

The RAF's Harrier GR1s (this is an early production example) began their first-line service with No 1 Squadron, based at Wittering, in 1969.

The Harrier AV-8A entered service with the US Marine Corps in 1971 and the Spanish Navy and Indian Navy acquired some in the mid-1970s. Although developed for land-based operations in order to circumvent the vulnerability of fixed bases to nuclear attacks, the Harrier was tested for ship-compatibility early in its career – and the Sea Harrier was eventually developed for the Royal Navy.

When the Argentine forces invaded the Falkland Islands in April 1982, Sea Harriers (which had been developed in the nick of time), together with a number of RAF Harrier GR3s, gave excellent service in the South Atlantic. Second generation Harriers began entering service in 1985 – the AV-8B in the US and the equivalent Harrier GR5 (and later the GR7) with the RAF.

"We have to get away from the Harrier being seen as an aircraft which flies twenty minute sorties out of a wood" – these words spoken by a senior Harrier pilot as the GR7 was entering squadron service in 1992 appeared to deny the *raison d'etre* of the Harrier. In truth, however, there was no contradiction. After more than two decades of service and in the context of the collapse of the Warsaw Pact, the Harrier has grown, matured and adapted to the new world, with better performance and improved avionics.

Despite the fact that it is now almost thirty-five years since the first Harrier entered service, no other high performance V/STOL aircraft has been produced on the same scale.

The RAF's No 1417 Flight in Belize adopted the 'sailfish' badge flanked by red and blue bars on its Harrier GR3s when officially designated in 1979. The GR3 featured a Laser Ranger and Marked-Target Seeker nose.

They had to see a vertical landing. I concluded that I could only just land vertically with not more than 300lb of fuel, and I was aware that the temperature over the concrete runway might be +3deg on the quoted OAT."

"After some brief manoeuvres for the assembled Navy I disappeared round the back of the horizon for a quick 360deg turn on final approach to get rid of 250lb of fuel to end up with a vertical landing with just under 300lb remaining. However, there were smiles all round and I tried to look unconcerned – I had been on the limit at touchdown. After a two-hour stay at Pratica I departed for Sicily and Sigonella. I was quite well occupied, but had time to admire the Italian coast and caught sight of Mount Etna above the haze some 100 miles away."

"We spent a full week at Sigonella, which proved ideal for the purpose. Not only were the temperatures well up to predictions, but the flying conditions were excellent. On the day we chose for the 'hot soak' tests the temperature touched +42deg C and we rigged up an umbrella to protect the cockpit, otherwise entry would have been a painful process. The umbrella later became

a standard piece of equipment."

"This early trial proved that the Harrier's cockpit conditioning system was powerful and effective, thanks to the experience gained in clearing the Hunter for tropical use some years before. In fact once airborne the Harrier cockpit was the most comfortable place to be during the trials. Minor modifications were made to the engine oil and fuel cooling systems as a result of flying in those extreme conditions."

"The return flight to Dunsfold was slightly more eventful than the outboard journey. Conditions for the let-down and approach to Nice were not as forecast and I was thankful to get the Harrier safely on the ground, only to find that I had an oxygen leak. There were no compatible facilities for oxygen at Nice so I was obliged to spend the night armed with a pair of pliers and a piece of locking wire to lock the valve open, so that I could fly along to the French base at Istres at low level. With the help of the 'Standard NATO' connection the oxygen was topped up, and (leak or no leak) I was on my way back to Dunsfold."

CHRONOLOGY

22 February 1979
The US Navy took delivery of its last McDonnell Douglas A-4 Skyhawk, which had been in production for 25 years in many variants.

9 March 1979
Dassault flew the prototype of its Super Mirage 4000 multi-role combat aircraft.

3 June 1979
The prototype PZL Swidnik Kania first flew – a turbine-engined conversion of the Mil Mi-2.

10 July 1979
The first full production standard Tornado GR1 made its initial flight at Warton.

27 October 1979
The Tornado ADV prototype first flew at Warton.

25 March 1980
The Boeing AGM-86B was selected to equip SAC's B-52 Stratofortresses in a stand-off role, to provide greater penetration capabilities in an operational role and extend the mission life of the aircraft by removing it from the worst air defence threats.

3 June 1980
Designed for close air support duties against ground targets, the AGM-65E laser-guided Maverick was fired from an aircraft for the first time.

1 July 1980
The first Tornados were delivered to the Tornado Tri-National Training Establishment (TTTE) at RAF Cottesmore.

12 July 1980
McDonnell Douglas flew the first KC-10A Extender – a military inflight refuelling/cargo aircraft for the USAF – derived from the DC-10-30CF civil transport.

18 July 1980
McDonnell Douglas flew a modified FSD F-15B to demonstrate the ground attack capabilities of the Eagle. This dual role 'Strike Eagle' had a redesigned front cockpit and the rear cockpit equipped for use by a Weapons System Operator (WSO).

24 August 1980
The prototype F-15B Eagle made the first unrefuelled transatlantic flight by a jet fighter.

20 April 1981
The considerably re-designed Sukhoi Su-27 'Flanker-B' made its first flight. Production commenced the following year.

8 May 1981
The Dassault-Breguet Atlantic Nouvelle Génération (later designated ATL2) advanced anti-submarine patrol aircraft made its first flight.

NASA'S REUSABLE SPACE SHUTTLE

A former American Airlines Boeing 747-123 was acquired by NASA in 1974 and modified by Boeing to serve as the Shuttle Carrier Aircraft (SCA).

For many years the Americans had a desire to have as functional hardware a reusable vehicle that could be launched into Earth orbit, have the ability to manoeuvre in space, and which could then re-enter the Earth's atmosphere to land conventionally on an airfield runway. This led to the design of the Space Shuttle Orbiter (SSO), with a thick section of double delta planform, whose power was provided by three Rocketdyne SSME rocket engines in the rear fuselage.

An ex-American Airlines Boeing 747-123 was converted by Boeing as a Shuttle Carrier Aircraft (SCA) to enable an SSO to be carried on a purpose-built rig on top of the fuselage.

CHRONOLOGY

7 June 1981
Despite US insistence that the aircraft should only be used for defence purposes, Israeli Air Force F-16As, escorted by F-15s, launched a devastating attack on Iraq's nuclear plant at Osirck, near Baghdad.

18 June 1981
The initial flight was made by the multi-faceted Lockheed F-117 from a special facility in the Nevada desert. Originally developed under the code name *Have Blue*, Lockheed was given the contract for the production of a derivative aircraft described as CSIRS (covert, survivable, in-weather, reconnaissance/strike), subsequently identified as the F-117A Nighthawk 'stealth' fighter.

1 August 1981
The first example of the Lockheed TR-1A – an advanced single-seat tactical reconnaissance aircraft, with electronic sensors, based on the airframe of the single-seat U-2R, made its first flight.

1 September 1981
The Indian Air Force took delivery of the MiG-25 'Foxbat'.

15 September 1981
The F-111Fs based with the 48th Tactical Fighter Wing at RAF Lakenheath became equipped with the Pave Tack weapons delivery system (comprising a pod housing a laser transmitter/receiver and a precision optical sight).

2 October 1981
President Reagan announced the resumption of the Rockwell B-1 programme, pending the secret development of what would become the Northrop B-2 'stealth' bomber.

20 November 1981
The Mirage F1-CR, the photographic reconnaissance version of the F-1 single-seat fighter, made its first flight in France.

5 February 1982
The unorthodox Northrop *Tacit Blue* stealth technology demonstrator aircraft was flown for the first time. It went on to make a further 135 test flights, before its retirement to the USAF Museum.

On 13 August 1977, *Enterprise* and its crew were launched in free flight from the SCA at a height of 22,800ft to make a gliding and unpowered flight to a conventional landing at Edwards AFB, CA.

It was four years later, on 12 April 1981, that spacecraft OV-102 *Columbia* lifted off from Cape Canaveral on its first orbital mission, returning to earth for an unpowered landing on Rogers Dry Lake at Edwards. The craft's capacity for delivering or launching satellites and 'weapons' and return to earth for re-use, gave it a unique capability and unprecedented military potential.

SEA HARRIER GOES TO WAR

Right: A Sea Harrier FRS1 takes-off from HMS *Hermes* to carry out a CAP sortie. Its primary role was as a fleet air defence fighter, with secondary roles including strike and anti-shipping missions, armed with BAe Sea Eagle anti-ship missiles.

The *Atlantic Conveyor* off Ascension Island on 6 May 1982, with the forward deck filled with Sea Harriers, RAF Harrier GR3s and helicopters ready for the last stage of its journey to the Falkland Islands.

The Royal Navy's introduction of the Sea Harrier FRS1 was with 800 Naval Air Squadron that formed at RNAS Yeovilton on 1 April 1980, followed by 801 NAS on 26 February 1981. After the commissioning of the brand-new HMS *Invincible*, 800 Squadron embarked for its first major deployment on 28 September 1980 and remained aboard until 31 March 1981. The unit's place on *Invincible* was shortly afterwards taken by 801 NAS, which began its first deployment on 21 May 1981. On 13 July 1981, 800 NAS went to sea aboard the ageing HMS *Hermes*, and this allocation of the two FAA operational Sea Harrier units to the two RN carriers was still in force at the time of the Falklands conflict.

When Argentine forces invaded the Falklands on 2 April 1982, RAF Harriers had been operational for more than a decade (in fact, the old analogue nav-attack system was due for replacement by a modern digital one), but the Sea Harrier FRS1 and the *Invincible* were still quite new. Some Sea Harriers were still lacking their Blue Fox radars, and none of them had clearance to employ the BAe Sea Eagle anti-ship missile.

In essence, the Sea Harrier had been developed just in time for the Falklands conflict, and Britain's Task Force sent to recover the islands could not have sailed without it. But in early 1982 its operational capability was still severely limited.

Despite its maturity, the RAF's Harrier GR3 was cleared only to fire its 30-mm Aden cannon, drop 1,000 lb (454 kg) bombs and BL755 cluster weapons, and fire 68 mm SNEB rockets, which were regarded as incompatible with the electromagnetic radiation level of a carrier deck. It had no clearance for the AIM-9 Sidewinder, laser-guided bombs, or anti-radiation missiles.

At the start of hostilities, Argentina was reckoned to have anything from 120 to 200 combat aircraft, some of which (certainly the MB339, Pucará, and Beech T-34C, and possibly even the A-4P and Mirage) could be deployed to the 4,250 ft (1,300 m) runway at Port Stanley, where there was a brand-new Westinghouse TPS-43 radar. The British Task Force also faced the threat from shadowing Boeing 707-320Bs, Neptunes and Electras, and of attacks by A-4Q Skyhawks and Exocet-armed Super Etendards from the carrier *Veinticinco de Mayo*. The Argentine Air Force had two KC-130H tankers, each with two drogue units for refuelling A-4 Skyhawks and Super Etendards.

Against this Argentine force sailed a carrier battle group with both *Hermes* and *Invincible*. The ships carried a total of 20 Sea Harriers and 45 helicopters. Encouraged by somewhat misleading talk of our fixed-wing aircraft being outnumbered by 10:1,

reinforcements followed, taking the eventual total to 28 Sea Harriers and 14 RAF Harrier GR3s (and 175 helicopters). With reference to the RAF claim in the 1960s that no RN aircraft carriers were necessary because the fleet could be provided with land-based air cover, it may be noted that the Falklands are approximately 3,250 nm (6,000 km) from Ascension Island, which would have made for a rather long sortie by a Tornado F3. On the other hand, they were only 400-500 nm (750-925 km) from the three main air bases in the south of Argentina, which placed the British ships and landing force within easy reach of attack aircraft flying HI-LO sorties.

Since the two operational Sea Harrier squadrons each had a nominal strength of six aircraft and normally went to sea with only five, it was quite an achievement to have embarked 20 aircraft within three days of the invasion.

RAF pilot training prior to deployment was limited to use of the RN's ski-jump at RNAS Yeovilton, with the requirement for three take-offs being quickly reduced to one. Air combat training was not considered necessary, since RAF pilots had achieved respectable results in exercises with their French Mirage counterparts. Clearance trials were carried out with the AIM-9 Sidewinder, the Navy's two-inch (5-cm) rocket, and the 1,000 lb (454 kg) Paveway laser-guided bomb.

The air war had begun on 1 May, when an early morning bombing raid on Port Stanley airfield by an RAF Vulcan flying from Ascension was followed by a dawn attack by the 12 Sea

CHRONOLOGY

5 April 1982
The main elements of a UK task force were despatched to the Falkland Islands, following their invasion by Argentina. It included the two remaining British aircraft carriers, HMS *Hermes* and HMS *Invincible*, with Sea Harriers and Sea Kings. Simultaneously an air-bridge to Ascension Island was established by freight-carrying Hercules C1s/C3s.

22 June 1982
The first BAe VC10 K2 tanker conversion was flown at Filton. The conversions, providing extra tankage and in-flight refuelling equipment, were made from ex-civil VC-10s.

3 July 1982
The single-seat General Dynamics F-16XL was flown for the first time – it featured a 'cranked arrow' composite wing and a lengthened fuselage, together with a greater weapon-carrying capability.

The Royal Navy's employment of the Sea Harrier FRS1 followed more a decade after the RAF's introduction of the Harrier GR1, with 800 Naval Air Squadron forming at RNAS Yeovilton on 1 April 1980.

CHRONOLOGY

4 August 1982
The first re-engined Boeing KC-135R Stratotanker had its maiden flight fitted with CFM-56 turbofans in place of turbojets giving significant performance improvements.

30 August 1982
The Northrop F-5G (later F-20) Tigershark made the type's first flight.

1 September 1982
US Air Force Space Command was activated.

16 December 1982
The AGM-86B air-launched missile (ALCM) reached Initial Operational Capability (IOC). Sixteen B-52Gs were modified to carry twelve ALCMs on wing pylons.

7 January 1983
The McDonnell Douglas F/A-18 Hornet naval strike fighter became operational with the US Marine Corps.

27 January 1983
The first of eight BAe Sea Harrier FRS51s was handed over to the Indian Navy.

18 June 1983
First launch of the LGM-118 'MX' Peacemaker ICBM. A total of 50 were subsequently deployed.

15 July 1983
The first Boeing E-4B (E-4A upgrade) was delivered to the USAF Electronic Systems Division. One E-4B was airborne at all times, with a crew of up to 94, with a senior officer onboard capable of assuming command of US forces in extreme emergency.

29 August 1983
Maiden flight of the Anglo-American AV-8B. BAe-built versions for the RAF were to be known as Harrier GR5s.

15 September 1983
First of four prototypes of the Italian Agusta A129 Mangusta light anti-tank, attack and advanced scout helicopter made the type's first flight.

26 October 1983
The Lockheed F-117A attained Initial Operational Capability. All F-117 flights were made at night until November 1988.

16 November 1983
The first Bell AH-1T+ Super Cobra, intended for the US Marine Corps, made its initial flight.

26 January 1984
First production AH-64A Apache was delivered to the US Army.

Harriers of 800 Squadron operating from *Hermes*, with the eight aircraft of 801 NAS providing fighter support. Nine of the attack aircraft struck at Port Stanley airfield, and the three reserves then bombed the grass airstrip at Goose Green. There were no losses on the British side.

The point is worth making that although the Sea Harriers were able to provide a useful degree of air cover for the vessels of the task force and later for British forces on the ground, this was far from an impenetrable shield. Faced with the threat of flight-refuelled Super Etendards armed with Exocet anti-ship missiles, the two aircraft carriers were generally held back about 150 nm (280 km) to the east of the Falklands. For the dawn attack on May Day, the carriers came in to within 90 nm (165 km) of the islands, but this was not standard practice.

However, the British side was also suffering losses. On 4 May, Lt Nick Taylor of 800 Squadron was killed when his aircraft (XZ450) was destroyed by AAA while attacking the Goose Green airstrip. On 6 May, Lt Cdr John Eyton-Jones and Lt Alan Curtiss of 801 Squadron were killed when their aircraft (respectively XZ452 and 453) evidently collided while descending through cloud. Until the reinforcements arrived on 18 May, the Sea Harrier total was reduced to 17 aircraft (eleven on *Hermes* and six on *Invincible*).

Following those three early losses, the employment of the Sea Harrier increasingly

Falklands air war

A Sea Harrier pilot wrote of the Falklands Conflict:
"Deploying south with the Task Force, rapidly assembled after the personal intervention of the First Sea Lord to the Prime Minister, as many Sea Harriers as possible were taken by the Royal Navy who had suddenly appreciated their importance in a theatre of war eight thousand miles away. Armed at the last moment with the latest Sidewinder missile from the US, the AIM-9L, the combination of aircraft and missile proved deadly to the Argentine Air Force. Flown by many of our highly experienced pilots who had introduced the aircraft to service, the Sea Harrier became known as the 'Black Death' to the Argentineans, who despite fighting bravely, suffered heavy losses."

"Operating from carriers proved the concept of V/STOL air operations in independent amphibious operations. HMS *Invincible* remained at sea for 166 days during the conflict, establishing a new record for continuous carrier operations, and her jets remained serviceable for 95% of this period. Forced to fight a war in a narrow inlet instead of the open sea, the Royal Navy lost one ship for every four enemy aircraft, and it is certain that without our Sea Harriers the conflict would not have had a successful outcome."

"No aircraft were lost in air combat, although several were destroyed by enemy action or the appalling weather conditions prevalent in the South Atlantic. The Task Force returned to the UK, triumphant but with many lessons to be absorbed."

The First Sea Lord, Admiral Sir Henry Leach, later said: "Without the Sea Harrier there would have been no Task Force." – a clear indication of the Sea Harrier's pivotal role in the conflict.

The Royal Navy's carrier-based Sea Harriers played a crucial part in the successful outcome of the Falklands conflict.

concentrated on air defence. In this task it was to provide an outer defence layer for the amphibious force that landed at San Carlos Water on 21 May, a second layer being represented by two ships forming a 'missile trap', and the third (innermost) layer by a 'gunline' of three or four ships.

The Sea Harrier defensive screen may have been far from impassable, but it was nonetheless taking a toll of incoming aircraft that was quite remarkable in the circumstances, with seven Argentine aircraft destroyed on 21 May alone. That day began with 801 Squadron's Lt Cdr 'Sharkey' Ward in XZ451 shooting down Pucará A-511 with 30 mm cannon fire. An hour later, 800 Squadron's aircraft were engaging Argentine Air Force A-4s – Lt Cdr Neil Thomas in XZ492 destroying C-309, and Lt Cdr Mike Blisset taking out C-325. Some 90 minutes later, the same squadron's Rod Frederiksen (now a BAe test pilot at Dunsfold) in XZ455 eliminated

Armed with Sidewinder AAMs, a Sea Harrier FRS1 of 809 NAS is marshalled on the flight deck of HMS *Hermes* during the Falklands conflict.

CHRONOLOGY

24 February 1984
The F-15E Strike Eagle was selected as the two-seat, dual-role fighter rather than the F-16XL.

31 March 1984
The last operational RAF V-bomber squadron was disbanded – ending over two decades of service.

12 May 1984
The Pilatus Britten-Norman ASTOR (Airborne stand-off radar) Defender made its first flight.

19 June 1984
The improved F-16C was first flown – it featured a GEC wide-angle HUD and Hughes APG-68 multi-mode radar. It entered USAF service on 19 July.

2 July 1984
The first Mirage 2000s of the French Air Force were declared operational.

Dagger C-409. The next wave of Daggers was successfully intercepted by 801 Squadron, Lt Steve Thomas in ZA190 destroying C-404 and C-403, and Lt Cdr 'Sharkey' Ward in ZA175 eliminating C-407.

Two days later (23 May 1982) Argentine fixed-wing activity appears to have subsided, but the Sea Harriers of 800 Squadron were now after helicopters. One of the seven RAF pilots on exchange postings, who had sailed with the Sea Harrier force in the initial deployment, Flt Lt Dave Morgan in ZA192 destroyed Puma AE-503 with his aircraft's wake, then downed Agusta A109 serial AE-337 with 30 mm fire. Later that afternoon Lt Martin Hale in ZA194 disintegrated Dagger C-437.

On the following day 800 Squadron's CO Lt Cdr Andy Auld, in XZ457, destroyed Daggers C-419 and C-430, and Lt Dave Smith in ZA193 shot down Dagger C-410. The Sea Harriers had consistently failed to intercept night-time Hercules missions to and from Port Stanley, but on 1 June Lt Cdr Ward of 801 Squadron shot down a C-130 (TC-63) in daylight, using an AIM-9L and then cannon fire.

On the final day of air combat, 8 June 1982, Sea Harriers of 800 Squadron were again in action against Air Force A-4s, Flt Lt Dave Morgan downing C-226 and C-228, and Lt Dave Smith in XZ499 following on with C-204.

In the course of three months, RN Sea Harriers had averaged 55 flight hours per month, more than twice their peacetime rate, flying over 2,514 hours and 2,197 sorties. The latter figure includes 1,000 combat air patrol sorties (which produced 23 kills) and 90 that were dedicated to offensive support. The conflict had been short, and it had revealed some shortcomings in both Harrier variants. On the other hand it had demonstrated beyond any doubt the unique operational versatility of the family. They had been flown, not only from relatively small carriers, but also from a container ship, the helicopter pads of the assault ships *Fearless* and *Intrepid*, and a short runway of aluminium planking that had been laid immediately after the amphibious landing.

ADVANCED TRAINER

The BAe Hawk has superb handling through a wide range of manoeuvres and has been in RAF service with No 4 FTS at Valley for advanced pilot training for over two decades.

CHRONOLOGY

17 December 1984
A C-5A Galaxy set a national record for taking off at the highest all-up weight – becoming airborne with a total of 920,836lb (418,562kg).

26 February 1985
The first McDonnell Douglas F/A-18 Hornet assembled in Australia made its initial flight prior to delivery to the RAAF.

4 March 1985
An F-16 Fighting Falcon began flight tests with a TERPROM (terrain profile-matching) navigation system – developed jointly by GD and BAe.

1 May 1985
Successful guided test launch of the AIM-120A AMRAAM (Advanced medium-range air-to-air missile) was accomplished from an F-16.

27 July 1985
The first Rockwell B-1B Lancer swing-wing bomber was delivered to the USAF.

6 August 1985
The USAF Aeronautical Systems Division carried out the first full operational flight test of the precision location strike system (PLSS) using three Lockheed TR-1A reconnaissance aircraft, together with ground support stations.

13 September 1985
An F-15 Eagle launched an ASAT (anti-satellite) missile and destroyed a target in space for the first time.

20 November 1985
First flight of the initial production Tornado F3 – the definitive air defence fighter variant. It also had provision for automatic wing sweep.

31 December 1985
Reversing the Pentagon decision of January 1982, McDonnell Douglas was awarded a contract to design and develop the C-17A long-range, heavy-lift cargo transport. The aircraft was required to be able to lift a C-5A Galaxy-size payload into rough-field areas normally accessible only to the C-130 Hercules.

The most successful modern, two-seat, advanced jet trainer produced in western Europe, the British Aerospace Hawk has gone on, in its second generation, to become an equally successful weapons platform. The original ideas included the importance of a baseline for the aircraft's development. Subsequent perseverance by engineers and marketeers, demonstrations by test pilots and RAF pilots, including the *Red Arrows*, has resulted in 16 world air arms operating the Hawk today.

The initial production aircraft for the RAF have equipped No 4 Flying Training School at RAF Valley for two decades and provided an advanced flying training aircraft highly regarded by students and instructors alike.

The Hawk T1A, with its systems for weapons delivery, and Sidewinder air-to-air missiles was used very effectively by the Tactical Weapons Units at Brawdy and Chivenor and as a supplement for the UK's air defence force. Today the RAF's advanced flying and tactical weapons training at Valley is augmented by a wider use of the Hawk for target facilities flying and navigator training by No 100 Squadron at RAF Leeming and the Royal Navy's Fleet Requirements and Direction Unit at RNAS Culdrose.

In the public eye, the Hawk has equipped the RAF's aerobatic team the *Red Arrows* since 1980, replacing the previously flown HS Gnats. The red-painted aircraft, with their eye-catching smoke, have entertained airshow audiences in Britain and across Europe, North America and the Middle East on countless occasions. The team has consistently demonstrated the high qualities of the Hawk wherever they have displayed. This highly visual promotion of the aircraft has undoubtedly assisted the manufacturer in securing overseas interest and sales.

In its service career, the Hawk has fulfilled – and in many cases exceeded – the objectives of the design team. The aircraft has proved to be safe, rugged, reliable and highly adaptable and to date has over 700,000 flying hours with the RAF. As for adaptability and mission flexibility, the Hawk's service record speaks for itself. Having begun life as an advanced flying and weapons training aircraft, it was soon adapted for display flying with the *Red Arrows*. In addition to its tactical weapons training role, the TWU Hawks were given a front-line role

CHRONOLOGY

17 January 1986
The USAF began operational testing of the first Martin Aerospace LANTIRN (low-altitude navigation and targeting infrared system for night) targeting system.

14 April 1986
The USAF was involved in co-ordinated air strikes on targets in Libya, mounted from bases in England under Operation *El Dorado Canyon*.

26 April 1986
A major accident occurred at the nuclear power station at Chernobyl in the Ukraine. Boeing EC-135Hs, RC-135Us and WC-135Bs operating out of RAF Mildenhall were involved in gathering details of the explosion and collecting air samples.

1 June 1986
The LGM-118A Peacemaker missile entered service. They were designed to be cold-launched from existing Minuteman III sites, of which 200 were spread over 5,866 acres of Wyoming.

Flying the Hawk

Squadron Leader D. A. Wyatt, a former Deputy Chief Instructor with the Royal Air Force with over 2,500 hours experience in the Hawk, recalled his views on the type:

"My first contact with the Hawk was as a student pilot at RAF Valley in 1981 – but since then I have instructed on the type at both RAF Chivenor and RAF Valley. I also spent three years with the *Red Arrows* aerobatic team, first as 'Red 8' and then as one of the 'Synchro Pair'."

"My experience of the Hawk took in advanced flying training, weapons training and formation display flying. The Hawk was a big step up from the Jet Provost – particularly in terms of speed – and the tandem cockpit really gives you the impression of being on your own in a single-seat aircraft."

Left: Modified to carry AIM-9 Sidewinder air-to-air missiles underwing, these RAF Hawk T1As were flown by Nos 63 and 151 'Shadow' Squadrons at Chivenor for close air defence, in the late 1980s.

"Ergonomically, the aircraft was a magnificent step-up from the JP, with a well laid-out cockpit, where everything falls nicely to hand. Positive aspects are the aircraft's outstanding manoeuvrability, the exceptional view from the rear cockpit and the fuel economy of the Adour engine - particularly at altitude. On the negative side I disliked the cockpit windscreen arch – which creates an obstruction during formation flying and low-level tactical weapons training."

"At medium altitude, the Hawk handles superbly and an extensive range of aerobatic manoeuvres can be demonstrated, including inverted flight. One must pay particular attention to engine power settings, in order to avoid over-stressing the airframe or causing the engine to flameout, through extreme manoeuvring at low speed."

"Stalling can be demonstrated with the Hawk, as it is quite docile, with adequate warning of the onset of the stall. Recovery is almost instantaneous, once back pressure on the control stick is released. Spinning too can be demonstrated, but requires positive control inputs to overcome the aircraft's

natural reluctance to spin. Spinning characteristics can vary but, in all cases, recovery is effected by centralising the controls."

"In the circuit, events happen quickly. The initial downwind leg is flown at 190kt as the aircraft is turned on to base leg. Turning on to final approach, speed decays to 130kt, with a target speed of 110kt (plus 1kt for every 100kg of fuel remaining)."

"For the approach, a minimum power setting of 70% is always selected to minimise engine response time, should an overshoot be necessary. Because of its twin-spool design, the Adour engine is relatively slow to accelerate and flight idle to full power can take as long as eight seconds."

"At low level, the Hawk T1 can comfortably operate at speeds of up to 500kt and is highly manoeuvrable. However, the aircraft's wing loading makes it susceptible to turbulence, and this can lead to a bumpy ride."

"Any future Hawk replacement should have a one-piece F-16-style canopy, a more powerful engine (especially when carrying external stores) such as the Adour 871, and a modern 'glass' cockpit."

and allocated to 'shadow squadrons' that would, in times of crisis, be capable of carrying out limited combat missions. Originally, the aircraft operated restricted ground attack missions but the decision was taken in 1980 to extend this role to include a limited air defence capability. Between 1983 and 1986, 88 Hawk T1s, including the aircraft flown by the *Red Arrows*, were modified by British Aerospace to carry AIM-9 Sidewinder air-to-air missiles, for close air defence of vital assets such as airfields and radar installations.

Three RAF Hawks in different configurations – a T1 of No 4 FTS, RAF Valley in training scheme; a T1A with underwing Sidewinders and a centreline gun pod from No 208(R) Squadron; and a black-tailed T1A of No 92(R) Squadron at Chivenor, with rocket launcher pods.

THE RED ARROWS

Nine modified Hawk T1s were delivered to RAF Kemble in 1979 for use by the RAF's aerobatic team, the *Red Arrows,* that was still flying the Gnat through the 1979 display season. These Hawks, painted in the team's distinctive red colour scheme, incorporated modifications to the fuel system of the Adour turbofan engine, allowing a shorter throttle response time. On the fuselage centreline they carried a 70 Imp gallon smoke pod containing separate tank compartments for diesel oil and red and blue dye. When fed into the hot jet efflux, the diesel on its own creates white smoke, whilst injecting red or blue dye creates coloured smoke. The *Red Arrows* gave their first display with the new Hawks at RAF Kemble in November 1979 before invited members of the press, but it was not until April 1980 that the team gave its first public displays.

Today, acting as international ambassadors for Britain, they are renowned for their professional displays around the world. Before the start of the 2000 season, the *Red Arrows* had performed in 42 different countries – bringing the total of their public displays to over 3,500.

Illustrating the international nature of their displays, this dramatic photograph shows the *Red Arrows* over the Victoria Falls during a visit to Africa.

A flight with the RAF's premier aerobatic team

Michael Scarlett recalls a never-to-be-forgotten passenger flight in a Hawk with the *Red Arrows*:
"From the ground the formations look so neat, so precise – but in the midst of that red swarm maintaining position is obviously no easy job. As the aircraft fly through turbulence they move about, pitching and rolling like a fish in a rapid. I am now aware of the team talking to each other, or rather the team leader giving the orders. It had been 'Rolling, go' to initiate the simultaneous take-off. Now it was simply 'Pulling up' – and we swerve upwards, horizon sinking abruptly from sight to be replaced first by sky and then the sun, then sky again. My corset pneumatically inflates to clamp my belly, as 340kt horizontally changes to 330kt upwards, pulling me down into my seat."

"After the climb the world reappears into view, upside down and seemingly above me. I feel a delightful neutral near-floating sensation which lasts until the view ahead is filled entirely with fields, a road, and part of the aerodrome. According to the airspeed indicator we had been travelling at 130kt at the top of the *Red Arrows* arrival loop. But now I cannot take my eyes off the ground as seven tons of efficient arrow shape falls, pointing vertically, in company with eight other arrows."

"The recovery from that dive causes the g-suit to squeeze hard, the g-meter tells me that we have undergone 5g. As the g force eases, so the corset relaxes its embrace and we streak across the runway we had only taken off from minutes earlier."

"The leader's terse orders name each sequence,

timing manoeuvres from start to finish, or ordering smoke on and off. The other team members answer the moment they rejoin or complete a formation change. The chatter is difficult for an outsider to follow and it made me wonder how they understand each other."

"Now we are flying low and fast along the runway once more. The two aircraft in front suddenly shoot upwards, twisting out of formation to roll over back into life. Then it was our turn. Although the leader had warned me about this manoeuvre, that twisting roll banged my helmeted head against the canopy side."

"As we rolled inverted, I could first see the runway and then a hangar roof seemingly brush past my head. The varying speeds during each formation change are fascinating and the precision of the flying is well demonstrated every time we cut through the smoke trail left at the beginning of a loop, as we pull up at the bottom of the manoeuvre. This precision is best experienced by riding with one of the synchro pair."

"Our aircraft turns hard, wings vertical, the g meter registering 5g, smoke trailing. Our opposite number does the same thing, though his turn will be delayed by one second per knot of crosswind, if need be. I am clamped once more into my seat, eyes straining to peer upwards for a sight of the other converging aircraft. It is not recognisable as such at first, just a red dot with a white tail tapering behind but moving at an incredible speed into my field of view. It appears to tighten its turn towards us as though it is deliberately trying to collide with us, then flashes below us. Our aircraft thuds horribly as we hit the other aircraft's slipstream – our combined speed around 700mph. This is one of the few moments when one senses real speed, the majority of the other manoeuvres suggesting great velocity when heading for or flying close to the ground."

"After we had landed I climbed out slightly dazed, my stomach very uneasy. In spite of that I felt blissfully happy. I cannot think of any other experience that touches flying with the *Red Arrows*."

Above and right: Keeping each formation shape cohesive demands intense concentration from all the team members throughout the whole of the display.

239

END OF THE CENTURY
1990–1999

Panavia Tornado GR4A

SUKHOI'S FORMIDABLE FLANKER

T he Sukhoi Su-27 'Flanker' family of fighter aircraft is, alongside the MiG-29 'Fulcrum', one of the most successful series to emerge from the former Soviet Union – a jewel in the Soviet aerospace industry's crown.

The big, twin-turbofan Su-27 was originally designed to meet the challenging requirements of the IA-PVO – the Soviet long-range air defence arm. It was conceived during 1969, after the Sukhoi OKB won a design contract for an all-weather interceptor and long-range bomber escort to replace the Tu-128 'Fiddler', Su-15 'Flagon' and Yak-28P 'Firebar'. Despite serious problems with the original T-10-1 prototypes, together with a lengthy and difficult development period, Sukhoi eventually produced the pre-eminent Soviet fighter of the latter Cold War period.

At the design stage, Sukhoi was given a directive that the Su-27 had to outperform the USAF's F-15 Eagle in air-to-air combat. The increasing use of stand-off weapons made it necessary to intercept targets at very long range – preferably before their weapons could be launched – and to be capable of intercepting low-flying missiles.

First flown in prototype form on 20 May 1977 and entering service in December 1986, the Su-27 has a very large internal fuel capacity to enable an unmatched radius of action. It features an effective multi-spatial suite of sensors, with radar, infrared and laser rangefinding. It has twin vertical tailfins, together with ventral fins, widely-spaced underslung AL-31 turbofans, fly-by-wire control systems, a highly-blended wing/forebody, high-lift wing with ogival leading-edge root extensions, leading edge slats and a large dorsal airbrake. For a fighter it has great 'combat persistence' with up to twelve hardpoints for a range of sophisticated air-to-air missiles, including up to eight beyond-visual-range R-27 missiles, a laser rangefinder set allowing passive target detection and engagement, and rounding off with a reliable Zhuck look-down/shoot-down radar.

With a helmet-mounted weapon cueing system, the Su-27 is a formidable opponent in close-in dogfighting and, if well flown, can match the very best Western fighters.

Code named 'Flanker' by NATO, the fighter's superb manoeuvrability has been demonstrated since 1992 at airshows around the world by Anatoli Kvotchur, senior pilot at the Gromov Flight Test Institute at Zhukovsky near Moscow, giving performances which no Western front-line jet could emulate. These displays also demonstrated the predictable and safe handling characteristics at the extremes of the flight envelope, which, for example, gives the pilot unparalleled agility in low-speed flight.

A modified, stripped-down version – adapted from one of the T-10S prototypes (under the designation P-42) – shattered twenty-seven world records for time-to-climb and level speeds between 1986 and 1988, taking most from a similarly modified F-15 Streak Eagle. Particularly impressive was the amazing

Right: The Sukhoi Su-27K naval version of the 'Flanker' carries streamlined ECM pods on the wingtips, with white-painted dielectric fairings covering antennas fore and aft. On the ground below the aircraft is an ASM-MSS anti-ship missile.

Below: This pair of Sukhoi Su-27Ps of the Russian 'Test Pilots' display team were built to a special order, with no military systems. The aircraft have been frequent visitors to Western air shows.

Above: The Su-32FN, with two seats side-by-side, is a long-range maritime strike fighter with Russian Naval Aviation, but is land-based.

Below: The latest production Sukhoi Su-30MKI has thrust-vectoring engine nozzles and canard foreplanes, giving exceptional combat manoeuvrability.

record climb to 49,210ft in 70.33 seconds, almost seven seconds faster than a similarly prepared F-15 Streak Eagle.

The variety and ever-changing complexity of designations given to Su-27 variants underlines the design's versatility. Early production single-seat 'Flanker-Bs' for use by the Soviet Air Force were designated Su-27P and have subsequently been exported to China, Ethiopia, India, Syria, Ukraine and Vietnam as the Su-27SK (Series Kommercial). The Su-30 (or Su-27PU) was the production two-seat interceptor which has been further up-graded (Su-30MK) as a multi-role two-seater with new radar, canards and two-dimensional thrust vectoring nozzles and a fly-by-wire flight control system. First flown in 1996 as the Su-37, this variant has been ordered by India, as the Su-30MKI.

Development of a navalised, shipborne version of the Su-27 was launched at the same time as the Soviet carrier programme. The Su-27K was developed from the basic air force Su-27, with double-slotted, full-span, trailing edge flaps – the outboard sections of which operate differentially as drooping ailerons at low speeds – and an arrester hook. Originally designated by Sukhoi as the Su-33, the production Su-27K 'Flanker-D' is today the standard carrier capable air defence fighter version for the Russian Navy and equips the carrier *Kuznetsov*. This version has folding wings, canards, strengthened undercarriage, refuelling probe and arrester hook.

Originally known as the Su-27M, the Su-35 is fitted with canard foreplanes and has upgraded turbofans. It features a reprofiled nose (for a larger radar) and the tailcone houses a rearward-facing radar. A retractable inflight refuelling probe, taller squared-off fins (each containing an auxiliary fuel tank) and twin nose wheels are fitted.

The side-by-side two-seat Su-27IB was originally designed for the Russian Air Force as a fighter-bomber, while the Su-32FN was the Russian Naval Aviation land-based version. The current Su-32FN is a long-range maritime strike fighter that features a maritime search radar, sonobuoy launcher, MAD, laser rangefinder, wingtip ECM pods and seven LCD screen EFIS cockpit, while the Su-34 is a two-seat air force version intended for long-range strike, to replace older types such as the Su-17, MiG-27 and Su-24 'Fencer'. The Su-34 has twin nosewheels, tandem main undercarriage units, canards, AL-35F turbofans, a Leninetz phased array multi-function terrain following radar, a retractable inflight refuelling probe, broader chord tailfins and modern avionics. Behind the two crew seats in the humped fuselage is a small galley and toilet.

Sukhoi continues to develop its 'Flanker' family despite Russia's current economic crisis. Upgraded early models remain in service, together with later variants - and remain potent adversaries. The most recent Su-27 variants are radical developments of the original 'Flanker' interceptor – their evolution has been shrouded in some confusion and not a little mystery – but they do feature a deadly combination of long-range 'reach' and attack punch. Although few firm sales have been achieved, the West has been reminded that Russia can still produce fighters equal to the latest Western designs.

Looking to the future, the Sukhoi S-37 with its radical swept-forward wings, displayed to the public for the first time at Zhukovsky in August 1999, is testimony to the advanced designs still evolving from Sukhoi.

The experimental Sukhoi S-37 Berkut is a radical design with swept-forward wings and canard foreplanes. The aircraft was displayed to the public for the first time at Zhukovsky, near Moscow in August 1999.

CHRONOLOGY

15 January 1990
In South Africa, the Atlas Corporation rolled out its XH-2 Rooivalk two-seat ground support and escort helicopter.

26 January 1990
The Boeing VC-25A 'Air Force One' presidential aircraft made its first flight.

6 March 1990
A Lockheed SR-71A Blackbird set four records when it made its last USAF flight.

14 March 1990
The first two-seat AMX International AMX-T two-seat operational trainer and maritime attack aircraft made its first flight in Italy.

1 June 1990
US Strategic Air Command FB-111As were assigned to Tactical Air Command.

1 July 1990
The first of seven E-3D Sentry AEW1s arrived with the RAF to join No 8 Squadron.

2 August 1990
The Iraqi Air Force supported an unprovoked invasion of Kuwait.

8 August 1990
The first US combat aircraft, ordered to defend the Gulf States against aggression from Iraq, arrived in Saudi Arabia.

11 August 1990
RAF Tornado F3s on APC in Cyprus relocated to the Saudi Arabian Air Force base at Dhahran. On the same day, Jaguar GR1As departed the UK for the Omani Air Force base at Thumrait. Operation *Granby* had commenced.

20 August 1990
The first of a major deployment of F-117A stealth attack aircraft was made to Saudi Arabia.

27 August 1990
Initial flight of the YF-23A – the first of two advanced tactical fighter contenders.

29 September 1990
The first prototype Lockheed/General Dynamics/Boeing YF-22A made its maiden flight.

10 October 1990
The first of four Boeing E-3F AWACS aircraft was delivered to the French Air Force.

21 November 1990
The NAMC/PAC K-8 two-seat basic trainer and light ground attack aircraft made its first flight in China.

FIGHTING FALCON

When considering the Lockheed Martin F-16's operational career, the Gulf War of 1991 must rank as the high point, as *Desert Storm* witnessed the type's combat début in USAF service. Despite the fact that the F-16 Fighting Falcon possesses genuine multi-role capability, and could therefore have contributed to the task of maintaining continuous combat air patrol (CAP) cover throughout the war, this mission was entrusted to dedicated air superiority fighters like the F-15 Eagle. Their exploits quickly resulted in the threat posed by Iraqi interceptors being all but eliminated during the first few days of the

A quartet of early production F-16As flying with the USAF's 347th TFW. These aircraft were later modified as 'Air Defence Fighters' for service with the Air National Guard.

Right: This Turkish Air Force F-16 was one of 26 Fighting Falcons that took part in Exercise *Determined Falcon* on 15 June 1998, when NATO put on a massive show of force over Albania and Macedonia.

aerial onslaught, which meant that the F-16 could be employed predominantly on air-to-ground missions throughout the conflict.

In the process, it made a significant contribution in preparing the way for the hugely successful and swift ground war that culminated in the liberation of Kuwait and also decimated Iraq's potential to wage effective warfare. With almost 250 examples operating from a handful of bases in the Gulf region and Turkey, the F-16 was by far the most numerous USAF tactical aircraft in the theatre and it is hardly surprising that it won the distinction of being described as both the 'workhorse' and the 'backbone' of the Coalition air effort.

While it may not have claimed any aerial victories in the 1991 confrontation, subsequent developments in the Gulf area have resulted in further shows of strength and US warplanes have been called into action several times, particularly in the Balkans throughout the 1990s.

However, when it comes to the art of knocking adversaries from the sky, the Israeli Defence Force/Air Force (IDF/AF) has repeatedly demonstrated that it has few peers, with most informed sources acknowledging that at least 45 aircraft and helicopters have fallen victim to F-16s flown by personnel of the IDF/AF since 1982, although the tally could possibly be even higher.

CHRONOLOGY

17 January 1991
Operation *Desert Storm* began with a strike by F-117As on targets in Baghdad and southern Iraq.

19 January 1991
The second Rockwell/MBB X-31A manoeuvrability demonstrator aircraft made its initial flight, following attachment of thrust-vectoring paddles.

22 January 1991
F-111F Aardvarks used laser-guided 'smart bombs' for the first time, against hardened aircraft shelters at Al Asad AB in Iraq.

10 February 1991
Service début of Tornados with TIALD (Thermal Imaging and Laser Designation) pods.

18 April 1991
USAF completed the first successful flight test of the Martin Marietta/Boeing ICBM (small version). The flight trajectory was 4,000 miles from Vandenberg AFB to the Pacific Island target area at the Kwajalein missile range.

23 April 1991
The USAF selected the YF-22A as its advanced tactical fighter.

Into Desert Storm

General Colin Powell, Chairman of the Joint Chiefs of Staff said, "the people who designed and made…M1 tanks and F-16 aircraft…gave our troops the decisive edge". The following account from an F-16 pilot underlines the impact that the Fighting Falcon had on the conflict. Lt Col William C Diehl, USAF, at that time Commander of the 17th Tactical Fighter Squadron based at Shaw AFB, SC, spoke of his deployment to Al Dhafra, Sharjah, UAE where his squadron formed part of the 363rd Tactical Fighter Wing (Provisional).

"On 7 August 1990, we were alerted for deployment to Saudi Arabia. We began deploying our people and equipment two days later on C-5 Galaxy and C-141 StarLifter aircraft, with intermediate stops en route to the Persian Gulf. As for deploying the aircraft; 24 of our jets took off at 5 o'clock in the afternoon for a long 16-hours or so non-stop flight with ten air refuelings. The sun went down as we began flying across the Atlantic and came up as we entered the Mediterranean at Gibraltar. We flew south over Egypt and across Saudi Arabia before landing at our destination, just prior to sunset."

"Our deployment was unprecedented for a large-scale movement of fighter aircraft. We broke several records; never before had a fighter squadron successfully launched and recovered all its aircraft, without any air spares, on this long a flight. Prior to our deployment the F-16 aircraft had never flown this long a mission. It was truly a challenge for both man and machine. I wish you could have seen our pilots climbing out of their jets after this gruelling flight and helping each other chock and pin the aircraft with a look of exhaustion yet excitement in their eyes."

"We were the first from the Wing in-country and had to park, bed-down, and secure the jets ourselves. The rest of our people started arriving the next day. Eight days after Saddam's troops invaded Kuwait, our squadron was in place, loaded, and on alert."

"Now for the war. On the morning of 16 January, we got the word that we were to execute Operation *Desert Storm* early the next morning. It was not at all a surprise, but we all swallowed hard when told that we were actually going to do it. The Wing could not have been better prepared. We had started planning the first day's missions four and a half months earlier."

"To accomplish the mission planning, we had a top secret room built within our intelligence office, only an absolute limited number of our people were briefed on

A 363rd TFW (Provisional) F-16C landing back at Al Dhafra after a mission over Iraq.

what was going on. Not a word was mentioned about this operation outside the top secret room. We conducted three different conferences with representatives from all the different units throughout the theatre to co-ordinate the most minute of details concerning the first missions of the operation."

"The Wing practised flying these missions on ranges in Saudi Arabia some twelve times. The majority of our pilots were not told they were practising the mechanics of the mission they would soon be called upon to fly for real. We had actually briefed the 'Day One' afternoon mission during four separate general officer visits and to the Secretary of the Air Force."

"Finally, one week before the war, we briefed the Chief of Staff of the Air Force. Following the briefing, he called CinC CENTAF and told him we were the most combat-ready and best prepared Wing in the Command.

That was a real confidence builder for us as we prepared for what we would soon have to do. Although we didn't think so at the time, our being over here five months early was a real blessing. It enabled us to do intensive training, studying, and design of theatre specific tactics for large force employment that we would have never been able to do at home."

"On 17 January, our morning package took off hours before sunrise for a night rendezvous with their cell of tankers and their F-15 air-cover. The sun was just starting to light the horizon as the package crossed the Iraqi border. At sunrise, our bombs were smashing their targets, letting Saddam's military know 'the fight was on'. The morning attack was a complete success. I can't describe the almost overwhelming feeling of pride all of us on the ground felt as we watched the formations of aircraft return to base and pitch out overhead for landing. It seemed that the entire base turned out to welcome the morning pilots. Our afternoon fliers didn't have time to hear the combat stories for we had to immediately start our own mission briefing. We took off at mid-afternoon and rendezvoused with our numerous other airborne assets. Our target was located deep in the heart of enemy territory."

"The package pushed across the Iraqi border a half hour before sunset. Ten minutes across the border our airborne warning and control (AWACS) aircraft warned us of our first enemy reaction – two MiG-29 *Fulcrums* airborne, turned towards our formation. Within a few minutes our pre-strike sweep of F-15s were on them and blew them out of the sky. As we made our last turn and headed for our target, the on-board radar warning receiver started lighting up and indicated an array of surface-to-air missile systems (SAMS) and anti-aircraft artillery (AAA) covering both front quadrants – they knew we were coming."

"Although there was a broken cloud layer below, we were able to pick out our individual targets at around ten miles. SA-2 and SA-3 SAMs were launched to the left of our formation. As we rolled in on our target, I informed our trailing flights that the weather was good enough for our primary attack plan, meaning that they wouldn't have to use a weather

backup radar attack. Following release of our weapons, we checked back to see if anything was coming up from the target after us. Tremendous explosions were going off at all our assigned target locations and the sky was filling with 37 mm AAA white puffy airbursts."

"By the time our last aircraft pulled off target they said you could have gotten out and walked on the layer of flak left by the AAA. Sometimes it's good to be in and out first! Our package reformed and raced out of the enemy territory. We rendezvoused with post-strike tankers and returned home at night for another super welcoming. The mission went exactly as we had planned, briefed, and practised."

"The rest of the week was pretty much the same as that first day. During Vietnam, I thought I witnessed some great air battles over Hanoi, but the intensity of our first week exceeded anything I remember."

"I completed my 100th combat hour in the F-16 on 12 February 1991. Completing 100 combat-hours in less than a month was quite an accomplishment for me, but says even more for the aircraft and our aircraft maintenance folks. In the last 27 days, I flew 28 missions without a single ground or air abort, or even late takeoff. Twenty of the flights returned with a Code One (a discrepancy-free aircraft) and believe me, the aircraft was really being worked out in the target area."

Return to base – with its 2,000lb Mk.84 bombs gone, a 363rd FS F-16C taxies in to the dispersal. The unit deployed to the Gulf from Shaw AFB, South Carolina on 9 August 1990.

CHRONOLOGY

27 April 1991
The prototype Eurocopter Tigre anti-tank and ground support helicopter flew for the first time in France.

19 May 1991
The first Dassault-Breguet Rafale CO1 made its first flight in France.

1 June 1991
The improved MC-130H Combat Talon II Hercules entered active service with USAF Special Operations Command.

15 July 1991
A specially modified F/A-18 Hornet high-angle of attack research vehicle (HARV) was flown with thrust-vectoring nozzles and a closed-loop controlled, three-axis command system.

15 September 1991
First flight of the McDonnell Douglas C-17A Globemaster III heavy-lift transport aircraft.

15 September 1991
The prototype of the T-1 Jayhawk flew at Edwards AFB. In USAF service, the Jayhawk was to be used for specialised undergraduate pilot training.

12 December 1991
Maiden flight of the Dassault Rafale M.

1 January 1992
USAFE activated the 100th Air Refueling Wing at RAF Mildenhall and began preparations to accept the first of nine permanently resident KC-135R Stratotankers destined for service with the European Tanker Task Force (ETTF).

4 March 1992
Two B-52 Stratofortresses landed in Russia on a friendship mission, demonstrating that the Cold War was over. This was the first landing by US bombers in Russia since WW2.

24 March 1992
The US joined 24 other nations in signing the Open Skies Treaty, which allowed unarmed aerial reconnaissance flights over any signatory nation.

6 July 1992
RAF Tornado F3s flew via Ascension Island to the Falklands, where they replaced Phantoms.

6 September 1992
RAF Tornados flew to Dhahran to assist US forces upholding the air exclusion zone over southern Iraq, south of the 32nd Parallel.

18 January 1993
The USA, Britain, France, Canada, Germany and other nations airlifting relief supplies to Sarajevo, Bosnia, established a joint air operation cell in Zagreb, Croatia.

DYNAMIC EAGLE

Spawned from the long-range air combat requirements of the Vietnam War, and proved by the Israelis in dogfights and escort missions, the McDonnell Douglas F-15 Eagle is one of the world's greatest post-war all-weather day/night superiority fighters.

The original F-X requirement had called for a single-seat, twin-engined aircraft to perform the fighter sweep, escort and CAP missions – and it was suggested that it had to be twice as good as the F-4E Phantom in terms of rate of climb, acceleration and radius of turn. It had to achieve absolute superiority by deflecting the advanced fighter threat in any and all types of aerial combat, at minimum weight and cost.

The F-15 received formal approval in January 1970 – being the first completely new fighter developed specifically for the USAF since the F-101 Voodoo, which first flew on 29 September 1954. The first F-15A had its maiden flight on 27 July 1972, being followed by the two-seat F-15B on 7 July 1973. It had a relatively low-wing loading and a thrust/weight ratio in excess of unity – the first time so much power (the Pratt & Whitney F100 afterburning turbofans) had been installed in a non-V/STOL aircraft.

Armed with the well-proven General Electric M61 Vulcan gun (that arms most contemporary US fighters) the F-15 received the Hughes APG-63 X-band pulsed Doppler radar with an all-aspect, look-down, shoot-down capability, in combination with AIM-7F Sparrow and AIM-9L Sidewinder missiles.

In several respects the F-15 bears a strong family resemblance to the preceding F-4, despite being a completely new design. The highly tapered fixed geometry moderately swept

Eagle CAP

Captain Anthony Schiavi, an Eagle pilot with the 33rd Tactical Fighter Wing's 58th Tactical Fighter Squadron describes a successful fighter combat air patrol nine days into the Gulf War, as recorded in 'Gulf War Debrief', (Aerospace Publishing 1991):

"We're running our intercept against the second group of MiG-23s to take off from H2. They're at low altitude. They're below 1,000ft. On our radar, as awesome as it is, at 80 miles we're painting these guys and we can see them at low altitude. It's so funny. Here, war is happening. And it's just like training. There's three blips on your screen. They're in standard 'Bic' formation."

"We're coming in about 30 miles from the merge. We punch our wing-tanks off, but keep the centreline tank on. Okay, so we have better manoeuvrability now if we get an engagement in this thing. If the man decides to engage us and our missiles don't work or whatever, we'll be able to turn more tightly without those tanks."

"The critical decision as you get within 20 miles is, 'Okay, who's going to target who?'"

"That's Captain Draeger's job as Number One to decide. So he does that. He says, 'Okay' – his philosophy is that, hey, I'm going to take the map-reader first, and that's usually the guy that's leading the thing, everybody else will go, 'Oh, shit, what do we do now?' – so he targets the leader, or the map reader as he calls him."

"He targets me as Number Two on the northwestern trailer. Draeger and I are One and Two. Now there's only one (Iraqi) left so he says, 'Okay, Three and Four, both of you take the southernmost guy.'"

During the Gulf War more than 2,200 missions were flown by F-15s (totalling some 7,700 hours of combat time), resulting in 32 aerial victories.

"We acknowledge. I say, CHEVRON 2, sorted. 270. 25 miles. It's just like William Tell. If they were closer together, it might be necessary to refer them by using a BRA call, meaning bearing, range and altitude – but that's not necessary."

"So we're coming in and the other thing we're looking at is, are we spiked or not spiked (locked up by the other guy)? That's our other indication of whether they know we're there, our RWR scope. At this point, there's no indication – but you can never be sure your system is working accurately."

"So the flight lead has called the target plan and now we have to do is lock the guy we're supposed to lock, and shoot. Like I said, we got an early 'bandit, bandit' call on these guys at about 35 or 40 miles so we know these guys are bad, which takes a lot of guesswork out. We take our shots, Captain Draeger shoots first. We're now well inside 20 miles. He shoots. His missile comes off. I shoot next. Just a couple of seconds after him. Because Bruce and Rico are offset from us, they have to wait a little longer before they get in range so it's probably several more seconds before you hear Rico fire."

"As the missiles start flying off, we pick up the first tally-hos (visual sightings) about 10 miles from the merge. We can see the 'Floggers' running across the desert, fast. A lot of times you can see the missile, you can keep a tally-ho on that missile."

"Captain Draeger's missile hits his man, hits him right in the back – the old 'Flogger' running across the ground, there – and he's flying so low you can see the dust kick up around it. He calls, 'Splash'. Then he looks again. The airplane flies right through the fireball and comes out the other side. It hit him but didn't just knock him out of the sky. He's burning but not down. Captain Draeger goes to a heater (prepares to fire a Sidewinder heat-seeking missile), to put some heat on this big fire. But before he can do this, the fire reaches the wing root and it suddenly explodes in a huge fireball. I'm so busy watching this guy blow up – so amazed by the damage the warhead did, that I've almost forgotten my own missile."

"Right about then, my missile (hits) my guy, I call a second, 'Splash'. There's another big fireball. After the first guy blows up, the other two guys do a hard, right-hand turn, right into us. Whether they picked up late

The F-15 Eagle has been the USAF's premier fighter since the late 1970s, subsequently undergoing many improvements to keep it at the forefront of the air superiority role.

visual on us, and saw us, and were coming down through the clouds, or what, I don't know – but what they were doing was too late and my missile hit him."

"As for what the MiG-23s looked like, they were camo'd and they were two-and-a-half to three miles in front of us when they actually blew up, so we saw them pretty well. Number Four's missiles were maybe two seconds late, so Number Three, Captain Rodriguez, got the kill."

"There was a road right underneath them. I think they were navigating following the road. The first guy blows up and the other two blow up on the side of the road – three fireballs right in a row. My guy blows up, zoom, and a moment later I hear Rodriguez call the third 'Splash'."

"We call AWACS and tell them that we've splashed three fireballs. AWACS says, 'Say type,' and that's when we say, 'Floggers'. We didn't use any code word. We just said 'Floggers'."

For many years, the standard missile armament of the F-15 comprised four AIM-9 Sidewinders on the wing launch rails and four AIM-7 Sparrows on the fuselage 'corner' stations. The Eagle's internal M61 AI cannon is provided with 920 rounds.

CHRONOLOGY

1 March 1993
Six RAF Tornado F3s were deployed to Italy to help UN forces monitor the 'No Fly Zone' over Bosnia.

14 March 1993
The first flight took place of an EF-111A Raven upgraded by the System Improvement Programme – the first major upgrade for EF-111As since delivery in 1981.

1 April 1993
USAF units in Alaska participated in the first joint exercise with the Russian Air Force – a search and rescue exercise in Siberia.

29 July 1993
First flight of the Tornado GR4 development aircraft for the GR1/GR1A Mid-Life Upgrade (MLU) programme.

1 July 1993
RAF Jaguars were deployed to Italy to enforce a 'No Fly Zone' over Bosnia, as part of Operation *Deny Flight*.

17 December 1993
The first B-2 Spirit, the USAF's first stealth heavy bomber, entered service.

25 January 1994
A USAF Titan II booster launched the unmanned space probe *Clementine I* towards the moon. This was the first lunar mission since Apollo 17 in 1972.

7 February 1994
A Titan IV missile boosted the first Military Strategic and Tactical Relay satellite into geostationary orbit.

24 February 1994
The first Slingsby T-3A Fireflies were accepted for service with the USAF Air Education and Training Command.

13 March 1994
The first Taurus booster launched two military satellites.

27 March 1994
The prototype Eurofighter DA1 made its first flight from Manching, Germany.

1 April 1994
The USAF removed the last of 150 LGM-30F Minuteman II missiles from Ellsworth AFB, implementing part of the Strategic Arms Reduction Treaty between the United States and Russia.

wing is broadly in line with F-4 practice, although it is set high on the fuselage and avoids the need for the steep outboard dihedral of its predecessor. Another important consideration was all-round view, and the F-15 provided one of the best rear view of any fighter since the F-86 Sabre, with the pilot seated high in a bubble canopy.

Combat effectiveness also benefitted from the use of an advanced head-up display (HUD) and the fact that most of the control functions needed in combat can be carried out without the pilot removing his hands from the control column and throttles (HOTAS – hands-on-throttle-and-stick). The Eagle entered USAF service in November 1974.

Eagles have also been supplied to the air forces of Israel (under the *Peace Fox* programme), where they went into action on 27 June 1979, Japan (*Peace Eagle*) and Saudi Arabia (*Peace Sun*). In December 1999 it was revealed that some USAF F-15Cs were being further developed and fitted with a new active-array radar to gain operational before the F-22 Raptor enters service. This Raytheon APG-63(V)2 radar has a longer detection range and can track multi-targets, including incoming cruise missiles.

TORNADO GOES TO WAR

T he RAF's Panavia Tornado GR1 quickly found its niche in the Gulf War coalition war effort and contributed much to the successful outcome. Three reinforced squadrons – averaging fifteen aircraft and twenty-four crews each – were based at Tabuk and Dhahran in Saudi Arabia and Muharraq on Bahrain.

Initially the Tabuk aircraft were operated in the defence and suppression role, making their combat débuts fitted with BAe ALARMs (Air-Launched Anti-Radiation Missiles). Subsequently five aircraft had provision for TIALD (Thermal Imaging And Laser Designation) pods. In addition, six Tornado GR1As were based at Dhahran for reconnaissance. A total of 60 Tornados took part in the bombing and reconnaissance campaign.

At the start of Operation *Desert Storm* the Coalition formulated a programme of airfield denial with the GR1 and its purpose-designed Hunting JP233 airfield-denial bomblet dispenser as a key element, together with the task of attacks against *Scud* launchers. These were flown at very low level where the Tornado's multi-role, terrain-following ground-mapping radar provided excellent service.

Despite the early collapse of the Iraqi Air Force's air operations, the ground defence took its toll. Four Tornados were lost while on low-flying missions during the opening phase of the air war. After a few days it was decided to move attacks up to medium altitude – above 20,000ft, where only the larger SAMs and AAA could reach. By early February 1991, when total air supremacy allowed regular daylight raids to augment those flown at night, dawn or dusk, these revised tactics had reduced both losses and accuracy – but precision returned with the arrival of laser-designators, initially provided by Pave Spike-equipped Buccaneer S2Bs.

The subsequent arrival of the TIALD-equipped Tornados allowed Tabuk to switch to precision guided munitions for its attack missions. Such operations were particularly successful against bridges and hardened aircraft shelters, command

Introduced hurriedly into service during the Gulf War, the ALARM anti-radar missile was carried by Tornado GR1s of No 9 Squadron. They are still carried by RAF Tornados when deployed to the Gulf or the Balkans.

Right: RAF Tornado GR1s equipped with JP233 airfield denial weapons, which were used to good effect during the early days of the Gulf conflict.

CHRONOLOGY

6 April 1994
The BAe-constructed British prototype of the Eurofighter 20000 made its first flight at Warton.

7 April 1994
First flight of the two-seat BAe Harrier T10.

22 June 1994
Russia joined NATO's 'Partnership for Peace' programme and detargeted its strategic missiles away from western countries.

1 August 1994
F-16C Fighting Falcons successfully launched twelve AGM-88 High-Speed Anti-radiation missiles in an air-to-ground weapon system evaluation programme conducted at the Utah Test and Training Range.

2 August 1994
Two B-52 Stratofortresses set a world record for circumnavigating the earth during a Global Power mission to Kuwait. The 47hr flight involved five aerial refuellings.

4 October 1994
USAF F-16 Fighting Falcons replaced the last F-4 Phantom *Wild Weasel* aircraft performing the suppression of enemy air defence missions.

An RAF Tornado GR1 carrying a TIALD (Thermal Imaging and Laser Designating) pod returning from a mission over Iraq. Also prominent are the 2,250-litre underwing fuel tanks borrowed from the Tornado F3 force.

bunkers, fuel/ammunition stores and runways/taxiways. Throughout the laser-bombing phase only one Tornado was shot down (by a pair of SA-2 SAMs) at medium altitude.

The Tornado GR1 force flew over 1,600 bombing sorties, during which it delivered over 100 JP233s and some 4,250 free-fall bombs and 950 LGBs. They were certainly among the busiest of Allied warplanes during the campaign.

The Tornado's small, variable geometry wing gave its two-man crew a very comfortable ride in most flight regimes – especially during high-speed, low-level missions. During *Desert Storm* all wing pylons were occupied by pods or fuel tanks and the Tornado's offensive load was carried almost exclusively under the fuselage.

The combined reconnaissance unit which operated in the Gulf theatre achieved notoriety as the 'Scudbusters' yet its success was far from assured when it had departed Europe a mere two days before the start of hostilities. The Tornado GR1A represented a major departure from standard recce practice in dispensing with traditional film. All its images are recorded on video tape from sensors which can

Desert Storm – Day One

An RAF Tornado pilot recalled his impressions at the start of Operation *Desert Storm*.

"After 0012hr GMT on 17 February 1991, the words 'Iraq' and 'enemy' became synonymous. The first RAF combat missions were launched weighed down by a pair of JP233 airfield-denial dispensers and extra large drop tanks. We dragged ourselves off the ground at an unaccustomed weight of 30.5 tonnes and turned towards the Iraqi targets."

"It was a very, very black night – probably one of the darkest I have flown on. Once you get out over the desert, especially over Iraq, there are no lights on the ground. You are flying very low. We saw the odd Bedouin encampment flash by on the left-hand side of the wing."

"Our appointment with the airfield defences was to be a lonely one, but we were far from being without friends as we cast off from the tanker and began descending to 200ft as enemy airspace was entered. Keeping watch over us were three E-3 Sentries, which would warn the attacking force of any air-threats."

"Hurtling over Talil at a height of 180ft on the radar altimeter, we scattered JP233s over the sprawling base's parallel runways and associated taxiways. It was absolutely terrifying. There's no other word for it. You are frightened of failure, you are frightened of dying, you are flying as low as you dare but high enough to get the weapons off. You put in as low as you can get over the target – just to get away as fast as you can."

"So ended the Tornado GR1's first 24 hours of *Desert Storm*, during which some 60 sorties were flown, including 44 with JP233s. The aircraft, the ALARM missile and the JP233 had all seen their combat débuts, but at the cost of two Tornados. Attrition of 3.3% was well below the double figures sustained at Bomber Command's darkest times in WW2 – but aircrew did not need a calculator to conclude that they could not survive a 'tour' of 30 missions if the wartime system was to be re-introduced."

"Day One was, for the Tornado, both a moment of supreme triumph and extreme tragedy. Those who said it could only get better were, for a change, right."

A GR1 in the Gulf with ALARM missiles on the fuselage launch rails, underwing fuel tanks and fitted with AIM-9L Sidewinders on the wing pylons, plus BOZ-107 chaff/flare pod and Sky Shadow jammer outboard.

operate at night with no artificial form of illumination. Beneath the GR1A's forward fuselage is the aperture for a Vinten 4000 horizon-to-horizon infrared linescan, whilst on each side, ahead of the intakes are BAe side-facing infrared sensors to provide a less distorted view of the middle distance. Six video recorders complete the package normally occupied by the two 27mm cannon.

At Night – by Stealth

The USAF's Lockheed F-117 Nighthawk 'stealth fighters' always struck at night. They were the only Allied aircraft to fly missions against the heavily defended targets in downtown Baghdad. Therefore it came as no surprise when revealed after the war that F-117s operated against 31% of targets in the first 24 hours of *Desert Storm*. Although assigned the most dangerous targets, no F-117 was damaged by the Iraqi air defences during the entire campaign.

Average F-117 missions were over five hours long and a number of in-flight refuellings

In addition to having a tiny radar signature, the F-117 Nighthawk has a very low infrared signature, due to the use of non-afterburning engines and its wide, diffusing engine exhausts.

'Black Jet' over Baghdad

USAF Lieutenant Colonel Barry E. Horne of the 415th Tactical Fighter Squadron wrote this account of his 'Wobblin Goblin' missions in the Gulf.

"Our guiding principle was that we concentrated on high-value, heavily defended targets – which lent themselves to the use of precision-guided munitions. Because of our stealth characteristics we were able to loiter over the targets, thus ensuring our weapons hit home. We scored 80-85% bomb hit rates (compared to 30-35% typical in Vietnam) – often against targets as small as windows and ventilation shafts."

"There were lots of communication targets. We wanted to cut Baghdad communications, but we were not sure where Saddam Hussein was running his war from. Combat missions could last up to six hours. It would start the day before, getting the tasking mid-to late-evening. Mission planning people would look at the task, co-ordinating with other agencies – like air defences, but most importantly with tankers."

"We'd plan to launch in daylight, late afternoon, wanting to use as much of the night over the target as possible. We might fly two or three waves a night. Some targets were close together, and we'd go in a package – while others were widely spread."

"Being the aircraft it is, the F-117 needed far less support on operations. Occasionally we had EF-111 Ravens and F-4G Phantoms, but the whole point about the 'Black Jet' is its ability to work in the face of the Electronic Warfare threats these aircraft were designed to counter – so our mission did not depend on them."

were essential. Its much-publicised 'stealth' properties allowed the aircraft to operate undetected over Iraq, while its dual infrared weapons system and laser-guided bombs gave it the ability to attack targets with great precision.

F-117s flew a total of 1,271 combat missions during *Desert Storm*, penetrating the massed defences of an estimated 3,000 AAA pieces and 60 surface-to-air missile sites. The GBU-27 Paveway III was the standard weapon, available with Mk 84 high explosive or BLU-10C penetration warheads.

CHRONOLOGY

28 October 1994
The first re-engined examples of the Lockheed U-2R, re-designated U-2S, were handed back to the USAF.

31 October 1994
Two B-1B Lancer bombers flew non-stop from the USA to a bombing range in Kuwait and back. The 25hr mission marked the first time that B-1s had flown to the Persian Gulf.

1 January 1995
The RAF E-3D Sentry AEW1 component of the NATO Airborne Early Warning (AEW) Force was declared fully operational.

17 January 1995
The C-17A Globemaster III entered operational service with Air Mobility Command.

1 February 1995
The first of the RAF's six new Sea King HAR3A Search and Rescue helicopters made its maiden flight.

24 March 1995
The last USAF Atlas Minuteman E booster, a converted ICBM from the 1960s, launched a satellite into polar orbit.

29 March 1995
The Tier III Minus Dark Star, a stealthy drone designed for high-altitude, long-duration reconnaissance missions over hostile enemy territory, completed its first test flight.

2 June 1995
Two USAF B-1B Lancer bombers flew around the world in a record 36hr 13min – refuelled in flight six times.

17 August 1995
The E-8C joint surveillance target attack radar system (J- STARS) aircraft began flight tests – the sophisticated radar aircraft that replaced the experimental version used during the Gulf War.

30 August 1995
NATO aircraft began air strikes on Serb positions in Bosnia in support of the United Nations – Operation *Deliberate Force*.

28 October 1995
Start of Operation *Vigilant Sentinel*, where the USAF first tested the Air Expeditionary Force concept, when F-16s deployed to Bahrain.

5 April 1996
Northrop Grumman delivered the first E-8C J-STARS to the USAF.

5 April 1996
The first of twenty-five Lockheed C-130J-30 Hercules IIs ordered for the RAF made its maiden flight at Marietta, GA.

ATTACK HELICOPTER

This AH-64A Apache displays a typical warload of Hellfires and two 19-round Hydra 70 rocket pods. The TADS/PNVS sensor array in the nose is evident.

There can be little doubt that the AH-64 Apache established itself as the world's premier attack helicopter with its notable achievements in the Gulf War. Conceived originally by Hughes, and developed by McDonnell Douglas, the Apache programme is now the responsibility of the Boeing Corporation.

Although the lineage of the attack helicopter in US service can be traced to Southeast Asia, the roots of the Apache lie firmly in Europe. First flown on 30 September 1975, the Apache did not enter service until 1984 and became operational in 1986. Significant design features include two shoulder-mounted GE T700 turboshafts, crew armour, aerobatic capability, a high degree of survivability and a nose-mounted AAQ-11 TADS/PNVS (Target Acquisition and Designation Sight/Pilot Night Vision Sensor.

Some 840 AH-64s were built for the US Army and for export. Many are now being upgraded to either AH-64D or Longbow Apache standard - ushering in a new era of the 'omnipotent' battlefield helicopter. The AH-64D features improved avionics housed

Apache on the attack

Lieutenant Colonel William Bryan of the US Army 2nd Battalion, 229th Aviation Regiment, described his attacks on Iraqi armour during Operation *Desert Storm*:
"The Iraqis showed little or no desire to fight. They had the equipment – but they did not have the resolve. Had the Iraqis been an armoured force we would have made stand-off attacks, but in this case we shot them

with 30mm cannon fire to get them stopped and the troops dismounted. Then we fired three Hellfires, which took out the three lead vehicles."

"From that point on we were able to finish them off with 30mm and 2.75in rockets. Hellfire is for point targets, something hard that has to be engaged with a precision munition with a lot of penetration. It is laser-guided, fired by the gunner in the front seat. You acquire the target, illuminate it with a laser and fire the missile.

The missile will hit the point illuminated by the laser, and will do it at ranges of more than five kilometres. The 2.75 is a good weapon if you have a lot of vehicles or personnel in a small area, and can strike from a good stand-off distance. They were extremely effective against trucks. The Chain Gun is in between– it is officially an area weapon, but it is extremely accurate and will penetrate light armour if you are within two kilometres."

"Our greatest concerns were the Iraqi shoulder-fired

Apart from the Longbow mast-mounted radar, this AH-64D is distinguished by the modified fuselage side fairings, which have been enlarged to cover the wing root and extend to the nose.

in enlarged cheek fairings, while full standard Longbow Apaches feature the Northrop Grumman mast-mounted millimetre wave radar, able to guide a radio frequency seeker Hellfire missile. The British Army is receiving the Longbow Apache in 2000, following the maiden flight of the first GKN Westland-assembled example, which took place on 26 August 1999. The 57 WAH-64s will replace the Army Air Corps' Lynx helicopters for anti-armour and battlefield gunship tasks.

air-defence weapons. By flying at low altitude and letting the ground clutter mask our signature, we could get around sophisticated long-range systems. But with the man-pack SAMs, one person in a hole in the ground can take you out."

"We flew a number of joint attack missions with A-10 Thunderbolts and F-16 Fighting Falcons. Normally we would be using artillery, but we were so far ahead that most of the time we were out of range. Generally we were at the greatest advantage over the Iraqis in combat at night."

"Any targets that we found were destroyed – over 800 tanks and tracked vehicles, 500 other military vehicles, 60 bunkers/radar sites, 14 helicopters, ten combat aircraft, plus innumerable artillery and AAA positions, were claimed by our Apaches. A total of 2,876 Hellfires were fired by our AH-64s and all aircraft damaged during fighting managed to return to base."

CHRONOLOGY

24 April 1996
An F-15 Eagle of the ACTIVE programme, equipped with thrust-vectoring engine nozzles, made its first supersonic 'yaw-vectored' flight.

30 April 1996
The *Tacit Blue* test aircraft, that was used secretly to test stealth technologies until 1985, was revealed by the USAF. It furnished the technology used to produce the B-2A Spirit bomber.

8 July 1996
It was revealed that the conventional warfare capability of the B-2A Spirit had taken a big step forward following delivery of the first seventeen (of an eventual total of 128) Global Positioning System-Aided Munitions (GAMS).

3 September 1996
The USAF received the Predator, an unmanned aerial vehicle designed for aerial surveillance and reconnaissance. Flights over Bosnia-Herzegovina helped the US to ensure a peace agreement there.

1 October 1996
After fifteen years in storage, both YC-15As were returned to service by McDonnell Douglas to act as technology test-beds for the development of future cargo aircraft.

1 January 1997
First production example of the AC-130U 'Spectre' gunship was issued to the USAF Special Operations Squadron.

1 April 1997
The B-2A Spirit obtained its Initial Operational Capability (IOC).

RUSSIA'S HIND

While the anti-armour attack-helicopter concept was being developed by Hughes/McDonnell Douglas in the USA, the Soviet Mil design bureau was working on a similar project at the same time, the Mil Mi-24 'Hind', first flown in 1973. The 'Hind' differs from US gunships in having a relatively large cabin volume, making it something of a hybrid between the pure attack helicopter and a troop carrier – neither does it display the obvious 'survivability features' which festoon Western combat

Under the nose of the Mi-24 'Hind' is the four-barrelled JakB 12.7-mm Gatling gun, which has a very high rate of fire of about 4,000 rounds per minute. The gun is manually aimed from the front cockpit.

helicopters, such as exhaust heat suppressors and separated engines. It does feature a package of sensors under the nose. The anhedral stub wings carry rocket launchers and launchers for anti-tank missiles.

The 'Hind', one of the most successful Soviet military aircraft of its generation, was also the most successful of all Soviet weapons in the Afghanistan War, when it proved highly resistant to the small-arms fire of the Mujahadeen rebels. The armed helicopter has proved almost invulnerable to ambush, unlike a ground force, and has been able to penetrate rebels' retreats in a manner wholly impossible for a fast jet attack aircraft.

In action, the Mi-24 appears to be used more like a fighter-bomber than a Western helicopter – firing missiles, unguided rockets and its gun at their maximum effective ranges in a high-speed diving attack, terminated by a sharp break at low level.

The Czech Air Force still operates 20 'Hind-D's with the 51st VRP at Prostejov. These battlefield helicopters played a key role in the air forces of the Warsaw Pact.

NEW GENERATION COMBAT HELICOPTERS

While the United Nations' arms embargo on South Africa was being maintained, the Denel (Atlas) CSH-2 Rooivalk (Red Kite) was designed to meet an Air Force requirement for a combat support helicopter. Development began in 1981 and the definitive Rooivalk prototype made its maiden flight on 11 February 1990.

Although it looks like an entirely new helicopter, the Rooivalk is based on the Aerospatiale SA330 Puma, using the same (though uprated) Turbomeca Makila 1A1 turboshafts. The fuselage is entirely new, incorporating some composite structural components, with stepped-tandem cockpits for pilot (rear) and co–pilot/gunner (front). It

Right: The third Eurocopter Tigre prototype in German UHT configuration as a multi-role anti-tank/support helicopter.

Below: Visible on the ADM (Advanced Development Model) Rooivalk are its infrared exhaust suppressors, weapons fit and revised rotor mast.

features extensive armouring, and a gyro-stabilised nose-mounted turret with FLIR and TV sensors and laser rangefinder which make up an automatic target detection and tracking system.

The cockpit is NVG-compatible, and night/all-weather capability is improved by twin redundant mission computers, twin weapon-aiming computers and a Doppler-based navigation system with moving map displays. It is heavily armed with an indigenous Armscor GA-1 Rattler 20mm cannon turret mounted under the nose.

The production representative EDM (Engineering Development Model) first flew in November 1996. One squadron of twelve helicopters has been ordered by the South African Air Force and deliveries began on 1 May 1999.

It has taken much longer in Europe for the attack-helicopter concept to be developed and a successful design put into production. The Eurocopter Tigre, a joint French/German venture (Aerospatiale and MBB) for a second generation helicopter, features a slender low-drag fuselage with two seats in tandem, stepped and offset to each side of the centreline. The structure is mainly of composites and has an advanced four-bladed composite semi-rigid main rotor. A fixed tricycle undercarriage is fitted and weapons are carried on anhedral stub wings. A cannon turret is fitted under-nose – though armament differs in the two versions – including SNEB 68mm rocket pods or Mistral AAMs. Some feature roof-mounted TV, FLIR, laser range finder and direct optics.

The prototype first flew on 14 February 1991. Tigre features include redundant electrical, fuel and hydraulic systems, two MTR 390 turboshafts and advanced cockpit displays. It is currently being developed in three versions – HAP, the French Army's escort/fire support version, with roof-mounted sight; HAC, the French anti-tank version, and the German Army UHT multi-role anti-tank/support helicopter.

CHRONOLOGY

12 May 1997
The new Sea King HAR3A Search and Rescue helicopter entered RAF operational service.

1 July 1997
A USAF F-16C recorded its 4,000th flight hour.

7 September 1997
The first Lockheed Martin/Boeing F-22 Raptor made its initial flight at Dobbins, GA.

25 September 1997
Sukhoi flew its forward-swept wing fighter prototype, the S-37, at Zhukovsky.

1 October 1997
First flight of the C-141C StarLifter – which included the installation of a 'glass cockpit'.

1 October 1997
The first Tornado GR4 conversion was delivered to the RAF.

1 December 1997
The British Defence Secretary signed the inter-governmental arrangements for the Eurofighter EF2000 Typhoon to go into full production.

MULTI-ROLE RAFALE

First deliveries of the interceptor/strike version of the Rafale are scheduled for 2002, for service with the French Navy on board the nuclear-powered carrier *Charles de Gaulle*.

The advanced multi-role Dassault Rafale has been designed as a replacement for a number of front-line French Air Force strike/interceptor and reconnaissance types including the Mirage F1, Mirage IVP and the Jaguar. When France withdrew as a participant in the Eurofighter consortium, it switched its attention to Dassault's Avions de Combat Experimental (ACX) design. As the Rafale A, the ACX demonstrator made its maiden flight on 4 July 1986, and was used to validate much of the design of the Rafale – including the airframe, all-moving canards, fly-by-wire system and SNECMA M88 turbofan.

The production Rafale is somewhat smaller than the Rafale A and features more composite construction, together with some stealth measures. It is being built in three versions – the single-seat Rafale C (which first flew on 19 May 1991) and the two-seat Rafale B ground-attack aircraft for the Armée de l'Air (which first flew on 30 April 1993), though both types have the generic Rafale D designation; and the navalised Rafale M single-seater for the French Navy. Notable features of the Rafale include its blended fuselage/wing airframe, comprehensive Spectra integrated defence aids sub systems, Dassault Electronique/Thomson CSF RBE2 radar, LCD cockpit displays, helmet mounted sight, voice commands, FLIR, IRST and laser rangefinder.

Stores stations can be used for up to eight MATRA MICA semi-active radar-guided or IR-homing AAMs, Aerospatiale AS30L laser-guided stand-off ASMs, MATRA Defence Apache stand-off munitions dispenser, and Aerospatiale AM39 Exocet anti-ship missiles.

Following operational experience with its Jaguars and Mirage 2000Cs during the Gulf War, which demonstrated the demanding workload in single-seat operations, the French Air Force has revived its Rafale D procurement plans to increase the proportion of two-seat operational versions.

Service entry is expected in 2002, with the first deliveries of the single-seat interceptor/strike version going to the French Navy, as its need is considered greater than that of the air force. These will equip the new nuclear-powered carrier *Charles de Gaulle*.

GLOBAL AIRLIFTER

The USAF issued a requirement for a new cargo airlifter in the late 1970s. This aircraft was to be capable of intercontinental range, but at the same time should also perform theatre resupply directly into a combat zone – and be capable of short-field performance. The McDonnell Douglas design was declared the winner in August 1981 with the designation C-17A being applied, and the new transport aircraft had its maiden flight on 15 September 1991. The C-17 is the newest, most flexible cargo aircraft to enter the US airlift force.

The ultimate measure of airlift effectiveness is the ability to rapidly project and sustain an effective combat force close to a potential battle area. Threats to Allied interests have changed in recent years and the size and weight of mechanised firepower and equipment have grown in response to improved capabilities of potential adversaries. This has significantly increased air mobility requirements, particularly in the area of big and heavy outsize cargo. As a result, additional airlift is needed to meet possible contingencies around the world.

Named Globemaster III, the C-17 is capable of rapid strategic delivery of troops and all types of cargo to man operating bases or directly to forward bases in the deployment area. It is also available to perform tactical airlift missions, when required. The C-17A is designed to be operated by a three-man crew - pilot, co-pilot and loadmaster. Cargo is loaded onto the

The design of the C-17 Globemaster III was driven by the need to carry heavy loads such as tanks and helicopters on strategic airlift tasks, whilst retaining the capability for tactical delivery missions into unprepared airfields.

C-17 through a large aft door that accommodates military vehicles and palletised cargo. It can carry virtually all of the US Army's outsize combat equipment, and is able to airdrop paratroops and outsized equipment, including the Low Altitude Parachute Extraction System.

It is able to operate through small, austere airfields and can take-off and land on runways as short as 3,000ft and only 90ft wide. The ability to perform short-field operations is primarily due to the incorporation of externally blown flaps, with the trailing edge being extended into the exhaust flow from the engines to create lift. Powerful engine reverse thrust capability enables the C-17 to back into narrow parking bays.

Without doubt, the Globemaster III has proved itself to be one of the most versatile airlifters ever designed.

Below: The USAF's C-17As flew many missions in support of NATO's Implementation Force (IFOR) in Bosnia and again during the Kosovo operations.

Operation Shining Hope

Maj Gen Wm S. Hinton Jnr, commander of USAFE's 3rd Air Force, reported on Operation *Shining Hope* and the key role played by the C-17 Globemaster III.

"Responding to the tidal wave of ethnic Albanians fleeing 'ethnic cleansing' operations in Kosovo, the US Air Force generated the largest humanitarian airlift in Europe in 50 years. Not since the Berlin airlift of 1948-49 have Europeans seen such a massive movement of food, medicine, tents and supplies."

"The airlift, part of NATO Operation *Shining Hope*, delivered to Kosovo refugees in the first month alone more than 3,150 tons of emergency supplies – 2,000 tons of food, 400 tons of shelter gear, 520 tons of support equipment, 140 tons of bedding, 30 tons of medical supplies and 60 tons of vehicles."

" The operation began on 5 April 1999. Airmen from the 86th Contingency Response Group, Ramstein AB, Germany arrived in Tirana, established a base camp at a local airfield, and made preparations for the relief force to follow. The C-17 Globemaster was the main workhorse and landed many tons of supplies, including thousands of pre-packed humanitarian daily rations, as well as support equipment. It provided a vital edge to NATO forces, delivering Army and Air Force equipment and personnel as part of a vast international refugee aid effort. USAF crews worked night and day to bring in food, supplies and equipment so desperately needed by uprooted and suffering Kosovar refugees."

"Flights by Globemasters originated not only in Europe but also from points in the United States. Supplies were offloaded in Albania and Macedonia, and also in Italy, where they were then transferred to ships for onward transport."

US military hardware being offloaded at Tirana in Albania. The C-17A can comfortably accommodate all current types of armour in the US inventory.

SPIRIT IN THE SKY

The Northrop Grumman B-2A Spirit is a stealthy, flexible, highly adaptive strategic weapons system that has the real-time decision-making and positive target-identification capabilities inherent only in a manned system. On entering service in 1993, it represented a dramatic leap forward in technology and the achievement of a major milestone in the US strategic modernisation programme.

The B-2's primary mission is 'deterrence across the spectrum of conflict'. It has the capacity to penetrate an enemy's most sophisticated defences and threaten its most valued targets, whatever they may be. The bomber received a 'stealth' label because it was designed to have low-observable characteristics to evade detection by hostile forces. One key to its stealth image is its flying-wing shape. Additionally, the aircraft is made of materials that help to reduce its radar signature. It has a crew of two – with provision for a third crew station – compared to the B-1B Lancer's crew of four and the B-52's six.

Work on the aircraft was undertaken in complete secrecy in the 1980s. Only the existence of the programme, and that the aircraft was a flying wing, had been officially acknowledged before the aircraft was rolled out in late 1988. Its maiden flight was on 17 July 1989 with the first production delivery being made in December 1993. With the end of the Cold War and a change in defence strategy, the US government slashed the number of B-2s ordered to twenty-one from a total of 133 that the USAF had planned to acquire.

The B-2A is powered by four GE F118-GE-110 non-afterburning turbofans and features fly-by-wire controls, two side-by-side internal weapon bays and a Hughes APQ-181 intercept radar. The bomber's armament is carried in two Boeing rotary launcher assemblies (RLAs) – one in each bomb bay – and can carry a total of sixteen AGM-129

The Northrop Grumman B-2 was developed in great secrecy as a stealthy radar-evading strategic bomber for attacking Soviet strategic targets with nuclear bombs and stand-off weapons.

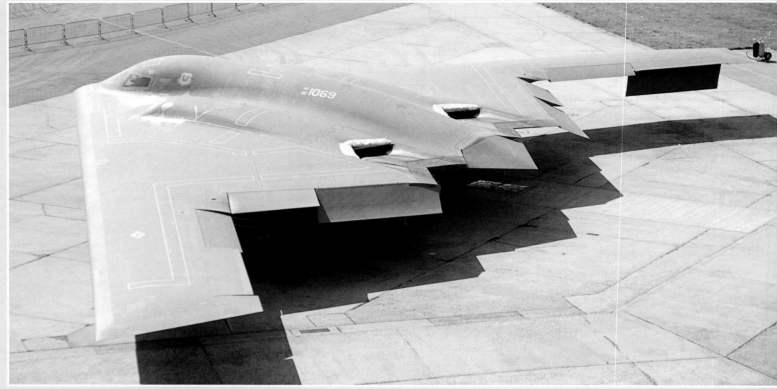

Global Reach

In a Pentagon briefing Maj Gen Bruce A. Carlson, director of operational requirements for the air staff, commented on the B-2:

"The B-2s are doing superbly in combat operations. The aircraft continues to improve in its maintainability. In fact, two of them landed the other day at Whiteman in driving rain – and they had flown thirty hours. The (low observables) maintaining was essentially routine. In other words, there were no major LO write-ups...that would have kept it from flying immediately thereafter. You put gas in it – and kept it running."

"So we think we're turning the corner on low observable maintenance on the B-2, and I think it has a great potential in the future. The B-2 is now the only penetrating nuclear bomber, the B-1 having been withdrawn from the nuclear mission".

"The B-2A has a pretty good signature. For the way we employ the bomber, it's adequate. Given the stealth work being done on the F-22 and JSF, there is confidence in the Air Force that stealth materials will soon get easier to apply and maintain. The B-2/JDAM combo was the 'absolute ultimate' in 'Global Reach, Global Power'."

The B-2A, obviously the focus of enormous debate for a number of reasons – cost, capability, need – over the last couple of decades, proved itself to be a decisive weapon in Operation *Allied Force*.

The B-2A's blended wing design necessitates a unique control surface layout. Moving inboard from the wingtip (in the plan view above) are a drag rudder/spoiler and then an elevator running along the same hinge line.

ACMs, or sixteen B61 tactical/strategic or B83 strategic freefall nuclear bombs – or a mixture of iron bombs. A GPS-Aided Targeting System (GATS) is used, together with the highly-detailed synthetic aperture mode on the aircraft's AN/APQ-181 radar.

The B-2A's combat début was on 25 March 1999, when they dropped JDAM bombs on high-priority targets during the Kosovo conflict. Two of the long-range aircraft struck a series of targets in Yugoslavia in the opening hours of Operation *Allied Force*. Making a round-trip of 30 hours duration from Whiteman AFB, MO, the B-2s used a combination of 32 JDAMs to strike 'a variety of soft and hard targets'. For the remainder of the conflict, B-2As were 'part of the mix' in almost every night of the air action in the Balkans, accounting for 11% of the bombload dropped in the conflict – although they flew less than 1% of the total number of sorties amassed by NATO aircraft.

HI-TECH HERCULES

The RAF purchased sixty-six Lockheed C-130K Hercules in the mid-1960s – and these have been in continuous service for over 30 years as its prime tactical transport aircraft. After hard use, and because technology has advanced considerably since they were delivered, they became due for replacement. By the mid-1990s the aircraft were showing their age, with corrosion and fatigue related problems leading to steadily escalating maintenance costs and decreasing reliability. After studying various options it was decided to replace twenty-five of them with the new Lockheed Martin C-130J.

To the casual observer, the latest model looks similar to the thousands of Hercules already in use around the world today. But under its skin lies a quantum leap in technology. Looks can be deceiving, and the new C-130J which flew for the first time on 5 April 1996 is a very different aircraft from the prototype Hercules that took to the air in 1954.

Although externally similar to previous versions of the Hercules, the new Allison AE2100 engines fitted with Dowty Aerospace R391 propellers give the Lockheed Martin C-130J a distinctive appearance.

269

Flying the C-130J

Author Peter R. March was one of the first journalists to be permitted by the manufacturer, Lockheed Martin, to examine the C-130J-30 Hercules and get first hand experience of it in the air.

In its overall structure, the new aircraft appears very similar to the C-130K. There is one less low-level cockpit window and no in-flight refuelling probe above the cockpit but until you look at the engines and propellers it is hard to distinguish new from old. The Rolls-Royce Allison powerplants, with their Westland manufactured nacelles, are smaller in profile and the scythe-shaped, six-bladed propellers, are certainly distinctive.

Climbing the steep ladder to the cockpit we entered a completely new world. The C-130J flight deck has been completely transformed from that of the older versions. The instrument panel, centre console and overhead panel are very different – only the two control columns, captain's nose-wheel steering wheel, parking brake and the two crew seats looked familiar. Two pairs of Lockheed Martin-designed, liquid crystal, colour, multi-function, flat panel display units are positioned in front of the two pilots. These provide all of the C-130J's basic flight, navigational and aircraft systems information including the Westinghouse low-power colour radar display. Apart from these four large colour displays, there are very few additional instruments on the main panel.

The displays are all compatible with night vision imaging systems, enabling the crew to operate the C-130J when 'special missions' dictate blackout conditions. Wayne Roberts, Lockheed Martin's Chief Test Pilot, commented: "The whole focus of the C-130J's development has been concentrated in the cockpit, with the integration of the mission computers, FADEC, digital avionics and MIL-Std 1553B Databus architecture.

On the console between the pilots, the four engine-control levers stand proud, with computer input panels on either side. The four Rolls-Royce Allison AE2100D3 turboprops, each flat-rated at 4,591 shaft horsepower (3,425kW), allied to the more efficient Dowty R391 six-bladed, composite propellers, generate up to 30% more thrust while using some 15% less fuel. The powerplants are equipped with the Lucas Aerospace full authority digital electronic control (FADEC), making engine management very easy and efficient. The throttles can be opened and closed as fast as the pilot chooses, FADEC ensuring that the powerplant responds effectively and safely. No juggling is needed to balance the engines in the cruise – it is done automatically.

Above: The US Air Force Reserve Command's 403rd Wing took delivery of six C-130Js at the beginning of 1999. The USAF plans to order at least 150 C-130Js, with further deliveries commencing in 2002.

The most significant of the many changes are the more fuel efficient Rolls-Royce/Allison AE 2100D3 turboprops and new six-bladed Dowty propellers. They give the 'J' a short take-off capability and the ability to climb rapidly to operational altitudes. There is extensive reliance on digital avionics to permit a two-person flight deck and the aircraft incorporates other modernised equipment, such as a 'glass' cockpit and fighter style controls on the control columns. The C-130J also features composite flaps and leading edge surfaces, and the external fuel tanks of earlier versions have been dispensed with.

The range, in many instances, is 50% greater than the 'K' model. It will deliver increased availability, lower operating costs and performance improvements for the RAF's transport fleet, often the cornerstone of numerous military exercises and operations worldwide.

The new C-130J is the first RAF transport (or large aircraft of any description) to have a head-up display (HUD). Able to show eight configurations of data, including failure

The most significant flight deck innovation is the Head-Up Display (HUD). Roberts explained that the full value of the computerised systems was being maximised by providing the C-130J's pilots with the first and most sophisticated HUD that could be developed for a modern tactical transport aircraft. The clear vision HUD screen folds down from the windscreen and locks in position in front of each of the pilots. The imagery is generated above the crews' heads and projected onto the screen in crisp green symbology.

With his checks completed, Roberts was ready to demonstrate a short-field/max-effort take-off. As the aircraft was relatively light, I expected an impressive performance. But I did not anticipate just how startling it would be. With the flaps set at 50deg, the pilot pushed the four power levers forward to the stops – the FADEC spooling up the engines very quickly. As soon as maximum power was reached, he released the brakes and we literally leapt into the air.

After the test mission had been completed I was invited into the right hand seat for the remainder of the sortie. Wayne Roberts re-briefed me on the Flight Dynamics HUD symbology as I took the controls. I was surprised at how quickly I could adjust to using this very clear information while maintaining my outside scan.

Roberts next demonstrated the clarity of the Westinghouse MODAR 4000 colour radar in its ground-mapping/ navigation mode and as a weather radar. This led us into the C-130J's next major feature, the CNI (Communication, Navigation and Identification) management system, with its dual embedded Honeywell Global Positioning System/ Inertial Navigation System (GPS/INS) feeding into the Flight Management System (FMS). In simple terms it meant that aircraft could be handed over to the computer systems with the integrated auto-navigation and auto-pilot controlling our heading, height and speed, making adjustments automatically and

relaying any supplementary information or warnings from the Ground Collision Avoidance System (GCAS) and Traffic-alerting Collision Avoidance System (TCAS), or indeed the missile and radar warning receivers, onto the HUD.

Then it was time for Roberts' *piece de resistance* – a tactical landing on a special 1,850ft concrete strip adjacent to Marietta's runway. This time a 4.5 deg approach was programmed into the HUD, which looked extraordinarily steep from the cockpit after my gentle approaches. With full flap set we crossed the threshold at 107kt and touched down firmly on the main and nosewheel at 101kt.

With no little assistance from the anti-skid system brakes and full reverse propeller pitch, the Hercules stopped in just under 1,500ft. "We've not yet fully exploited the C-130J's angle of approach potential", Roberts confided as we taxied off the strip. "I expect

we will be able to increase to about 7 deg before too long. Allison and Dowty have indicated that software changes will give us a steeper approach without having to resort to lower blade angles."

With its modern computer technology, more powerful engines and propellers and the resulting enhanced performance, the C-130J is undoubtedly the best (in fact the only) option available to the RAF at this time. This was ably summed up in the words of Lyle Schaefer, Lockheed Martin Chief Experimental Test Pilot: "It's a pilot's airplane that is a lot of fun to fly. I've been higher and faster than anyone in a C-130 – to 42,000ft, and it flies comfortably at 31-35,000ft with a standard load. Pilots will be able to fly wherever they want to in all kinds of weather and when they get into a drop zone, for example, they can designate where they want to drop something without too much external help and with very precise accuracy."

With the introduction of the 'glass cockpit', the C-130J's flightdeck crew can be reduced to two. Amongst an array of new systems and instrumentation, the new aircraft is fitted with a Head-Up Display (HUD) – the first to be fitted to a modern tactical transport.

warnings, the HUD will be the pilots' primary source of information for all stages of the flight. Twin autopilots lessen the workload and, although capable of Category 2 landings (100ft decision height, 1,300ft visibility) will actually be employed by the RAF down to the less demanding Category 1 (200ft/2,600ft).

Night or bad weather missions are assisted by new aids aboard the aircraft – the Ground Collision Avoidance System (GCAS) and the Traffic-alerting Collision Avoidance System (TCAS). For dropping large numbers of troops in close concentration, the C-130J has Sierra AN/APN-240B station-keeping, which is an updated (but still compatible) version of the APN-169 retrofitted to twenty Hercules C3s.

The first of 15 C-130J-30 Hercules C4s on order for the RAF was officially handed over at RAF Lyneham on 23 November 1999. They will be followed by ten 'short' C-130J Hercules C5s in 2001.

KOSOVO CRISIS

O ver 300 combat and support aircraft from 13 NATO nations assembled in the Balkans at the start of the Kosovo crisis in March 1999 – a total which had doubled within two weeks of the start of the campaign against Yugoslavia. In the words of the NATO Supreme Commander, General Wesley Clark: "We are going to systematically and progressively attack, disrupt, degrade, devastate and, ultimately, unless President Milosevic complies with the demands of the international community, we are going to destroy his forces and their facilities."

Italy provided eleven of the fifteen European air bases, together with 42 aircraft. Hungary's recent membership to NATO resulted in some Western military aircraft using its facilities for the first time. Germany fielded fourteen Tornados for the first post-WW2 combat operation. Armée de l'Air Mirage 2000Ds participated in NATO action for the first time. Other aircraft – mainly F-16s (which numerically was the most important warplane in the Allied forces inventory) – were deployed by Belgium, Canada, Denmark, Netherlands, Norway, Portugal, Spain and Turkey. Yugoslavia was only able to muster some 250 front-line aircraft that included MiG-21s, Soko Oraos, Galebs, Super Galebs and Jastrebs, though most were obsolete and in a poor state of serviceability.

Northrop Grumman B-2As, carrying JDAM bombs, were used in the opening days, flying direct from the USA. The RAF deployed Harrier GR7s, together with VC10s and Tristar tankers, plus three E-3D AWACS aircraft. USAF B-52H Stratofortresses, equipped with Boeing AGM-69C Conventional Air-Launched Cruise Missiles (CAL-CMs) operated from RAF Fairford, England, and were joined by B-1B Lancers which had received the latest Defensive System Upgrade programme (DSUP) – or Block D upgrade – for the campaign. A vital part of the electronic warfare/surveillance effort was the RC-135V/W Rivet Joint – operating from RAF Mildenhall.

Left: The RAF's major contribution to the air war over Kosovo was a force of Harrier GR7s based at Gioia del Colle in Italy.

Under the title of Operation *Trident*, the French Air Force contributed Mirage 2000s, based at Istrana.

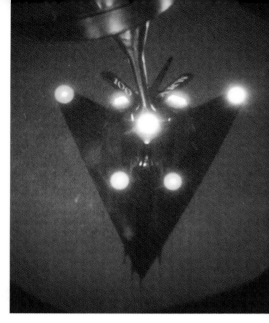

Above: The 24 USAF F-117A Nighthawks deployed to the Balkans flew mostly night missions against targets in Serbia.

Left: B-52H Stratofortresses were deployed from bases in the US, along with B-1B Lancers, to RAF Fairford, Gloucestershire from where bombing missions were launched against targets in Serbia and Kosovo.

On 28 March, one of the twenty-four F-117A Nighthawks deployed crashed near Belgrade, possibly brought down by a Yugoslavian SAM. From then on Allied aircraft were restricted to a minimum operating altitude of 15,000ft, except in special circumstances. Six RAF Tornado GR1s were eventually deployed and made their first attacks on Yugoslav targets on 4 April. Later, A-10 Thunderbolts and AH-64A Apaches (of Task Force *Hawk*) were deployed to the theatre. Other aircraft operating in the Balkans were F-14s and HARM-firing F/A-18s aboard USS *Theodore Roosevelt*. Royal Navy Sea Harrier FA2s from HMS *Invincible* operated CAPs over the Adriatic.

The use of eight unmanned air vehicles (TRW/IAI Hunters) for reconnaissance over Yugoslavia by the US Army was confirmed when it was revealed that one of them was lost during the campaign. They were used for transmitting data to AWACS and ground forces. General Atomic Predator drones were also used with synthetic-aperture radar to supplement two German-based E-8C J-STARS in supplying real-time battlefield surveillance and targeting data.

To prevent its vulnerable transports being exposed to AAA or shoulder-mounted SAMs (MANPADS), the USAF's C-141B StarLifters made food drops to refugees from 30,000ft – all landing within an area 2,000yd by 1,000yd.

Bad weather frequently grounded air operations. Later in the campaign, RAF Harriers used the 2,000lb Paveway III laser-guided bomb for the first time – a weapon whose absence up until that point had been the cause of some speculation. The second month of strikes was again frustrated on many occasions by continuing poor weather. Precision weapon deliveries were further affected by general restrictions placed on NATO aircraft to a minimum altitude of 15,000ft. Dwindling stocks of cruise missiles resulted in a decrease in their usage later in the campaign.

Use was also revealed for the first time of previously secret air-launched non-lethal weapons which incapacitated some 70% of Serbia's electrical supplies to command, control and communication centres, airfields and military installations. Also used were the cylindrical

CHRONOLOGY

24 June 1998
Weapons capability was enhanced when the first precision Joint Direct Attack Munition (JDAM) was delivered to the USAF by Boeing.

8 July 1998
Boeing launched the process of assembling the first example of what may ultimately provide the USAF with the core of its fighter force for much of the 21st century, the Joint Strike Fighter (JSF).

15 July 1998
First production Raytheon T-6A Texan II turboprop made its initial flight.

10 October 1998
The F-22A Raptor exceeded Mach 1 for the first time – in 'supercruise' flight, without the aid of afterburner augmentation.

29 June 1998
The second EMD Lockheed Martin F-22A Raptor made its maiden flight.

1 December 1998
The Royal Navy's EH101 Merlin HM1 ASW helicopter unit, No 700M, was formally commissioned.

12 December 1998
First operational use of a KC-135R featuring a *Pacer CRAG* upgrade, that enabled it to be operated by a crew of just three.

Left: Two USAF E-8C J-STARS, based in Germany, provided NATO forces with real-time battlefield surveillance and targeting information.

Below: A number of General Atomic Predator UAV drones with synthetic-aperture radar were flown by NATO over Kosovo.

parachute-retarded BLU-114B beer-can-sized sub-munitions which were scattered in large numbers from the GPS/INS-guided Lockheed Martin CBU-97 cluster-bomb Wind Corrected Munitions Dispenser (WCMD). These caused massive and destructive short-circuits in power stations, transformers and overhead cables – the graphite powder being particularly penetrative into delicate systems.

Air operations ceased on 17 June – Day 80 of the campaign. Over 35,000 sorties had been flown, of which some 10,000 had involved offensive roles. NATO had pressed home its attacks for over two months, aiming to hit Serb forces wherever they could be found in Kosovo, while disrupting the military and political infrastructure within Serbia itself.

Despite some serious setbacks, notably the inadvertent attacks on the Chinese embassy and refugee convoys, NATO's massive airpower forced the defiant Serbs to the negotiating table, allowing NATO ground troops to finally occupy Kosovo.

So the 20th century came to an end, with some of the West's most sophisticated aircraft, weapons systems and surveillance equipment coming together under the NATO flag to fight a major air war. It revealed the strengths and weaknesses of a dependence on modern technology and the fact that the underlying problems that exist today are much the same as they were 100 years ago. Operations over Kosovo were hampered by poor weather, inadequate information and human failure; they were strengthened by the careful employment of the best available equipment, a tested command and control system and a determination to succeed by all those on the front line.

CHRONOLOGY

16 December 1998
Air strikes by US and British forces against Iraq were resumed over four nights with the launch of Operation *Desert Fox*.

24 December 1998
The prototype 6.5-tonne Kamov Ka-60 utility helicopter for the Russian Air force made its first flight.

1 January 1999
RAF Mildenhall's 100th ARW absorbed the mission of the European Tanker Force.

30 January 1999
It was announced that the Grob G-115E was to be the replacement for the RAF's long-serving Scottish Aviation Bulldog trainer.

24 March 1999
Operation *Allied Force* commenced – the first aggressive NATO military action in the organisation's 50-year history – with air strikes against Serbian military targets in Kosovo and Yugoslavia. Over 300 combat and support aircraft from thirteen NATO nations were assembled in the Balkans. Germany mounted its first post-WW2 operations.

25 March 1999
Combat début of the B-2A Spirit, which dropped JDAM bombs on high-priority targets in the Balkans.

1 April 1999
Production commenced of a 'stretched' CN-295M for the Spanish Air Force.

1 April 1999
First flight of the 'E210' Strike Eagle – the first F-15E Eagle to be built for the USAF since 1993.

BEYOND 2000

The European fighter for the new millennium – the Eurofighter Typhoon has the potential to become the most flexible and effective air weapons system the RAF has ever put into service.

The Eurofighter Typhoon is one of the world's biggest collaborative military aircraft programmes and is a key element in the future air defence of both Britain and its European neighbours.

The RAF started out on the protracted road to Eurofighter in May 1979, with the requirement for a possible replacement for the Harrier, Jaguar and Tornado F3. On 8 August 1986, the EAP technology demonstrator made its first flight – with the UK, Germany, Italy and Spain joining together to form the European Fighter Aircraft programme (France had already cut adrift in July 1985) – and rapid progress was made towards completing project definition. The Eurofighter consortium was then formed in June 1986 to manage the EFA.

Eurofighter had the misfortune to be born at a time of great political change and a situation for which NATO had long striven. Dramatic political events were unfolding in the East which were soon to lead to the re-unification of East and West Germany and the dissolution of the Warsaw Pact.

In December 1992, EFA was re-named the Eurofighter 2000 ('EF2000' for short). The German DA1 made its maiden flight on 27 March 1994 and the UK prototype (DA2) flew on 6 April 1994 – both initially using the Tornado-type RB199 engines for expediency.

The first priority for the delivery of Eurofighter is to the interceptor squadrons of the air arms that have ordered it. Despite protracted development and controversy over its high price tag, the Eurofighter should prove to be a highly capable fighter, armed with an internal 27mm Mauser gun and up to ten air-to-air missiles. Features include its specially developed EJ200 engines, canard configuration, ECR 90 radar, an infrared search and tracking system (IRST), and an advanced Defensive Aids SubSystems (DAAS), together with an advanced cockpit with helmet mounted sight and Direct Voice Input (DVI) controls.

Pilots will be the first in the RAF to have helmet-mounted sights for point-and-shoot launching of missiles at visual targets. Night-capable, the sight will be complemented by the usual HUD, which will be of wide-angle type and additionally will display images from the PIRATE. It is the purpose of these screens to replace the multitude of dials and indicators found in most current RAF aircraft, displaying the data required for each stage of the sortie. Overriding priority is given to providing the pilot with a clear view of the complete tactical solution, combining inputs from all sensors.

Eurofighter from the cockpit

Observations from British test pilots Peter Weger and Chris Yeo:

"Never seen such an elegant airplane and such a nice airplane to fly."

"We will open it up step-by-step and I think it will be a perfect airplane."

"It is going to be a fighter pilot's aircraft. It accelerates rapidly, its clearly going to turn quickly, and the rate of climb is going to be spectacular."

Squadron Leader Simon Dyde, RAF Eurofighter project:

"It was an absolute joy from start to finish. Take-off was brisk with a prompt rotation and, once airborne, it was easy to fly. I could not believe this was reversionary flight control laws...it flies much better than any other fighter I have flown... a tremendous field of view...on approach to land, I could control the speed to within one knot...landing was as easy as all other phases of the flight and the first landing was the greatest I have ever done."

Left: RAF procurement of the Typhoon will include 37 two-seat trainer versions (as DA4 pictured here) out of a total of 232 aircraft on order.

CHRONOLOGY

1 April 1999
The first RC-135 Rivet Joint intelligence aircraft to be fitted with the new CFM International F108-CF-100 engines made its first flight.

29 April 1999
Initial flight of the two-seat Sukhoi Su-27KUB carrier-based combat-trainer for the Russian Navy.

1 May 1999
Delivery of the first of twelve production Denel AH-2A Rooivalk attack helicopters was made to the South African Air Force.

1 June 1999
Raytheon was awarded the contract for the British joint Army/RAF airborne stand-off battlefield surveillance radar system (ASTOR) aircraft.

1 July 1999
The prototype navalised Rafale MO2 completed its first ever flight-deck operations from the new nuclear aircraft carrier *Charles de Gaulle*.

25 August 1999
Boeing's new CH-47SD 'Super-D' Chinook made its maiden flight.

26 August 1999
The first WAH-64 Apache helicopter for the British Army was flown by GKN-Westland.

1 September 1999
The first of four ex-USAF KC-135A tanker/support aircraft were delivered to the Republic of Singapore Air Force.

1 October 1999
Delivery of the first of three Dassault Falcon 50 Surmar aircraft for the maritime surveillance role with France's Aeronavale.

12 October 1999
The first WC-130J was delivered to the USAF Reserve Command's 53rd WRS at Keesler AFB.

17 October 1999
The first of three new EC-130J 'Combat Solo' aircraft were assigned to the USAF's 193rd SOW, Pennsylvania ANG.

Above all, Eurofighter will *be* a fighter. Emphasis has been placed on low wing loading and high thrust-to-weight ratio for manoeuvrability, good all-round vision from the cockpit and computer-managed flight controls to ensure 'care free' handling.

The Eurofighter is both light and strong because of modern techniques of construction. No less than 70% of the surface area is of carbon fibre composites and a further 12% comprises glass reinforced plastic. Metal skimming accounts for just 15%. As on the F-16 Fighting Falcon, intakes are located under the fuselage to ensure a supply of air to the engine when flying at a steep angle of attack and low speed.

Eurofighter is intended to remain in service over a 30-year/6,000 flying hours lifetime. The ability to operate Eurofighter with the minimum of support whilst on lengthy overseas deployments has been an important factor that has influenced its design.

At the heart of the Eurofighter is a quadruplex fly-by-wire flight control system and an extensive, totally integrated avionics suite which employs seven duplicated high-speed databases for the transmission of information between individual systems and equipment.

Given the name Typhoon in 1998, it will enter service with the RAF between 2004 and 2008. The first aircraft will be delivered to the RAF Operational Evaluation Unit at BAE Systems, Warton in 2002 and the Operational Conversion Unit will form at RAF Coningsby, Lincs two years later, where the first operational squadron will also be based. Further squadrons will be formed at RAF Leeming, Yorks in 2006 and the final Tornado F3 replacement by Typhoons will be at Leuchars, Fife in 2008.

SHAPE OF THE FUTURE

The Lockheed Martin/Boeing F-22 Raptor will be the first all-new air superiority fighter to enter service with the US Air Force in twenty-five years, if current plans reach fruition. It features advanced aerodynamics, 'supercruise' engines, fourth-generation stealth technology and the most advanced integrated avionics and computers needed to maintain US air dominance well into the 21st century.

The F-22 integrates a variety of new technologies to permit both virtually undetectable high-speed flight and combat capability. Basically, the Raptor will be able to fully exploit warfare while denying the enemy information about itself. Its radar involves a whole new technology – the AN/APG-77 is the first active-element, electronically scanned system to be incorporated in a US fighter.

Another first for the Raptor is the inter/intra-flight data link – which is part of the communication, navigation and identification (CNI) system. Using this data link, which cannot be accessed by enemy receivers, all F-22s can share data on weapons availability, fuel state and enemy aircraft without having to make any radio transmissions.

The Pratt & Whitney F199 engine is unique – it allows the F-22 to 'supercruise', or fly at high supersonic speeds without fuel-consuming afterburners. In addition, they are more infrared-stealthy, so better equipped to evade detection in the event of pursuit by a heat-seeking missile. It will also use thrust vectoring to give the pilot air combat advantages.

Raptor '002' taking off from Edwards AFB, California in October 1999 for another flight in the demanding test programme that is demonstrating the qualities of this new technology fighter.

Four bays carry the weapons. Two – one each side of the aircraft where the leading edge of the wing meets the fuselage – carry a single AIM-9 Sidewinder, later to be replaced by the AIM-9X. A third, larger bay under the aircraft can carry six AIM-120C AMRAAMS or two GBU-32 Joint Direct Attack Munitions (JDAMs) and two AMRAAMS. The Raptor also carries a 20mm M61 rapid-fire gun. It is likely to have four underwing hard points, each of which can handle an LAV-128 launcher. Each of the hardpoints will carry up to 5,000lb in weaponry or fuel tanks.

The F-22 is expected to be able to fly twice as many sorties in a given period as current fighters, needing only half the direct maintenance man-hours per flight and will require only two-thirds the turnaround time before the next mission.

Reporting in October 1999 on progress in meeting the five goals set by the Department of Defense that had to be reached by the end of the year, Brig Gen Michael Mushala, F-22 Program Director, was confident that they would be surpassed. "In July, the Air Force's next-generation fighter hit supercruise, or sustained speeds greater than Mach 1.5, without afterburner in full combat configuration and at 50,000ft. This ability to supercruise will allow the F-22 larger patrol areas. It will permit the Raptor to enter and exit hostile areas in quick fashion, reducing the time that a pilot spends over enemy territory."

"There's more. In August, Raptor flights achieved 60-degrees angle of attack. The current frontline air superiority fighter, the F-15 Eagle, can reach only 30 degrees angle of attack. High angle of attack, or high alpha, testing clearly proved that the F-22 can double such performance, verifying its agility and manoeuvrability strength. Moreover, it met requirements to complete high alpha post-stall manoeuvring with thrust vectoring."

"The Raptor continues to surpass our expectations", said Bob Rearden, Lockheed Martin's F-22 Program General Manager. "Supercruising in less than 275 flight hours and reaching 50,000ft a full year ahead of schedule validates its maturity at this early stage of flight test."

At the end of 1999, the Lockheed Martin/Boeing/Pratt & Whitney consortium producing the F-22 was set further specific targets to meet by the end of 2000. A total of 17 F-22s, nine development and eight pre-production aircraft, had been ordered and success in meeting the systems and performance targets will ensure that the Raptor goes into full production.

When the Raptor was conceived, the USAF was looking ahead to the threat posed by advanced Soviet fighters that were backed by integrated air-defences and able to strike Allied aircraft at their bases. But when the Raptor enters service, the F-15 will have been operational for 30 years, and the threat its replacement has been designed to counter, might well have changed substantially. The consortium has a difficult task ahead in making its product the 'must have' fighter for the 21st Century.

An underside view of Raptor '001' showing the port weapons bay door open, revealing two of the six AIM-120C AMRAAMs that can be carried.

Widely regarded as the most advanced fighter in the world, the Raptor combines a major leap in technology with reduced support requirements and maintenance costs. A total of nine development aircraft are to be completed for the programme, followed by eight pre-production examples.

BIBLIOGRAPHY

Andrews C.F. and Morgan E.B., *Supermarine Aircraft since 1914*, Putnams (1981)

Andrews C.F. and Morgan E.B., *Vickers Aircraft since 1908*, Putnams (1988)

Baker, David, *Flight & Flying: A Chronology*, Facts on File (1994)

Beamont, Roland & Reed, Arthur, *Typhoon & Tempest at War*, Ian Allan (1974)

Beamont, Roland, *Testing Years*, Ian Allan (1980)

Bickers, Richard Townshend, *A Century of Manned Flight*, Quadrillion (1998)

Bishop, Chris., *The Aerospace Encyclopedia of Air Warfare II: 1945 to the present*, Aerospace Publishing (1997)

Bowyer, Chas., *Pathfinders at War*, Ian Allan (1977)

Boyne, Walter J., *The Smithsonian Book of Flight*, Sidgwick & Jackson (1987)

Braybrook, Roy, *Harrier: The Vertical Reality*, RAF Benevolent Fund Enterprises (1996)

Braybrook, Roy, *V/STOL The Key to Survival*, Osprey (1989)

Bruce, J.M., *The Aeroplanes of the Royal Flying Corps (Military Wing)*, Putnams (1982)

Carey, Keith, *An Illustrated History of the Helicopter*, Patrick Stephens (1986)

Clark, Ronald W., *The Role of the Bomber*, Sidgwick & Jackson (1977)

Cole, Christopher & Chessman E.F., *The Air Defence of Britain 1914-18*, Putnams (1984)

Cooksley, Peter G., *Air Warfare: Encyclopedia of 20th Century Conflict*, Arms and Armour (1997)

Dean, Sir Maurice, *The RAF and Two World Wars*, Cassell (1979)

Donald, David & Lake, Jon, *Encyclopedia of World Military Aircraft Vols I & II*, Aerospace Publishing (1994)

Donald, David, *American Warplanes of WW2*, Aerospace Publishing (1995)

Donald, David, *Warplanes of the Luftwaffe*, Aerospace Publishing (1994)

Donovan, Frank, *Bridge in the Sky: The Story of the Berlin Airlift*, Robert Hale & Co (1968)

Dorr, Robert & Bishop, Chris, *Vietnam Air Warfare Debrief*, Aerospace Publishing (1996)

Duke, Neville, *The Crowded Sky*, Cassell (1959)

Duval, G.R., *British Flying Boats*, D. Bradford Barton Ltd (1973)

Ege, Lennart, *Balloons and Airships*, Blandford Press (1973)

Flintham, Victor, *Air Wars & Aircraft: A Detailed Record of Air Combat*, Facts-on-File (1990)

Franks, Norman, *RAF Fighter Command 1936-1968*, Patrick Stephens (1992)

Frawley, Gerard, *The International Directory of Military Aircraft 1998/99*, Aerospace Publications, Australia (1998)

Goulding, James & Moyes, Philip, *RAF Bomber Command and its Aircraft 1941-45*, Ian Allan (1978)

Gunston, Bill, *Chronicle of Aviation*, Chronicle Publications Ltd (1992)

Gunston, Bill, *Encyclopedia of Russian Aircraft 1875-1995*, Osprey (1995)

Gunston, Bill, *World Encyclopedia of Aero Engines*, Patrick Stephens (1986)

Gunston, Bill & Gordon, Yelfin, *Yakovlev Aircraft since 1924*, Putnams (1997)

Halley, James J., *The Squadrons of the RAF & Commonwealth*, Air Britain (1998)

Harris, Sherwood, *The First to Fly: Aviation's Pioneer Days*, Tab Aero (1970)

Ireland, Bernard, *The Rise and Fall of the Aircraft Carrier*, Marshall Cavendish (1979)

Jackson A.J., *Avro Aircraft since 1908*, Putnams (1965)

Jackson A.J., *De Havilland Aircraft since 1909*, Putnams (1962)

Jackson, Robert, *Canberra: The Operational Record*, Airlife (1988)

Jackson, Robert, *F-86 Sabre: The Operational Record*, Airlife (1994)

Jackson, Robert, *High Cold War: Strategic Air Reconnaissance and the Electronic Intelligence War*, Patrick Stephens (1998)

Jackson, Robert, *The Guinness Book of Air Warfare*, Guinness Publications (1993)

James, Derek N., *Gloster Aircraft since 1917*, Putnams (1987)

Jarrett, Philip, *Biplane to Monoplane: Aircraft Development 1919-39*, Putnams (1997)

Kosin, Rüdiger, *The German Fighter*, Putnams (1983)

March, Daniel J. & Heathcott, John, *The Aerospace Encyclopedia of Air Warfare I: 1911-1945*, Aerospace Publishing (1997)

March, Daniel J., *British Warplanes of WW2*, Aerospace Publishing (1998)

March, Peter R., *Brace by Wire to Fly by Wire: 75 years of the Royal Air Force 1918-1998*, RAF Benevolent Fund Enterprises (1993 & revised 1998)

March, Peter R., *Confederate Air Force, Celebrating 40 Years*, Confederate Air Force Inc (1997)

March, Peter R., *Eagles – 80 Aircraft that made History with the RAF*, Weidenfeld & Nicholson (1998)

March, Peter R., *Freedom of the Skies: An Illustrated History of Fifty Years of NATO Airpower*, Cassell (1999)

March, Peter R., *Hawk comes of Age*, RAF Benevolent Fund Enterprises (1995)

March, Peter R., *Sabre to Stealth: 50 years of the United States Air Force 1947-1997*, RAF Benevolent Fund Enterprises (1997)

Mason, Francis K., *The British Bomber since 1914*, Putnams (1994)

Mason, Francis K., *The British Fighter since 1912*, Putnams (1992)

Morse, Stan, *Gulf War Debrief*, Aerospace Publishing (1991)

Morse, Stan (Ed), *The Encyclopedia of Aviation*, Aerospace Publishing (1985)

Moyes, Philip J.R., *Supermarine Spitfire Remembered*, Wingspan

Murphy, Daryl E., *The Aviation Fact Book*, McGraw-Hill (1998)

Nemecek, Vaclav, *The History of Soviet Aircraft*, Willows Books (1986)

Payne, A/Cdr L.G.S., *Air Dates*, Heinemann (1957)

Peacock, Lindsay, *On Falcon Wings: The F-16 Story*, RAF Benevolent Fund Enterprises (1997)

Peacock, Lindsay, *Mighty Hercules*, RAF Benevolent Fund Enterprises (1994)

Penrose, Harald, *British Aviation: Ominous Skies*, HMSO (1980)

Penrose, Harald, *Architect of Wings*, Airlife (1985)

Penrose, Harald, *British Aviation: Widening Horizons 1930-34*, HMSO (1979)

Philpott, Bryan, *English Electric/BAC Lightning*, Patrick Stephens (1984)

Philpott, Bryan, *History of the German Air Force*, Hamlyn (1986)

Philpott, Bryan, *Meteor*, Patrick Stephens (1986)

Rabinowitz, Harold, *Conquer the Sky: Great Moments in Aviation*, Metro Books (1996)

Ransom, Stephen and Fairclough, Robert, *English Electric Aircraft and their Predecessors*, Putnams (1987)

Rawlings, John D.R., *The History of the Royal Air Force*, Temple Press (1984)

Robertson, Bruce, *British Military Aircraft serials 1911-1979*, Patrick Stephens (1964)

Smith, Alan, *Schneider Trophy - Diamond Jubilee: Looking back 60 years*, Waterfront (1991)

Sowinski, Larry, *The Pacific War*, Conway Maritime Press (1981)

Swanborough, Gordon & Bowers, Peter M., *United States Military Aircraft since 1909*, Putnams (1963)

Swanborough, Gordon & Bowers, Peter M., *United States Navy Aircraft since 1911*, Putnams (1968)

Taylor, John W.R., *A History of Aerial Warfare*, Hamlyn (1974)

Taylor, John W.R. & Munsen, Kenneth, *The Battle of Britain*, New English Library (1976)

Taylor, Michael J.H., *The Aerospace Chronology*, Tri-Service Press (1989)

Taylor, Michael, *Naval Air Power*, Hamlyn (1986)

Taylor, Michael J.H. & Mondey, David, *Milestones of Flight*, Jane's (1983)

Taylor, Michael J.H. & Mondey, David, *The Guinness Book of Aircraft Records, Facts and Feats*, Guinness Publishing (1988)

Terraine, John, *A Time for Courage: The RAF in the European War*, Macmillan (1985)

Thetford, Owen, *Aircraft of the Royal Air Force since 1918*, Putnams (1988)

Thetford, Owen, *British Naval Aircraft since 1912*, Putnams (1977)

Thetford, Owen & Gray, Peter, *German Aircraft of the First World War*, Putnams (1962)

Tillman, Barrett, *Corsair: The F4U in WW2 and Korea*, Patrick Stephens (1979)

Walker, Percy B., *Early Aviation at Farnborough*, MacDonald (1971)

Winton, John, *Air Power at Sea: 1945-today*, Sidgwick & Jackson (1987)

Wragg, David W., *Speed in the Air*, Osprey (1974)

Magazines

Aircraft Illustrated, Ian Allan Publishing

RAF Yearbook Bomber Command Special, RAF Benevolent Fund Enterprises (1991)

RAF Yearbook Coastal Command Special, RAF Benevolent Fund Enterprises (1992)

RAF Yearbook Fighter Command Special, RAF Benevolent Fund Enterprises (1990)

RAF Yearbook Gulf War Special, RAF Benevolent Fund Enterprises (1991)

Royal Air Force Yearbooks 1988-1999, RAF Benevolent Fund Enterprises

United States Air Force Yearbooks 1989-1999, RAF Benevolent Fund Enterprises

PICTURE CREDITS

PHOTOGRAPHS

The photographs in *Warplanes* have kindly been supplied by the following photographers,
collections and organisations, and printed on the pages, as indicated below:

Graham Finch
8/9, 102/103, 214 (bottom) and 226

Jeremy Flack/Aviation Photographs International
247, 272 and 273

Derek N. James
70, 71, 72 (both), 107 (top), 110 (top) and 139

James D. Oughton: 208

RAF Museum:
38 (Neg P000937), 49 (Neg P021747), 58 (Neg P011383), 61 (Neg P007557), 62 (Neg P016849), 62 (Neg P000335),
68 (Neg P015332), 69 (Neg P019267), 79 (Neg P015291), 84 (Neg P012122), 87 (Neg P009362), 91 (Neg P009495),
96 (P016645), 98 (Neg P003822), 110 (Neg P0131113), 112 (Neg P011931) and 120 (Neg P1016373)

All remaining photographs appear courtesy of:
Army Air Corps, BAE Systems (Gordon Bartley, Phil Boyden, Geoff Lee and Chris Ryding), Boeing, Lockheed Martin,
McDonnell Douglas, Andrew P. March, Daniel J. March, Peter R. March, NATO, Panavia, PRM Aviation, RAF Red Arrows,
RAF Public Relations (Rick Brewell, John Cassidy and Jack Pritchard), The Royal Air Force Benevolent Fund archives,
Rolls-Royce, Brian S. Strickland Collection, US Army and US Air Force (JCCD).

ILLUSTRATIONS

The following six paintings are reproduced courtesy of The Royal Air Force Benevolent Enterprises and the artists,
having first appeared in the publications *Brace by Wire to Fly by Wire: 75 years of the Royal Air Force 1918-1993* (RAFBFE 1993)
and *Sabre to Stealth: 50 years of the United States Air Force 1947-1997* (RAFBFE 1997).

Keith Ferris *Gallant Beginning* (Page 18)
Wilfred Hardy *Operation Chastise* (Page 128) and *Hawker Hunter F1s* 1954 (Page 180)
Henry Godines *Fueling the Orange Beast* (Page 150)
Robert G. Smith *Berlin Airlift* (Page 153)
Bob Cunningham *'Gabby' Scores Again* (Page 160)

INDEX